AFRICAN-AMERICAN RELIGION

Dr. Musa's book is a noteworthy piece that covers a topic little attention has been historically paid. With this work, he provides the field of religious studies with an important connection and understanding of the influence of African Traditional Religions on the Christianization of Africans brought to the U.S. through the slave trade. Providing stories, experiences, and histories, this is a foundational text for understanding African-American Religion. His thorough coverage of the history provides insights not previously available in the literature. This should be required reading for those pursuing religious studies; understanding the influence of the Church in African American communities is necessary.

Danielle Geary
Professor of Social Work
Carthage College, Kenosha, Wisconsin.

Professor Musa's masterly book, African-American Religion: A Confluent of African Traditional Religion and Christianity, is rapidly becoming a must-read for all serious scholars of African American history generally, and most especially for scholars of American church history. No other contemporary study so capably probes the influence of African traditional religion upon the hearts and minds of plantation slaves confronted with the unfamiliar religious traditions of the new world. Summoning a wide array of documentary evidence, Musa unlocks the mystery of American slaves' cool response toward well-intended Anglican proselytization in contrast to their vibrant reception of the teachings and spirit of the two Great Awakenings. This new understanding offers every educated reader unparalleled insight into the religious life of this cruelly displaced population, and also witnesses to their extraordinary resilience fueled by their enduring spirituality.

Rom Maczka
Professor and former Head of the Religion Department
at Carthage College, Kenosh, Wisconsin

AFRICAN-AMERICAN RELIGION

A CONFLUENT OF AFRICAN TRADITIONAL RELIGION AND CHRISTIANITY

David Musa

authorHOUSE®

AuthorHouse™
1663 Liberty Drive
Bloomington, IN 47403
www.authorhouse.com
Phone: 1 (800) 839-8640

Published by AuthorHouse 06/26/2015

ISBN: 978-1-5049-1367-6 (sc)
ISBN: 978-1-5049-1368-3 (e)

Library of Congress Control Number: 2015908049

Print information available on the last page.

CONTENTS

TABLES

FOREWORD

One cannot talk for too long with African-Americans about the formative influences in their lives without religion, especially Christianity, coming to the fore. It is a well-known fact that religion plays a critical role in understanding all aspects of African-American life. A Pew Research Center report of 2009 found that "While the U.S. is generally considered a highly religious nation, African-Americans are markedly more religious on a variety of measures than the U.S. population as a whole, . . ."

This is not a new phenomenon. Even at the beginning of the 1900s centuries since the beginning of the slave trade, when W.E.B. DuBois wrote the <u>Souls of Black Folk</u>, he said, "The Negro has already been pointed out many times as a religious animal,--a being of that deep emotional nature which turns instinctively toward the supernatural. Endowed with a rich tropical imagination and a keen, delicate appreciation of Nature, the transplanted African lived in a world animate with gods and devils, elves and witches; full of strange influences,--of Good to be implored, of Evil to be propitiated." The religiosity of the slaves was not the result of becoming Christians. They were religious before they encountered Christianity. On the subject of the religion of the slaves, he said that the church was not only the social center for the slave life but also "the most characteristic expression of African character". In other words, the church or their religious life was not just about what they did, it was who they were.

DuBois explained that the religious identity of the slaves is best explained by an understanding of the context from where they were taken. He says, "the social history of the Negro did not start in America. He was brought from a definite social environment, . . . under the headship of the chief and the potent influence of the priest." Though DuBois astutely noted the connection between the religion of the slaves and African Traditional Religion, subsequent scholarship did not explore this path further. Rather it was assumed by many that the slave masters suppressed African religious practices as heathen. Only dancing which is considered the most primitive form of religious expression survived. But nothing could be further from the truth.

The African philosopher, John S. Mbiti, describing contemporary African life says Africans are "incurably religious." There is a congruence between Mbiti and DuBois' description of these Africans many centuries apart. If these descriptions are accurate, then wherever Africans are, they will display this almost innate characteristic. There is ample evidence to suggest that this is what happened. When they were brought into the new world, they came with their religion and organized themselves and continued to practice it in some form before they converted to Christianity. In some places like Brazil and Haiti, African Traditional Religions survived slavery into the modern times albeit in new forms but the connection with African Traditional Religions is irrefutable.

Though the role of religion in African American life is incontestable, there is a dearth of literature on the relationship between African traditional religious heritage of the slaves and their Christianity. Dr. David Musa's work, <u>African-American Religion: A Confluent of African Traditional Religion and Christianity</u> has done us a great service by contributing to fill this deep, embarrassing and ugly ditch in American religious literature.

He argues that "while innovation and creativity of the Africans played crucial roles in the origin, development and practice of African-American Christianity, the residual African cultures, including the slaves' native African traditional religious heritage, also played significant roles in their response to the new religion of the masters." This book is helpful in understanding the American religious landscape. DuBois says, "the study of Negro religion is not only a vital part of the Negro in America, but no uninteresting part of American history." Musa brings a rich first hand knowledge of African Traditional Religions to this study thus he is able to see natural connections that may elude one who knows African Traditional Religions only through literature. Anyone who wants a better understanding of the sources of African-American religiosity, especially Christianity, and the forces that shaped it will find this book helpful.

Bulus Galadima
La Mirada, California
June 2015
Soli Deo Gloria

Dr. Bulus Galadima is the Dean of the Cook School of Intercultural Studies at Biola University, La Mirada, California.

References

- Du Bois, W. E. B. 1903. *The Souls of Black Folk.* Chicago: A.C. McClurg & Co.
- Mbiti, John S. 1969. *African Traditional Religions and Philosophy.* Heinemann Educational Publishers, Oxford, 1969.
- *A Religious Portrait of African-Americans* www.perforum. org/2009/01/31/a-religious-portrait-of-african-americans/

ABSTRACT

Literature on North American slavery is vast but negligent of the religious culture of the slaves, most especially African-American Christianity. As noted in Robert Handy's insightful article,[1] for several decades African-American Christianity appeared only as incidentals in the general historiography of American Church history. Considering the immeasurably positive role of the Church in the lives of African-Americans, this oversight is almost inexcusable.

Even where studies of slave Christianity have been attempted one would search in vain for any substantial discussion of the mutual effects of the slaves' original African religion and Christianity.

Thus this study is a contribution to recent explorations into that vital aspect of the history of African slaves in North America-- their Christianization. The study focuses on the question of why the slaves were apparently more responsive to Christianity in the Great Awakenings than during previous evangelization efforts by Anglican missionaries. I propose that the continuities as well as discontinuities between Christianity and African Traditional Religion were key among determinant factors in the slaves' response to Christianity. Basically, the slaves responded to the type of Christianity in which these factors were more prominent, the Great Awakenings vis-à-vis the Anglican version.

The first chapter of this study highlights the problem of past inattention to slave Christianity, especially as it relates to African Traditional Religion. In chapter two, I argue for both West Africa as the original home of most of the slaves and African Traditional

---

[1]   Robert T. Handy, "Negro Christianity in American Historiography," in <u>Reinterpretations in American Church History</u>, ed. Jerald C. Brauer (Chicago: University of Chicago Press, 1968), 91-112.

Religion as the predominant religious culture of that region. The Third chapter describes the process, personnel, and problems encountered in slave Christianization. Chapters four and five analyze and evaluate the impact of Christianizing efforts by Anglican missionaries and revival evangelists respectively. Chapter six summarizes and discusses the value of my findings for the African-American Church and evangelical missions in general. The study contains suggestions for further research.

Dedicated first and foremost, to the glory of God and to my family. To Ndidiamaka: my beloved wife; Ndiloma, Ukejeh and Ngozi: our Children. Also, to the memory of Dr. Timothy Philips of the Wheaton Graduate School, Wheaton, Illinois, who selflessly worked with me on this project, undeterred by his terminal illness

.

ACKNOWLEDGMENTS

I am indebted to many people for their various contributions in making this project a reality.

First, to Dr. Thomas Nettles, my mentor and first reader, without whose encouragement and guidance this study may not have materialized. I am also grateful to Dr. Bruce Fields, my second reader, for his candid corrections and suggestions. My sincere thanks Dr. John D. Woodbridge for his encouragement and solid pieces of advice. I am further indebted to Dr. Bulus Galadima for his willingness to step in as external reader on very short notice when we lost Dr. Timothy Philips. Thanks to my best "buddy," Carew, for his invaluable technical assistance.

Without the help, encouragement, and sacrifice of my family, this study could hardly be done. Hearty thanks to my wife, Ndidi, for your love and support in the tough periods of this journey. To Ndiloma, Ukejeh (UK), and Ngozi, our Children: I acknowledge the huge debt I owe you for allowing me to divert several precious moments and attention from you for the sake of this study. You will always have a special place in my heart.

CHAPTER 1

INTRODUCTION

The Negro Church is the only social institution of the Negroes which started in the African Forest and survived slavery; under the leadership of priests or medicine man, afterward of the Christian pastor, the Church preserved in itself the remnants of African tribal life and became after emancipation the center of Negro social life. So that today the Negro population of the United States is virtually divided into church congregations which are the real units of race life.[2]

Statement of the Problem

The effects of African-American slavery are indelibly stamped on many facets of American life, most especially American Christianity. "Nowhere else in the World has Negro slavery exercised such large influence upon the Christian Church as in the United States,"[3] asserts William Sweet, a noted American Church historian. Elaborating on his point, Sweet affirms that

---

[2]   William E. Burghardt DuBois, ed. <u>The Negro Church</u> (Atlanta Ga.: The Atlanta University Press, 1903; (New York: Octagon Books, 1968), 3.

[3]   William Warren Sweet, <u>The Story of Religion in America</u> (New York: Harper & Brothers, 1930), 285.

all of the great American Churches grew in more or less
intimate contact with the institution of slavery and all of them
were of necessity greatly affected by it. The most important
of the schisms that have occurred among American churches
were those growing out of Negro slavery, while some of the
most difficult problems facing the Churches today are due
to the Negro and the bitter conflicts which have arisen in
the Churches because of him.[4]

Sadly, not too many American Church Historians seem to have had
the insights and perceptions of Professor Sweet. For until very recently,
hardly any attention was paid to African-American Christianity, or
Church life as a whole, notwithstanding the tremendous volume of
literature available on the institution of slavery.[5] Such neglect prompted
the very insightful comment by Robert T. Handy that; "American
church historiography has regarded the history of Christianity among
Negroes as a 'special topic,' to be treated in connection with certain
definite crisis or to be handled by those with a particular interest in
that subject." In the same train of thought Handy claims that "in the
main general historical interpretations of American Church life, Negro
Christianity has been treated rather incidentally, even casually."[6]

This is an unfortunate oversight, because the story of American
Christianity would be incomplete without a treatment of the interaction
between Christianity and slavery. In addition, a centerpiece would be
missing in the story of African-American slavery, and to a large extent,

---

[4] Ibid., 285.

[5] In their massive work, <u>A Dictionary of Afro-American Christianity</u> (New York:
    Greenwood, 1967), Randall M. Miller and David Smith suggest that "the
    literature on slavery is so vast and production so prolific that a scholar can no
    longer pretend to master it within a lifetime. Non-specialists and general readers
    often face confusion and frustration in trying to sort through the many and
    varied books and articles on slavery."

[6] For a more extensive discussion of the neglect of African-American Christianity
    in the general treatment of American Church history, see Robert T. Handy,
    "Negro Christianity and American Church Historiography," in <u>Reinterpretations
    in American Church History</u>, ed. Jerald C. Brauer (Chicago: University of
    Chicago Press, 1968), 91-112.

the total experience of African-Americans in their sojourn in America, if the mutual effects of Christianity and slavery were not properly articulated. This is especially crucial considering the seemingly firm consensus among scholars of African-American religion that even before emancipation and thereafter "black religious institutions have been the foundation of Afro-American culture."[7] This has been observed at several levels, notably: the role of the Church in African-American life as "an Agency of social control, a source of economic cooperation, an arena for political activity, a sponsor of education, and a refuge in a hostile white world."[8]

Hence one of the goals of this study is to investigate that generally neglected but very vital aspect of the African experience in North America--the Christianization of the African slaves. Not only am I interested in the mechanics of the Christianization of the slaves but my curiosity also extends further into the mutual interaction between the slaves' original African Traditional Religion and Christianity, from the 1600s to the time of emancipation. As one of its benefits, it is my hope that this study will contribute to a deeper understanding of the genesis of the African-American Church. I also hope it will foster a healthy appreciation for the nurturing and supporting role which evangelical Christianity, as a body of confession, played in the transformation of African-Americans from African slaves to American citizens.

I also envisage a subsidiary contribution of this study to be the exposition of the intricate relationship between African Traditional Religion and Christianity. Lessons learnt from that relationship, as played out in the context of North American slavery, could lead to more relevant approaches and methodologies in evangelism and evangelical missions.

---

[7] Albert J. Raboteau, <u>Slave Religion: The Invisible Institution in the Antebellum South</u> (New York: Oxford University Press, 1978), 9.

[8] Ibid. Other key writers in this field like W. E. B. DuBois, Carter G. Woodson, and E. Franklin Frazier, to mention just a few, share this view.

Description of the study

For several decades, the general historiography of American slavery tended to fit into four periods: the period of the Post-war polemics, the period of the nationalist historians, the period of the scientific historians and lately, the period of the economic approach.[9] According to Miller and Smith, a historical conflict over African-American slavery followed immediately after the civil war, at which time the debate polarized into the old pro and anti-slavery camps.

Instead of the interest in slavery abating with emancipation, it seemed to have only ignited keen and fresh interest in the institution. The polemics were largely between North and South, black and white. It is estimated that over "600 books and articles on slavery were published in the year 1865-1899" and "slavery also ran like a leitmotif through post-bellum writings on the 'Negro problem'[10] and race relations"[11]

It is understandable that at this time most Southerners, especially Whites, tended to describe slavery in glowing terms. Many of them held the belief that slavery was actually beneficial, not only for the South as a whole, but for the slaves also. Pro-slavery arguments included the idea that racial order and harmony thrived better in slavery days than in the post-slavery South. Unlike the post-slavery times, argued pro-slavery writers, slaves were better fed, clothed and housed in the antebellum South. In fact, the argument continued, "slaves reaped humane treatment from their paternalistic masters. Cruel, abusive slaveholders were rare."[12] Robert Collins' book, Essay on the Treatment and Management of Slaves published in Boston, in 1853, is typical of sentiments expressed by those in favor of slavery. His presentation concludes with the following words:

> Under this system of management and treatment, which I have attempted to detail and which differs but little from

[9] Ibid. An elaboration on this periodization can be found in A Dictionary of Afro-American Christianity, ed. Randall M. Miller and David Smith.
[10] Ibid.
[11] Ibid.
[12] Ibid., 326.

the common practice of the country in its main features, the owner receives a good income upon the property, and the slaves are generally a happy and contented people. They have but few cares on their minds, and no provisions to make for tomorrow. The thought of a starving family never disturbs their dreams, for they have the strongest guarantee in the direct interest of their owner, that they will be provided for, both in food and raiment.[13]

To underscore his point, Collins refers to other writers who shared his views thus:

Another eminent writer of extensive information in regard to Negroes in Africa says: the greatest blessing that could be bestowed upon them would be to transport them across the Atlantic to the shores of America. Though they might be perpetual bondsmen, still they would emerge from darkness into light - from barbarism to civilization - from idolatry to Christianity - in short, from death to life. Then it may well be asked, of what has the slave of the South, or his true friend, to complain? There is no country, and no place upon the face of this earth, where the Negro race have such security for wholesome living, as in the United States.[14]

This mentality that slaves were better off in bondage than freedom in America or even in their native Africa was the backbone of the pro-slavery rhetoric. On the other side of the post-war polemics on slavery, some Northerners, including, former abolitionist, blacks, and friends of freedmen, "condemned slavery as a blot on American civilization and identified vestiges of the institution in the black codes of reconstruction, and later, in sharecropping, convict labor, peonage and Jim Crow laws."[15] The ability of these writers to capture and accurately describe

---

[13] Robert Collins, Essay on the Management and Treatment of Slaves (Boston: Eastburn's Press, 1853), 15.

[14] Ibid., 17.

[15] Ibid., 327.

the long-lasting influence of slavery on American racial thought was remarkable. Some of those effects, in the form of White domination and racial conflicts, not only remained quite alive in the South even after emancipation, but are still with us today. Stanley M. Elkins offers a succinct discussion of this debate in his book, <u>Slavery: A Problem in American Institutional and Intellectual Life</u>. He also provides a list of helpful titles of some of the literature that came out in that period.[16]

The Nationalist period in general slave historiography roughly covers the years 1890 - 1920. Miller and Smith suggest that "more than 2,000 slavery items, including many Theses and Dissertations appeared"[17] in this period. The focal point in the study of slavery became a keen interest in the institution from a historical perspective. Under the strong influence of nationalist motivations and scientific methodology, some historians of slavery became obsessed with the ideas of objectivity and impartiality. Some of the influential writers at this time were "Herman E. von Holst, James Schouler, John Bach McMaster, James Forde Rhodes and Albert Hart."[18]

The Nationalist historians also tended to emphasize the "institutional features of slavery," and in their bid to present a "truly national history, they interpreted slavery and the Civil war as national tragedies."[19]

They exercised every caution not to cast any blame on the South, but still their criticism of slavery was almost of equal fervor to that of the abolitionists. In fact they wrote with enough moral underpinnings to warrant the comment from Miller and Smith that; "the Nationalist historians were no more impartial than the old abolitionists or

---

[16] Stanley M. Elkins, <u>Slavery; A Problem in American Institutional and Intellectual life</u> (Chicago: The University of Chicago Press, 1959). In a footnote on page 2, Elkins lists the following as some of "the most widely circulated of the polemical material: Albert Barnes, <u>An Inquiry into Scriptural views of Slavery</u> (Philadelphia: Perkins & Purves, 1846); James G. Birney, <u>A Collection of Valuable Documents, Being Birney's Vindication of Abolitionists</u> (Boston: James G. Birney 1836); George Bourne, <u>A Condensed Anti-Slavery Bible Argument</u> (New York: S. W. Benedict, 1845).

[17] Ibid., 327.
[18] Ibid., 326.
[19] Ibid., 327.

post-bellum neo-abolitionists."[20] Nevertheless, they were precursors or catalysts for the scientific historians of slavery.

It is noted in Miller and Smith that the "Scientific" approach to the history of American slavery started with scholars at the Johns Hopkins University.

They approached the issue from a legalistic and factual stance. Using primary sources like Newspapers, government records and manuscripts, they came up with questions previously overlooked by other historians. Their investigations centered mainly on questions of the origins of slavery and race in America.

In an attempt to break with their predecessors, these historians simply described and did not judge "the evolution of slavery's various institutional features."[21] In terms of their meticulous quest for detail, these researchers brought a new dimension to the study of slavery. However, their rigid and impersonal methodology prevented them from looking at slavery from a humanitarian point of view. In most cases they ended up losing their desired objectivity and siding instead with the slaveholders. Their influence, nonetheless, is said to have been very strong on prominent historians of slavery like Ulrich Bonnell Phillips. Phillip's book titled, American Negro Slavery,[22] published in 1966, was a pivotal work in the study of African-American slavery, but his southern background did not permit him to write without undue prejudice against the slaves. Thus he tends to portray slavery from the old Southern pro-slavery perspective. Not only did he portray blacks as biologically inferior and culturally backward, but presented their life on the plantation as normal. According to Phillips, "In the actual regime severity was clearly the exception and kindliness the rule."[23] His interpretation of slavery was mostly in terms of economics and he earned the reputation of being one of the first historians to propound

[20] Ibid., 328.

[21] Ibid.

[22] Ulrich Bonnell Phillips, American Negro Slavery (Baton Rouge, Louisiana State University Press, 1966).

[23] Ibid., 306

the theory that considering the cost of feeding and maintaining the slaves, the institution was economically unprofitable.

An earlier work by Kenneth Stampp by the title, The Peculiar Institution,[24] which was published at the time of the Civil Rights movement in the 1960s, held a radically different position from Phillps'. Stampp wrote from the presupposition that "the slaves were merely human beings; that innately Negroes are, after all, only white men in black skins, nothing more, nothing less."[25] From this perspective, he proceeds to defend the dignity of the slave and condemn slavery as not only cruel and dehumanizing, but a profitable enterprise for the masters.

With the availability of more efficient research tools like complicated computing mechanisms, studies in African-American slavery took a new turn in the 1970s. Aided by new advances in technology, researchers have been able to discover and use resources they could hardly use before. For example, the use of folklore, material culture, music, ex-slave narratives and biographies became more popular.

Of late the stress seems to be increasingly laid on the social and cultural lives of the slaves. This innovative approach tends to evaluate the slaves "on their own terms, not just as victims of bondage."[26] The emphasis seems definitely to have shifted from the traditional approach of focusing on the ante-bellum plantation to focus on slavery and human progress. Time on the Cross: The Economics of American Negro Slavery, written by Robert William Fogel and Stanley L. Engerman, published in 1974, is typical of this new trend.

In this momentous work, there is obviously a keen interest in presenting an economic perspective on slavery. The authors' basic thesis consists of a ten-point correction to the "traditional characterization of slave economy." One of the crucial claims in the work of Fogel and Engerman is that slavery was generally a profitable enterprise; it was not on the verge of collapsing due to bad economics on the eve of the civil war, as some had maintained. Rather, even up until the eve of the civil

---

[24] Kenneth M. Stampp, The Peculiar Institution (New York: Alfred A. Knopf, 1963).
[25] Ibid., 7.
[26] Ibid.

war, slave owners were still anticipating tremendous profit from slavery. Slave agriculture was never inefficient in comparison to free agriculture. Slaves were not typically lazy, as the old tradition suggested, but hard working and efficient.

The slave family was not destroyed by slave promiscuity, but rather was viable under slavery, insists Fogel and Engerman. The material conditions of slaves were favorable, compared to free industrial workers. The economy of ante-bellum South grew considerably, instead of stagnating, the argument goes.

From such general perspectives on African-American slavery, attention has just begun to be focused on a long neglected but very important aspect of slave life in America: slave religion. The customary references to slave religion as an "Invisible Institution" and the black Churches after emancipation as the "Visible Institution" no longer carry any persuasive weight among recent scholars. Albert Raboteau, for example, believes that; "we should speak of the 'invisibility' of slave religion with irony: it is the neglect of slave sources by historians which has been the main cause of this invisibility."[27] Raboteau cites John Blassingame's The Slave Community and Slave Testimony, Eugene Genovese's Roll, Jordan Roll and Lawrence Levine's Black Culture and Black consciousness, among others, as demonstrations of "the fallacy in assuming that slaves left no articulate record of their experience."[28] It is becoming increasingly clear that several sources exist for a meaningful study of African-American religion and many eminent scholars have already availed themselves of this opportunity.

Among scholars who have shown considerable interest in the study of African-American religion, two schools are easily distinguishable:

---

[27] Albert J. Raboteau, Slave Religion: The "Invisible Institution" in the Antebellum South (New York: Oxford University Press, 1978), 10.

[28] Ibid. The following are annotations of the works cited by Raboteau: John Blassingame, The Slave Community: Plantation Life in Antebellum South (New York: Oxford University Press, 1972) and idem., Slave Testimony (Baton Rouge: Louisiana State University Press, 1977); Eugene Genovese, Roll, Jordan Roll: The World the Slaves Made (New York: Pantheon Books, 1972); Lawrence Levine, Black Culture and Black Consciousness (New York: Oxford University Press, 1977).

The old School, led by DuBois and the New School led by Raboteau. A key distinguishing mark between the two schools is that while the older folk merely contented themselves with narration and little or no interpretations of the story of African-American religion, the newer breed or new school usually takes a more interpretive approach. The old school tends towards telling stories of the various denominations, as found in the writings of Carter Woodson, for example.

The earliest and most comprehensive account of the African-American Church was by DuBois in 1903. It was part of a series of a decade-long studies "into the Negro problem" by Atlanta University. DuBois published his account under the title: The Negro Church,[29] in which he provides very valuable insights into the origins and development of the African-American Church. Backed by tremendous amounts of statistical data, DuBois outlines the weaknesses and strengths of various black denominational associations. His select bibliography, focusing mainly on works which dealt more with the slave rather than with the system was a crucial innovation in the way previous historians had treated African-American slavery. DuBois' work remains unsurpassed as one of the best pioneering attempts at shedding light on the crucial role religion played in the lives of African slaves in America.

In another early effort by DuBois, titled Soul of Black folk, published in 1903, the suggestion was first made that "the study of Negro religion is not only a vital part of the history of the Negro in America, but no uninteresting part of American history." Here the author describes the African-American Church not only as "the social center of Negro life" but also as "the most characteristic expression of African character"--the community spirit. Further, DuBois clearly articulates the key ingredients, which characterized the religion of the American slave: "the Preacher, the music and the frenzy."[30] These to him are strong cords, which tie the African-American church to a definite historical African social foundation.

---

[29] William E. B. DuBois, ed. The Negro Church, The Atlanta University Publications No. 8 (Atlanta, Ga.: The Atlanta University Press, 1903).

[30] W. E. B. DuBois, The Soul of Black Folk (New York: A. C. McClurg, 1903; reprint, New York: Penguin Books, 1989), 155.

Perhaps, the greatest contribution of DuBois is his focus on the historical African social environment as foundation for the African-American Church. Thus to understand the African-American Church, DuBois invites his audience to realize that

> no such institution as the Negro Church could rear itself without definite historical foundations. These foundations we can find if we remember that the social history of the Negro did not start in America. He was brought from a definite social environment,--the polygamous clan life under the headship of the chief and the potent influence of the priest. His religion was nature-worship, with profound belief in invisible surrounding influences, good and bad, and his worship was through incantation and sacrifice.[31]

While DuBois sees the continuity between the African-American Church and its African Traditional religious roots, he fails to recognize that there are also discontinuities between the two systems. It is one of my contentions in this study, that it was not only the continuities but also the discontinuities between Christianity and African Traditional Religion that largely determined the response of the African slaves to the various attempts at their Christianization.

Another pioneer among writers on African-American religion was Carter G. Woodson. His book, The History of the Negro Church, was first published in 1921, followed by a revised edition in 1945. A third edition of the same work became available in 1972.[32] Woodson's goal was to present a comprehensive story of the Negro church by synthesizing fragments of individual denominational histories. It is a useful historical sketch of African-American Churches in the United States, with strong emphasis on the lives and achievements of mainly Baptist and Methodist clergy. The absence of footnotes or bibliographies in all editions of Woodson's book leaves readers wondering about the

---

[31] Ibid., 159.
[32] Carter G. Woodson, The History of the Negro Church (Washington, D.C.: Associated Press, 1921, 1945).

author's sources. He is concerned with telling the story of the black denominations, and unlike DuBois, shows little concern for the possible historical connections between African-American Christianity and the original religions of the slaves.

While DuBois and Woodson represent the older approach to African-American religious studies, E. Franklin Frazier stands as a link between the old and the new. His sociological approach to the study of both the Negro family and the Negro Church has earned him an important place among scholars of African-American religion.

Frazier's views of the African-American religion were contained in a lecture series he gave in England in 1953. These were later published in 1964 under the title, The Negro Church in America.[33] With reference to the link between the Africa-American Church and its native African background, Frazier makes the very insightful observation that "there is one element in their African heritage that was able to survive capture in Africa and the 'middle passage'--dancing, the most primitive form of religious expression."[34] He concedes that "in the 'Shout songs' on the Sea Islands off the coast of South Carolina and Georgia, one may discover the remnants of the African religious heritage" but denies that any "African religious cults became established on American soil," because the Whites did every thing possible to suppress these heathenish practices.[35]

Whether African religious cults were established on American soil or not, there is still ample evidence to suggest that the previous religious background of the slaves was a crucial factor in the way they responded to the various brands of Christianity presented to them while in captivity. This is partly my thesis in this book. The new School in African-American religious studies probably holds views similar to but not identical with Frazier's.

Clearly, one of the best representatives among recent scholars on African-American religious history is Raboteau. In his book,

---

[33] E. Franklin Frazier, The Negro Church in America (New York: Schocken Books, 1974).
[34] Ibid., 86.
[35] Ibid., 87.

Slave Religion: "The Invisible Institution" in the Antebellum South, Raboteau attempts to tackle questions such as: "What were the origins of black religion in America? What aspects of African religions did the slaves retain? How did the evangelization and conversion of Africans to Christianity take place? What was the nature of the religion to which the slave was converted? What, if anything, was distinctive about religion in the slave quarters?"[36] These and similar questions are representative of the primary preoccupations and concerns of recent scholars of African-American religion.[37] Their Interpretive approach is well demonstrated in African American-Religion: Interpretive Essays in History and Culture,[38] edited by Timothy Fullop and Albert Raboteau. A common bond among these devoted researchers of African-American religious history seems to be the conviction that

> the study of the religious history of the United States has been for too long an examination of the institutional and intellectual development of American Protestantism-especially in the Northeast--and it is not the least contribution of much recent work in Afro-American religious history that has helped break this mold. Students of American religious history generally are slowly--but, one hopes, surely--coming to see that Africans were as much a part of the earliest history of the Atlantic world as Europeans were, that the American story begins as much in the South as in New England, or the Middle Colonies, and that through out that history

---

[36] Ibid., 11.

[37] From the 1970s to the present, very helpful scholarly works focusing wholly or partly on African-American Christianity have not been lacking. Among so many are: Carol V. R. George, Segregated Sabbaths: Richard Allen and the Rise of the Independent Black Churches 1760-1840 (New York: Oxford University Press, 1973); Milton Sernett, Black Religion and American Evangelicalism: White Protestantism, Plantation Missions, and the Flowering of Negro Christianity 1787-1865 (Metuchen N.J.: Scarecrow Press, 1975); Milton Sernett, ed. Afro-American Religious History: A Documentary Witness (Durham, N.C.: Duke University Press, 1985).

[38] Timothy Fullop and Albert J. Raboteau, eds., African-American Religion: Interpretive Essays in History and Culture (New York: Routledge, 1997).

the encounter of blacks and whites has been as central a
part of the American religious problematic as the heritage
of Puritanism or the diversity of Euro-American religion.[39]

Charles Joyner expresses a similar sentiment, though in a narrower
sense. He goes beyond a mere general acceptance of African-American
religious history as a valid part of the American religious heritage to
argue cogently for the originality of African-American Christianity.
Joyner believes, for example, that "the originality of African-American
Christianity...lies neither in its African elements nor in its Christian
elements, but in its unique and creative synthesis of both."[40] He further
elaborates on his statement as follows:

> To underestimate the Africanity of African-American
> Christianity is to rob the slaves of their heritage. But
> to overestimate the Africanity of African-American
> Christianity is to rob the slaves of their creativity. Africans
> were creative in Africa; they did not cease to be creative
> as involuntary settlers in America. The African-American
> Christianity that developed was neither a dark version of the
> Christianity preached by the slaveholders nor a continuation
> of African Religion disguised as Christianity. The story of
> the emergence of African-American Christianity is a story
> of emergent African-American culture as well as residual
> African cultures, a story of innovation as well as tradition, a
> story of change as well as continuity.[41]

I whole-heartedly endorse Joyner's appeal for balance in dealing
with the interaction of Christianity and the slaves' African Traditional
Religion, which ultimately resulted in African-American Christianity. It

[39] Albert J. Raboteau et al., "Retelling Carter Woodson's Story: Archival Sources for Afro-American Church History," Journal of American History, formerly The Mississippi Valley Historical Review 77, no. 1 (1990), 181-199.
[40] Charles Joyner, "Believer I Know: The Emergence of African-American Christianity" African-American Christianity," ed. Paul E. Johnson (Berkley: University of California Press, 1994), 7.
[41] Ibid., 19.

is, in fact, this "story of the emergence of African-American Christianity" as a "story of emergent African-American culture as well as residual African Cultures" that forms the backbone of this book. It is one of my goals to add an African perspective to the interpretation of that "story of innovation as well as culture, change as well as continuity,"[42] with its African background as the starting point.

My thesis is that while innovation and creativity of the Africans played crucial roles in the origin, development and practice of African-American Christianity, the residual African cultures, including the slaves' native African traditional religious heritage, also played significant roles in their response to the new religion of the masters. I also propose that the continuities and discontinuities between Christianity and African Traditional Religion were critical determinant factors in the Christianization of the slaves. On the one hand, the slaves' response to Christianity depended on which brand of the new religion contained elements akin to or which struck a familiar cord with the residual religious instincts of the slave. On the other hand, the discontinuities between Christianity and African Traditional Religion made the latter vulnerable and easily replaceable by the former.

This dynamic of the encounter between Christianity and the old religion of the slaves has been referred to here and there by scholars of African-American religion, but one looks in vain for an adequate explanation of the role the slaves' residual religious affinities played in their conversion. Nor is there satisfactory account for possible inherent weaknesses or strengths in the slaves' former religion that would cause it either to easily succumb to or resist a new alternative like Christianity. This book is an attempt to fill those gaps in the story of slave Christianization. Previous attempts at meeting this need are commendable but seriously inadequate.

For example, Albert Raboteau displays a keen awareness of the crucial nature of the encounter between Christianity and the residual African religions that the African slaves possessed and summarizes it in the following words:

---

[42]   Ibid.

In the encounter with European Christianity in its Protestant form in North America, enslaved Africans and their descendants encountered something new: a fully articulated ritual relationship with the Supreme Being, who was pictured in the book that Christians called the Bible not just as the Creator and Ruler of the cosmos, but as the God of History, a God who lifted up and cast down nations and peoples, a God whose sovereign will was directing all things toward an ultimate end, drawing good out of evil. As the transplanted Africans reflected on the evil that had befallen them and their parents, they increasingly turned to the language, symbols and worldview of the Christian holy book. There they found a theology of history that helped them to make sense of their enslavement.[43]

Like many of his contemporaries, Raboteau's articulate description of what happened when the slaves' residual religion encountered Christianity is very insightful, but he falls short on offering adequate reasons for the results of that encounter. For example, Raboteau offers no explanation for the Africans' transfer of allegiance from African Traditional Religion to Christianity. Why would the theology of history found in the Christian book be more helpful to the slaves in making sense of their enslavement than their previously held beliefs?

One explanation Raboteau offers for the fact that "during the first 120 years of black slavery in British North America, Christianity made little headway in the slave population" but slaves "were first converted in large numbers in the wake of the religious revivals that periodically swept parts of the colonies beginning in the 1740s,"[44] is that "the analogy between African and evangelical styles of worship enabled the slaves to reinterpret the new religion by reference to the old, and so made this brand of Christianity seem less foreign than that of the more

---

[43] Albert J. Raboteau, "African-Americans, Exodus, and the American Israel," in <u>African-American Christianity: Essays in History</u>, ed. Paul E. Johnson (Berkley: University of California Press, 1994), 1.

[44] Ibid., 4.

liturgically sedate Church of England."[45] This is clearly a very insightful observation but several questions still remain unanswered.

What, for example, were some of the analogies or points of contact between African and evangelical styles of worship that attracted the slaves? What were the points of reference in their old religion that the slaves saw in the revivals which made "this brand of Christianity seem less foreign than that of the more liturgically sedate Church of England"? Apart from the positive points of contact, what other elements in the slaves' native religions could possibly have made them disposable in favor of "the language, symbols and worldview of the Christian book"? These are some of the questions I will attempt to answer in this book.

Definition of Terms

The term "Christianization" or "Christianize" is used in this study to refer to "conversion to Christianity."[46] That is, the process of giving a Christian character to someone who was previously not a believer in Christianity.

In all its usages in this study, the word "Negro" should be understood to mean, "a member of the dark-skinned race, one of the three main anthropological divisions of mankind, living in Africa south of the Sahara or a descendant of this race living in the U.S.A, the Caribbean etc."[47] Due to the historically negative and derogatory connotations the term has acquired, I will limit its usage only to places where it occurs in direct quotations. A synonymous term, "African-American" will be preferred in this project.

African Traditional Religion(s) can be generally characterized as "nature worship, with strong belief in sorcery,"[48] or "Nature worship with profound belief in invisible surrounding influences, good and bad."[49]

---

[45] Ibid.

[46] The New Lexicon Webster's Dictionary of the English Language (New York: Lexicon Publications, 1989).

[47] Ibid.

[48] Ibid.

[49] Ibid.

The worship usually consists of incantations, pouring of libations, huge feasts, and sacrifice. Terms like "Juju," "fetish," "magic," "animism" and "ancestral worship" refer to vital aspects of African Traditional religion(s), but none of those terms by itself constitutes a comprehensive definition.

Limitations of the Study

This study is not intended to deal with the whole quagmire of the pro- and anti-slavery debate. It is not a general dissertation on slavery but limited to a specific aspect of the experiences of African slaves in America--their conversion to Christianity and how it affected their transition from African slaves to American citizens. I will discuss some but not every effect of Christianity on the slaves and slavery in general. That would require a series of dissertations.

Moreover, only the experiences of slaves on the North American main land constitute our study. Slaves held in the Caribbeans and other places outside North America are mentioned only for brief comparative purposes.

Also a treatment of African-American religion in its entirety is beyond the scope of this study. I am narrowly confined to the role of Christianity in the lives of the slaves. African Traditional Religion is studied only in an effort to identify continuities and discontinuities therein with Christianity. The study avoids extensive denominational histories.

The roles of various denominations in the conversion of the slaves will be discussed but a detailed denominational history of a particular black or white Church would be superfluous. I do not intend to write a history of the black Church per se but my central focus will be on the conversion of the slaves and subsequent birth of the African-American Church.

Because conversion is generally a personal experience, the study primarily relies for its sources, on slave testimonies. A careful reading of appropriate sections in the sixteen volumes of slave narratives was done. These massive works "containing about 10,000 pages and roughly

3.5 million words, are based on interviews with more than twenty-two hundred people in seventeen States."[50] Interviews for the narratives were prepared by the Federal Writers Project (FWP) in 1936-1938, and deposited in the rare book room of the Library of Congress in 1941. All or at least some volumes at a time are available in local libraries in many States. I found the volumes in the Indiana University (IUPUI) Library especially helpful for my study. The study also relies heavily on slave biographies.

For information on African Traditional Religion, I consulted major African Scholars like John Mbiti, who is one of the pioneering writers on the subject. Also, extensive use was made of the holdings of Africana Collections at the Indiana University, Bloomington Library and the Africana Library at Northwestern University, in Evanston, Illinois. I also made use of holdings at the Rolfing Memorial Library, Trinity International University, Deerfield, Illinois.

Procedure and Chapter Summary

Chapter one serves as an introduction to My thesis. Here I have endeavored to articulate the nature of the problem I wish to address in my study. It also contains a description of the study, definition of crucial terms, and the establishment of the limitations to the study.

---

[50] See Review Article by C. Vann Woodward, "History from Slave Sources," *American Historical Review* 79, no. 2 (1974): 470-81. In this article Vann Woodward carefully examines the origins and methods by which the interviews were gathered. He provides a very helpful evaluation of the materials based on what previous historians had perceived as problems with the Narratives. He mentions inherent problems such as the age range of the interviewees. Most former slaves interviewed were over eighty years old, which raises the question of memory loss or lapses. Moreover, most of them were children at the time of enslavement and probably did not actually have the same experience as adult slaves. The composition of the team of interviewers, being mostly southern white males, also made the materials suspect for several years. In spite of the apparent flaws, Vann Woodward comes to the conclusion that; "the slave narratives have their peculiarities, as all types of historical sources do, but they are not all that different from the norm. The norm for historical sources is a mess, a confusing mess, and the task of the historian is to make sense of it."

This chapter also discusses the procedures followed in the conduct of this research.

In chapter two, I lay the foundation for the rest of the discussion by asking: What area of Africa supplied the bulk of slaves involved in the Atlantic slave trade? What was the predominant religion of the region from which the slaves were captured? The goal will be to ascertain what exposure, if any, the Africans had to Christianity before their capture. Also, to determine whether the slaves had any knowledge of God prior to their arrival in North America.

In the third chapter I examine the process, personnel and problems that were involved in slave Christianization. The approach in this chapter is mainly descriptive rather than interpretive. In as much detail as my research could allow, the various attempts at converting or Christianizing the slaves are investigated and described. The obstacles encountered in the process are also investigated.

Chapter four looks at the progress or regress of slave Christianization. This chapter deals basically with the analysis and evaluation of the success or failure of Christianization attempts by the Church of England, through her various agencies and missionaries.

In chapter five the Christianization efforts of the evangelical revivals are assessed. Here I have attempted to explain slave conversions in the light of their previous African background, especially African Traditional Religion. The continuities and discontinuities between Christianity and African Traditional Religions are scrutinized for possible clues to the success or failure of Christianization methods.

Chapter six concludes the study with a summary and analysis of my findings. This chapter also summarizes the implications of my findings for the African-American Church and evangelical missionary enterprises in general. Suggested areas for further research are included in this chapter.

CHAPTER 2

THE PROVENANCE AND PROTO-RELIGION OF AFRICAN SLAVES IN NORTH AMERICA

Emil Ludwig is reported to have asked once when on a visit
to Africa: "How can the untutored African conceive God?"[51]

The exact number of Africans enslaved in North America and
other parts of the Western World during nearly four centuries of the
transatlantic slave trade is a hotly debated topic among recent scholars
of African-American slavery. After careful evaluation of the various
propositions in the "numbers game," it is safe to suggest that between
ten and sixteen million Africans were transported across the Atlantic
ocean into bondage in Europe, the Americas and several other locations
in the Atlantic World.[52] Scholarly interests in the number of Africans

---

[51] Geoffrey Parrinder, <u>African Traditional Religion</u> (West Port, Connecticut:
Greenwood, 1962), 9.

[52] A concise but very helpful summary of the "state of the debate over the Slave
trade" is found in Paul Lovejoy, "The Impact of the Atlantic Slave Trade on
Africa: A Review of Literature," <u>Journal of African History</u> 30 (1980): 365-94.
A landmark publication on the issue of volume is Philip Curtin's <u>The Atlantic
Slave Trade: A Census</u> (Madison, Wis.: University of Wisconsin Press, 1969).
For fuller appreciation of the intensity of the debate, see Paul E. Lovejoy's "The
Volume of the Atlantic Slave Trade: A Synthesis," <u>Journal of African History</u> 23
(1982): 473-501.

sold into slavery are useful and highly commendable, but probably more crucial for our purposes regarding the study of the slaves' native religion and its relationship to Christianization, is the provenance, and hence religious background of the slaves. For as Professor Melville Herskovits has observed:

> A knowledge of the provenience [sic] of the Negroes in the new World is basic to the study of New World Negro cultures, since to comprehend the cultural equipment with which these people entered upon their lives in the western hemisphere is essential in any successful attempt to utilize the materials gained from investigations of their present day life for an analysis of the processes of cultural change and of the results of culture-contact.[53]

This statement, in my opinion, applies even more succinctly to the religious life of the slaves. An ample understanding of the religious "equipment with which these people entered upon their lives in the Western hemisphere" is critical to deciphering not only the motives behind their Christianization, but also the processes by which they were Christianized, and eventually the effects of Christianization on them.

Hence we are faced with a two-fold task in this chapter: First, to determine as much as possible, the region or regions in Africa from which most of the slaves were captured; second, to investigate the predominant religious practices in the regions from which they originated. To determine the provenance of the slaves, I shall rely on slave shipping records, early ethnolinguistic inventories, personal testimonies of former African slaves, and eyewitness accounts of a former slave trader.

For the predominant religious practices of the slaves' region of origin, I shall sieve through the scanty literature available and also make use of my personal knowledge, being a born and bred West African. Knowledge of the predominant religious practices of the areas or regions from which the slaves were obtained will be helpful in providing answers

---

[53] Melville J. Herskovits, "On the Provenience of New World Negroes," <u>Social Forces</u> 12, nos. 1-4, (October 1933-May 1934): 247-62.

to crucial questions, such as the level of religious awareness, if any, that the slaves brought to North America. What was the nature of religion the slaves brought to the New World? Let us start with the slaves' origin.

The Provenance of African Slaves in North America

Africa is a huge and diverse continent, with the population estimated at about two hundred million.[54] It has been argued that both domestic and commercial slavery were rife among Africans even before the transatlantic trade blossomed.[55] For example, trade in slaves and gold from the successive western Sudanic Kingdoms of Ghana, Mali and Songhai, in exchange for commodities like salt from North Africa, was going on across the Sahara desert as early as medieval times.

Domestic slavery is known to have existed on the East coast of Africa at about the same time or even earlier.[56] It also was previously

---

[54]   See Simon and Phoebe Ottenberg, <u>Cultures and Societies of Africa</u> (New York: Random House, 1960), 17.

[55]   J. D. Fage, "Slavery and the Slave Trade in the context of West African History" <u>Journal of African History</u> 10, no. 3 (1969), 393-404. In this article, Professor Fage is mainly concerned with the slave trade in West Africa and discusses the three most widely held views about the origin of the trade. One of which according to Fage, is "that the institution of slavery was natural and endemic in West African society, so that the coming of foreign traders with a demand for labor, whether from Muslim North Africa or from countries of maritime Europe, led swiftly and automatically to the development by West Africans of an organized trade in slaves for export." While Fage agrees with the proposition, he nonetheless believes that the type of slavery referred to in West Africa was mostly domestic and nothing in comparison to the chattel slavery that existed on American plantations. He condemns the use of the prior existence of slavery in Africa as an excuse for the barbaric nature of the transatlantic slave trade.

[56]   See A. T. Groove, <u>Africa</u> (Oxford: Oxford University Press, 1978), 87-88; Ralph A. Austin, "The Trans-Saharan Slave Trade: A Tentative Census," in <u>The Uncommon market: Essays in the Economic History of the Atlantic Slave trade</u>, ed. Henry A. Gemery and Jan S. Hogendorn (New York: Academic Press, 1979). Ralph Austin suggests a volume of about 14 million slaves for the duration of the trans-saharan slave trade. This is probably a very tentative figure as the author himself readily admits.

believed that slaves were obtained from almost every part of Africa: "Central, South, East, as well as West Africa."[57]

However, recent evidence from slave shipping records, early ethnolinguistic inventories, personal testimonies of former African slaves, and eyewitness accounts of former slave traders suggests otherwise. It has now become clearer that the bulk of slaves transported across the Atlantic Ocean between 1400 and 1800 came largely from a sub-region of equatorial Africa, mainly south of the Sahara desert. This area is thus the focus of my investigation, beginning with its geographical location.

The Geography of the Slaves' Original Home

Three major subdivisions exist within the equatorial zone of Africa: The first subdivision is Central Africa, which "includes the Congo area, northern Angola, and the southern portion of French Equatorial Africa." The Guinea Coast is the second subdivision and the third is "the East African Highlands and the Ethiopian Highlands."[58] Of these three subdivisions, the largest supplies of slaves in the transatlantic slave trade were from the Guinea Coast and Central Africa.

Dense forests, heavy rainfalls, high humidity and constant high temperatures characterize these subdivisions of the continent. The part of Africa historically known as the Guinea Coast covers over a 2,000-mile span, "from Dakar in the west to the Cameroon in the east."[59] This region, which forms the bulk of the Atlantic coastline, exhibits a variety of features on the shoreline. Stretches of sandy beaches, interrupted by dense mangrove swamps at the mouths of large but unnavigable rivers, are the first features that greet the eyes of the maritime visitor. There are very few natural harbors on the coast, such as Freetown, Lagos and Dakar. A thick and almost impenetrable rain forest rises immediately from the shores, stretching for miles inland. "In these well-watered

---

[57] Albert J. Raboteau, Slave Religion: The "Invisible Institution" in the Antebellum South (Oxford: Oxford University Press, 1978), 7.

[58] For a more detailed description of these areas see: Simon and Phoebe Ottenberg, Cultures and Societies of Africa (New York: Random House, 1960), 8-16.

[59] Robert O. Collins, African History in Documents: Western African History, vol. 1 (Princeton: Markus Wiener Publishers, 1997), 144.

forests, shifting cultivation is practiced to support a relatively dense, sedentary population."[60]

According to the New Lexicon Webster's Dictionary, this region is the exclusive and original home of "one of the three main anthropological divisions of mankind--the dark skinned race called Negroes."[61] Thus based on the fact that almost all imported slaves from Africa into the Atlantic World were Negroes, it is safe to suggest that West Africa was their original home. Other evidences can be cited in support of this proposition. One example is shipping records.

Evidence from Slave Shipping Records

The Guinea Coast is generally accepted as the principal source of African slaves brought to North America.[62] Evidence gathered from shipping records of slave trading nations,[63] is one of the sources supportive of this position. The following tables from various sources would also serve to illustrate the point. Tables 1 and 2 were culled from Philip Curtin's The Atlantic Slave Trade: A Census, published by the University of Wisconsin Press, in 1969. Although Curtin's book was based mainly on previously published material, and his approach strongly revisionist, some have hailed it as "a landmark in the historiography, not just of the slave trade, but in the larger fields of slavery and migration."[64]

---

[60] Ibid.

[61] The New Lexicon Webster's Dictionary of the English Language (New York: Lexicon, 1989).

[62] The following are a representative sampling of such literature suggesting the Guinea Coast to be home to African slaves: Hugh Thomas, The Slave Trade (New York: Simon & Schuster, 1997); Philip Curtin, The Atlantic Slave Trade: A Census (Madison: University of Wisconsin Press, 1969).

[63] A typical example of such research is Jean Mettas's Repertoire Des Expeditions Negrieres Francaise Au XVIII Siecle, ed. Serge Daget (Paris: Societe Francaise D'Histoire D'outre-Mer, 1978).

[64] David Eltis and David Richardson, "The 'Numbers Game' and the Routes to Slavery," in Routes to Slavery: Direction, Ethnicity, and Mortality in the Transatlantic Slave Trade, ed. David Eltis and David Richardson (Portland, Oregon: Frank Cass, 1997), 1.

Table 1. Regional Distribution in Percentage of
Slaves Exported from Africa by Ships Known to the
British Foreign Office, 1817-43

Exporting Region	1817-20	1821-30	1831-40	1841-43	Total
Senegambia	-	*	-	0.2	*
Sierra Leone	-	0.4	0.5	1.8	0.6
Windward Coast	-	*	-	-	*
Gold coast	-	-	0.5	-	0.2
Bight of Benin	-	0.4	1.8	4.7	1.3
Bight of Biafra	-	4.4	0.9	-	2.6
Congo North	55.9	27.5	11.9	6.5	22.6
Angola	26.6	37.6	38.7	28.7	36.2
Mozambique	13.5	21.2	24.4	6.8	20.1
Sao Thome principe	-	0.1	3.6	0.3	1.2
Origin unknown	4.0	8.3	17.7	51.0	15.4
Total	100.0	100.0	100.0	100.0	100.0

Less than 0.05% Source: From Philip Curtin, Census, table 74, 258. Based on the Foreign Office sample of slaves imported into the Americas.

The names of places listed in table 1 unquestionably show the slaves originating from West Africa. Some of the places mentioned, such as Senegambia, Sierra Leone, the Windward Coast, Gold Coast, the Bight of Benin, sometimes known as the Slave Coast, the Bight of Biafra, Sao Thome, and Angola, are found only in what has been described as the Guinea Coast of West Africa.

This fact tends to tally with Basil Davidson's observation "that the areas from which slaves were consistently taken in great numbers were relatively few, and perhaps relatively small" and with the exception that "a few were taken from East Africa in the sixteenth century," Davidson also states that "most of the slaves were undoubtedly from Western Africa." "They were taken from a score of principal markets, and from many smaller ones, on a 3,000-mile coastline between Senegal

in the North and Angola in the South."[65] There are some, like Joseph
E. Inikori, who believe that Curtin's figures are an underestimation of
"the volume of slave exports from Africa to the Americas."[66] The value
and excitement in the debate over numbers can hardly be ignored. Our
interest, however, to this point lies not in the mathematical accuracy
of Curtin's figures but the origins of the slaves, which are repeatedly
mentioned in the shipping tabulations, as illustrated by table 1.

Table 2. Slave Departures (Thousands) from Outlets in the
Gold Coast, Bight of Benin, and Bight of Biafra, 1662-1863
(Listed from West to East)

	Slaves	Ships
Gold Coast		
Assinie	0.3	1
Axim	0.1	1
Quaqua	6.7	17
Kormantine	3.0	11
Elmina	2.4	9
Cape Coast Castle	38.9	191
Anomabu	53.9	196
Apam	1.2	5
Tantumquerry	0.4	1
Wiamba	0.2	1
Accra	7.1	24
Porto Novo	31.8	77
Christiansborg	4.7	14
Alampo	2.0	6
Total identified	120.9	477
Bight of Benin		
Keta	4.0	14
Little Popo	6.1	18

[65] Basil Davidson, *The African Slave Trade: Precolonial History 1450-1850* (Boston: Little, Brown and Company, 1961), 102-104.
[66] See Joseph E. Inikori, "Measuring the Atlantic Slave Trade: An assessment of Curtin and Anstey," *Journal of African History* 17, no. 2 (1976): 197-223.

Grand Popo	0.4	1
Popo (Unspecified)	11.3	36
Whydah	260.2	696
Jaquin (offra) (Ardrah)	38.8	106
Apa (Epe)	9.3	25
Badagry	21.0	57
Lagos	63.5	162
Costa da Mina	579.5	1,497
Benin	29.5	84
Total identified	1,055.5	2,773
Bight of Biafra		
Rio Nun	2.2	9
Formosa	0.2	1
Rio Brass	5.0	16
New Calabar	45.3	150
Bonny	240.4	678
Adony	0.8	3
Calabar (or Old Calabar)	196.5	633
Bimbia	1.1	4
Cameroons	22.7	63
Cameroons River	4.8	16
Corisco	0.3	2
Gabon	25.3	84
Cape Lopez	6.6	26
Total identified	522.2	1,686

Source: David Eltis and David Richardson, "West Africa and the Transatlantic Slave Trade: New Evidence of Long-run trends," in Routes to Slavery: Direction, Ethnicity and Mortality in the Transatlantic Slave Trade, ed. David Eltis and David Richardson, 23. (Portland, Oregon: Frank Cass, 1997).

Table 2 also lists some of the specific ports through which the slaves were exported.[67] Most of these ports are still identifiable on the current map of West Africa, suggesting the region to be the home of the slaves.

Another proof revealed by shipping records in support of West Africa as the original home of the Africans in North America comes from the names of the ethnic groups recorded (see table 3).

Table 3.   Projected Contribution of African Regions
and Ethnic Groups of the Northern and Transatlantic
Slave Trade, 1526-50

Region and Ethnic Group	Annual Average Exports	
	No.	%
Senegambia	499	37.6
Wolof	271	20.4
Fulbe	4	0.3
Tukulor	4	0.3
Serer	110	8.3
Malinke	110	8.3
Guinea-Bissau	543	40.8
Kassanga	23	1.7
Banyun	60	4.5
Biafada	249	18.7
Bram	211	15.9
Sierra Leone	56	4.2
Temne and related Peoples	56	4.2
Cape Mount to Cameroon	114	8.6
"Tierra Nova"	97	7.3
Sao Thome re-exports	13	1.0
Cameroon Coast (Ambo)	4	0.3

---

[67]   For a more detailed study of some of the key areas and ports in West Africa through which the slave trade was transacted, see: Douglas Chambers, "My own Nation: Igbo Exiles in Diaspora," in Routes to Slavery, ed. David Eltis and David Richardson (Portland, Oregon: Frank Cass, 1997), 72.

Congo-Angola	<u>82</u>	<u>6.2</u>
Bakongo	69	5.2
Tyo or Teke	9	0.7
Ambundu	4	0.3
Southeastern Africa	<u>32</u>	<u>2.4</u>
Total	1,330	100.0

Source: Philip Curtin, <u>Census</u>, table 28, 100. Please note the totals are the sum of the underlined regional figures only. Also, the percentages and totals have been rounded.

The list of ethnic names appearing in the table is far from exhaustive, but the fact that most, if not all the tribes named can still be found in West Africa clearly suggests that most of the slaves were taken from that area.

Evidence from Eyewitness Accounts of a Slave Trader

It must be quickly pointed out, however, that although the bulk of the slaves were sold by Africans to European traders stationed in coastal towns, and that the slaves were shipped through ports on the Guinea coast, the supply mostly came from considerable distances inland. Opinions vary as to the exact distance over which slaves were moved before their final sale on the coast. A.T. Grove suggests that

the slaves were procured from the hinterland by African traders who were careful to prevent the Europeans from travelling far inland. The Europeans stayed on the Coast, living in forts built along the rocky shores of the Gold coast, for example, or in hulks tied up in the creeks of the Niger delta.[68]

Grove's statement is authenticated by the eye witness account of John Barbot. Barbot was a seventeenth century slave trader and "Agent-General of the Royal Company of Africa and Islands of America, at Paris." He displays in his writings, a profound knowledge of how slaves were obtained and by which country. Barbot's records also indicate that slaves were normally brought to the coast "from very remote inland

---

[68]   A. T. Grove, <u>Africa</u> (Oxford: Oxford University Press, 1978), 91.

countries, by way of trade, and sold for things of very inconsiderable value." Along the Gold Coast, where Barbot had done considerable trading, his slave stock came mainly from prisoners of war. Thus in his own words; "when the inland country is at peace" he sometimes obtained no slaves at all. "As it happened to me in the year 1682, when having lain three days before Lay, I could not get one, nor was there any likelihood of it at that time..."[69]

Evidence from Former Slaves

Also, evidence from narratives of former slaves suggests considerable distances of travel, over several days. And sometimes the slaves passed through several hands by way of sale and re-sale, before their final delivery to the Europeans on the Coast. The stories of Olaudah Equiano, known in bondage as Gustavus Vassa and Samuel Adjai Crowther will serve as typical examples.

In his autobiography, Olaudah Equiano or Gustavus Vassa, a former Ibo Slave, recalls his home or area of initial capture as "that part of Africa, known by the name of Guinea, to which the trade for slaves is

---

[69]   John Barbot's narrative is found as "A Description of the Coasts of North and South Guinea, and Ethiopia Interior, Vulrarly Angola, being a new and Accurate Account of the western Maritime Countries of Africa" in Awnsham and John Churchill's Collection of Voyages and Travels (1732), vol. 5, 1-420. Cited and reprinted by Elizabeth Donnan in Documents Illustrative of the History of the Slave Trade to America, 1441-1700, vol. 1 (New York: Octagon Books, 1969), 282-301.

carried on, extends along the coast above 3,400 miles, from Senegal to Angola, and includes a variety of kingdoms"[70]

It must be granted that a time gap of over twenty years existed between Equiano's capture, enslavement, freedom and the writing of his story. During this time, he had gone through tremendous changes, including sale and re-sale by several masters. He traveled extensively and lived in many countries. He even lost his original African name in the process. Thus doubts have been raised concerning "the accuracy of his memories," but allayed by the fact that "the account he gives of Ibo society is generally very close to modern Ibo life, however, where it differs we might allow for changing conditions as well as inaccurate memories."[71] Apart from the very vivid accounts of his travels and enslavement, Equiano leaves no doubt in the minds of his readers as to the proximity of his home from the Coast. For he recalls originating from a province of the Kingdom of Benin, and that, "the distance of this province from the capital of Benin and the sea coast must be very considerable; for I had never heard of white men or Europeans, nor of the sea."[72] He also remembers after his capture, travelling "sometimes by land, sometimes by water, through different countries and various nations, till, at the end of six or seven months after I had been kidnapped

---

[70]   Olaudah Aquiano's story was published as: "The interesting Narrative of the life of Olaudah Equiano or Gustavus Vassa, the African, Written by himself." In 1789, in London. It has been reprinted and or edited in various forms such as: Paul Edwards, Equiano's Travels: His autobiography, The Interesting Narrative of the Life of Olaudah Equiano or Gustavus Vassa the African (New York: Frederick Praeger, 1966); James Walvin, An African's Life: The Life and Times of Olaudah Equiano, 1745-1797 (New York: Cassell, 1998); G. I. Jones, "Olaudah Equiano of the Niger Ibo," in Africa Remembered: Narratives of West Africans from the Era of the Slave Trade, ed. Philip Curtin (Madison, Wisconsin: The University of Wisconsin Press, 1968), 60.; James Albert Ukawsaw Gronniosaw, Slave Narratives (New York: The Library of America, 2000).

[71]   Ibid., 6.

[72]   Ibid., 70.

I arrived at the sea-coast."[73] Other former slaves like Samuel Adjai Crowther had similar experiences.

The Narrative of Samuel Adjai Crowther has been rightly described as "a preface to one of the greatest success stories of all time."[74] Unlike Equiano, who was enslaved in foreign countries for several years before purchasing his freedom, Crowther was rescued from his slave ship by the British Navy before he was taken to Europe. He was liberated at Freetown, Sierra Leone, on June 17, 1822. Under the guardianship of Church Missionary Society (CMS) missionaries, Crowther soon learned to read and write. He became the first student at Fourah Bay College, the oldest university in Africa, south of the Sahara, and later the first African Bishop of the Anglican Church.

Before his liberation by the British "Man of War," Crowther's story of capture from his Yoruba home town of Osogun, sale and re-sale by several owners and several months of travel before arriving at the port of Lagos, closely parallels that of Equiano's. Like Equiano, Crowther's journey to the Coast took several months and his shock at the first sight of the sea was almost beyond description. Neither had he seen any white man until he arrived at Lagos. While awaiting shipment in Lagos, Crowther narrates his first encounter with white men in the following words:

> One part of the town was occupied by the Portuguese and Spaniards, who had come to buy slaves. Although I was in Lagos more than three months, I never once saw a White man, until one evening, when they took a walk, in company of about six and came to the street of the house in which I was living. Even then I had not the boldness to appear distinctly to look at them, being always suspicious that they had come for me: and my suspicion was not a fanciful one;

---

[73] Ibid., 91. It must be noted that Equiano's reference to "different countries" and "various Nations" can probably be best interpreted as the tribes he encountered on his way to the Coast whose language and manners were unidentical to what he was used to.

[74] Ibid., 289. A more detailed account of Adjai Crowther's life and career can be found in Jesse Page, <u>The Black Bishop: Samuel Adjai Crowther</u> (London, 1910).

for, in a few days after, I was made the eighth in number of the slaves of the Portuguese.[75]

It is clear from this testimony that although the final sale of slaves took place on the coast, slave provenance included anywhere from a few miles off the coast to considerable distances inland. This is not denying the fact that some coastal inhabitants might have been sold as slaves, but that in the main, the coastal tribes only acted as intermediaries in the trade and for the most part desisted from selling their own people into slavery. They would rather wage war on inland tribes and sell the war victims as slaves on the coast. Typical examples are the kingdoms of Dahomey,[76] Ashanti and Oyo. These states grew and became powerful in the western Sudan as a result of the role they played in the Atlantic slave trade as middlemen. Basil Davidson succinctly sums up the situation:

> One may say that the strong peoples of the coast and its immediate hinterland raided or purchased northward, but not very far. They drew their regular supplies from the relatively abundant peoples of the forest belt and to a lesser extent from sparser peoples of the grasslands beyond the forest.[77]

The interesting revelation here is that hardly any West African tribe remained untouched by the Atlantic slave trade. This fact is underscored by early ethnolinguistic inventories of African tribes involved in the trade.

---

[75] Ibid., 310.

[76] See Archibald Dalzel, The History of Dahomey (London: Frank Cass, 1793); Robin Law, "Slave-Raiders and Middlemen, Monopolists and Free-Traders: The Supply of Slaves for the Atlantic Slave Trade in Dahomey c. 1715-1850," Journal of African History 30 (1989): 45-68, and The Oyo Empire c. 1600-1836 (Oxford: Oxford University Press, 1977).

[77] Basil Davidson, The African Slave Trade, 107.

Evidence From Ethnolinguistic Inventories

A nineteenth century ethnolinguistic study among recaptive slaves in Freetown, Sierra Leone, revealed a picture consistent with Davidson's observations. The research was carried out by the Rev. Sigismond Koelle, a Church Missionary Society (CMS) missionary, and published in 1854.[78] Rev. Koelle arrived in Freetown, Sierra Leone, a tiny British colony, in December, 1847. He was assigned to the African Languages Department at Fourah Bay College, then the only institution of higher learning in West Africa. The CMS already had on-going research and study projects of African languages, using Freetown not only as their first missionary base in Africa, but also as their first center for the study of the languages of the entire continent. The goal of the CMS in all of this was the evangelization of Africa, as Koelle himself testifies:

> The Church Missionary Society, who from a praiseworthy compassion for the most degraded portion of our race, made the evangelization of Africa one of their chief objects, have long ago felt the necessity of bringing to light, and making available by grammatical cultivation the languages of that mysterious continent, before they could reasonably expect to Christianize the tribes by which they are spoken. With this view they for many years urged their missionaries in Sierra Leone to study the native languages.[79]

Thus it must be pointed out that although this was not necessarily the original intent of the project, Koelle's research has become one of the most reliable sources for establishing the provenance of the African slaves. His motivation stemmed partly from his realization that despite the death of previous missionaries before him from the deadly malaria fever, "Sierra Leone, where slaves from almost every quarter of Africa have found an asylum of liberty, was too inviting a field to be left any

---

[78] Sigismond W. Koelle, <u>Polyglotta Africana</u>, ed. Paul Hair (London: CMS House, 1854; reprint, Freetown: University of Sierra Leone Press, 1963).

[79] Ibid., 9.

longer unoccupied."[80] Sierra Leone had indeed become such an "asylum of liberty" when the British, in their abolition efforts, decided to make the colony the home of recaptive or rescued slaves from slave ships. This readily made available for Koelle's study, about 160 African languages, gathered in an area of not more than 20 miles in radius.

Hence after near abortive attempts at mastering the individual Kanuri and Vai languages, Koelle devoted his attention to doing simply a linguistic analysis of every African language and tribe represented among the recaptives at that time. Thus his <u>Polyglotta Africana</u>, the first and most comprehensive comparative study of African languages was born.

The <u>Polyglotta Africana</u> contains notes on 210 informants, 179 of whom were ex-slaves and the rest were traders or seafarers who had voluntarily settled in the colony of Freetown. With the exception of two, all the ex-slaves interviewed were male. Koelle used several parameters in his inquiries, such as; the name or names of the informants, their ages and dates of capture, approximate time elapsed since they left their home country and an attempt to locate that country in Africa. The informants were also asked to supply information on the number of speakers of their language, present in Freetown at the time of the experiment. In most cases, Koelle also requested information on the circumstances under which the informants became enslaved.

Some critics of Koelle's work have charged that most of his informants had possibly forgotten their mother-tongue before they were interviewed. In other words, even though analysis of the data on informants show that four-fifths actually experienced slavery for only a short period of time before they were brought to Freetown, the time gap between the date of enslavement and that of the interview exceeded ten years for three-quarters of the ex-slaves and even twenty years for some. In this time lag, critics suggest, the informants might have forgotten their original languages.

Other historians of West Africa see it differently. For example, Paul Hair, a former History lecturer at Fourah Bay College, Freetown,

---

[80] Ibid.

finds Koelle's work to be of "proven dependability…not because Koelle caught his informants raw from their homelands" but for the fact that it shows "the persistence of the mother-tongue in the individual, even in an apparently hostile environment."[81] Another fact Professor Hair finds even more remarkable is "the relation between the collection of these vocabularies and the historical circumstance of the Atlantic slave trade."[82] For Koelle's time of interview was one unique period in history when probably the largest "group of Africans drawn from a wide range of tribes and linguistic divisions, assembled in their first generation in one place. This is doubtless one of the reasons Koelle's collection has remained unique for a century."[83]

It is probably due to its unique nature that so much use has been made of Koelle's information in studies related to slave provenance. Typically, in studies by eminent scholars like Hair and Curtin.[84] Apart from the very useful figures already borrowed from Professor Curtin, his Census (fig. 19) on page 246, uses Koelle's data to plot the origins of ethnic groups in Freetown on a map of Africa. The result is a near-perfect collaboration of previous suggestions that slaves involved in the

---

[81] Ibid., 14-15.

[82] Ibid.

[83] Ibid.

[84] See Philip Curtin, The Atlantic Slave Trade: A Census. In this work, Professor Curtin reproduces a fully analyzed and condensed form of Koelle's data as an appendix to his book under the title: "Koelle's Linguistic Inventory"; Philip Curtin and Jan Vansina, "The Sources of the Nineteenth Century Atlantic Slave Trade," Journal of African History 5, no. 2 (1964): 185-208. In this article, the authors attempted to analyze Koelle's notes on his informants in terms of provenance and presented their results as an indicator of the geographical origins of slaves in the Atlantic Slave Trade; Paul Hair, "The Enslavement of Koelle's Informants," Journal of African History 6, no. 2 (1965): 193-203. Here Hair utilizes notes from Koelle's Polyglotta to analyze the age and marital condition at enslavement, date of enslavement and age at interview, period of enslavement, and the manner of enslavement.; Hair, "Ethnolinguistic Continuity on the Guinea Coast," Journal of African History 8, no. 2 (1967): 247-268; E. M. Chilver and P. M. Kaberry, "Sources of the Nineteenth Century Slave Trade: Two Comments," Journal of African History 6, no. 1 (1965): 117-20.

Atlantic slave trade essentially originated from the forest region of West Africa. See a reproduction of Curtin's map in appendix A.

Hair also utilizes Koelle's data in his article on "Ethnolinguistic Continuities on the Guinean Coast."[85] The usefulness of this article lies in the fact that the author compares ethnolinguistic inventories from several early written sources on the Guinea Coast, including Koelle's inventory, of course, with a modern inventory of his own and finds "a striking continuity." This leads him to the conclusion that, "in the particulars compared", such as, "names of units, the boundaries of units, the language of each unit, the ethnolinguistic units of the Guinea coast have remained very much the same for three, four, five centuries."[86]

It is therefore reasonable to infer from this that other aspects of the Guinea Coast culture, such as the religious practices of the people, remained practically untouched until the arrival of Western Christian missionaries in the late nineteenth and early twentieth centuries. This religious climate of the equatorial forest zone of Africa, including the Guinea Coast, probably offers the most useful clues to the religious baggage African slaves brought to America in the course of the Atlantic trade. We shall look at the slaves' original religious orientations.

The Proto-Religion of African Slaves in North America

The slaves brought from Africa to North America did not exhibit a homogeneous religious culture in their state of captivity. This is an obvious indication that they were from diverse religious backgrounds. This could range from possible Islamic and Christian influences to African Traditional Religion.

---

[85] Ibid.
[86] Paul Hair, "Ethnolinguistic Continuity," 247-68.

Probable Islamic and Christian Influences

Although not in overwhelming numbers, the presence of Muslims had been reported among enslaved Africans in North America.[87] Muslim slaves were made conspicuous by their peculiar attire. Unlike slaves of other religious orientations, Muslims were easily recognizable by the "amulets" and "charms" worn by some. The case for "Christian slaves" coming from anywhere in Africa is not as clear-cut as that for Muslims. It is very possible that some of the slaves had had some contact with Christianity before they were taken from Africa and some could have even been baptized. Several reasons could be cited in support of this proposal.

In the first place, the presence of Christianity in Africa is generally assumed to pre-date the Atlantic slave trade or the nineteenth century Protestant missionary movement that brought Western missions to the continent. It has also been suggested, for example, that the Biblical account of the conversion of the Ethiopian eunuch is one evidence pointing to the fact that Christian presence in Africa "dates from the

---

[87] See Charles Joyner, "Believer I Know: The Emergence of African-American Christianity," in African-American Christianity: Essays in History, ed. Paul E. Johnson (Berkeley: University of California Press, 1994), 19-20. For more evidence in support of Islamic presence among the slaves, please see: Mahdi Adamu, "The Delivery of Slaves from the Central Sudan to the Bight of Benin in the Eighteenth and Nineteenth centuries," in The Uncommon Market, ed. Henry A. Gemery and Jan Hogendron, 163-80; Humphrey John Fisher, "A Muslim William Wilberforce? The Sokoto Jihad as an Anti-slavery Crusade: An Enquiry into Historical Causes," in De la Traite A'L' Esclavage, ed. Serge Daget Actes du Colloque International sur la traite des noirs, Nantes 1985, 2 volumes (Paris: L'Harmattan, 1988), 538-55; J. F. Ade Ajayi, "Samuel Crowther of Oyo," in Africa Remembered, ed. Philip Curtin, 299; Basil Davidson, The African Slave Trade, 8. Both Adamu and Fisher argue that for various reasons, by the second half of the eighteenth century, sale of Muslim slaves from central Sudan had been largely diverted from the northward route across the Sahara southwards to the Atlantic coast.

early decades of the first century."[88] Moreover, after the proclamation of the *Le Code Noire* by Louis XIV of France in the seventeenth and eighteenth centuries, it became mandatory for all slaves intended for the islands of French Americas to be baptized prior to their transportation.[89] Thus the influences of Islam, and probably to a much lesser extent, Christianity, among imported African slaves into the Americas is difficult to dismiss.

But by far, the most pervasive religious beliefs manifested by the slaves consisted of African traditional religion, hereafter referred to as ATR. Consequently, a knowledge of some aspects of ATR holds the key to understanding the crucial dynamics that came into play as the slaves encountered various brands of Christianity during their captivity. As we will demonstrate in subsequent chapters, the African traditional religious background of the slaves had a direct bearing on their rejection or acceptance of Christianity. It is in view of such a salient fact that we shall now devote some space and time to a discussion of African traditional religious backgrounds.

[88] John Parratt, <u>Reinventing Christianity: African Theology Today</u> (Grand Rapids, Michigan: Eerdmans, 1995), 3. See also, Jose B. Chipenda et al., <u>The Church of Africa: Towards a Theology of Reconstruction</u> (Nairobi: African Challenge Book Series no. 2, September 1991). Here, Andre Karamaga argues that "the story of Simon Niger (that is, Black) and that of Lucius of Cyrene (which is today's Tripoli in Libya), who was one of the 'Prophets and Teachers' at Antioch (Acts 13)" and the presence of Libyans and Egyptians among the 3,000 converts on the day of Pentecost, is indicative of early Christian witness in Africa.
Parratt is also in agreement with the tradition that credits St. Mark with the founding of the Church at Alexandria. See Eusebius, <u>Church History</u> 2, no. 16, cited by Parratt. Early Christian presence in the Congo Basin has also been suggested by C. R. beazley, "Prince Henry of Portugal and the African Crusade of the Fifteenth Century," <u>The American Historical Review</u> 16 (October 1910 to July 1911), 16. Also see: Josiah Young III, <u>African Theology: A Critical Analysis and Annotated Bibliography</u>. (Westport, Conn.: Greenwood, 1983), 8; Marie-Louise Martin, <u>Kimbangu, An African Prophet and His Church</u> (Oxford: Oxford University Press, 1975).

[89] Philip Hesse, "Le Code Noire: De L'homme et de L'esclave," in <u>De la Traite a l'Esclavage</u>, ed. Serge Deget, (Nantes: Actes du Colloque International sur la traite des Noires), 186. As a result of this law, it is possible that some slaves could have been baptized before shipment from Africa.

The study will be done in several stages; our first task is to define ATR, then take a look at its essential nature, including some peculiar characteristics, and finally, we will make some comments on its structure.

African Traditional Religion: A Definition

Literature on ATR is scarce. And even in what is available, a precise definition has often proved problematic. The elusive nature of a definition of ATR can be generally traced to two sources: the problem of numbers and the problem of terminology.

The problem of numbers basically deals with the question of whether or not one can speak of ATR in the singular or plural. That is, in view of its huge size and the apparently immense diversity of its peoples and cultures can one speak of a single indigenous religion for the entire African continent? There are no easy answers to this question, which nevertheless, deserves an attempt. Geoffrey Parrinder is one among many scholars who have tried to grapple with this problem. While affirming earlier general descriptions of Africans by colonial administrators as "incurably religious people," Parrinder raises the salient point that "amid the more than 200,000,000 people of Africa, however, there must be great diversity of religion." He then poses the following very provocative questions:

> Can one compare this with Hinduism or Islam? The desert nomad of Somaliland has little in common with the citizen of Dakar who knows no language but French, and the Cow Fulani of Nigeria must have a very different mentality from the miner of the Rand. Lacking a governing organization how can one speak at all usefully of African religion?[90]

To answer Professor Parrinder's questions directly, one has to concede, first of all, that diversity of African cultures and the sheer enormity of the continent are always daunting factors to deal with in the study of any aspect of African life. In many ways ATR is very

---

[90] Parrinder, <u>African Traditional Religion</u>, 10.

different from Hinduism, Islam or even Christianity. The absence of a "governing organization" in ATR, as Parrinder has indicated, could as well be one of those discontinuities. It must, however, be pointed out that such a statement as ATR lacking a governing organization should be taken with a pinch of salt. Viewed through the spectacles of a Western mind-set and by the side of Christianity, ATR is definitely more decentralized than any of the so called World religions, but that does not make it totally devoid of organization.

The point at issue here is that in spite of the apparent diversity in African cultures, "there is much more kinship between the various peoples of Africa than might appear at first sight" and that where variations seem to occur, "the resemblances are far more important than the differences."[91] As Darryl Forde has observed, "There can be no single 'blue-print' that will apply directly to all African cultures" but that "there are, however, recurrent themes and a number of main patterns of activity and interconnexion"[92] [sic] which are useful in understanding African cultures. Even though linguistic and ethnic variations in Africa are easily observable, Parrinder observes, however, that

> in religious beliefs there is great similarity between many parts of the continent that cuts across racial origins perhaps because of contacts over the centuries. Thus a Supreme Being is worshipped both by the Ashanti in the west and the Kikuyu in the East, there are divine kings in Nigeria and Uganda, witches in Dahomey and Botswana[93]

This position is not unique to Parrinder. Dominique Zahan is another scholar who believes that ethnic diversity should not be a problem in the study of African religion. In Zahan's own words,

> The diversity of African ethnic groups should not be an obstacle to such an undertaking since the variation in

---

[91] Ibid., 11.

[92] Daryll Forde, <u>African Worlds: Studies in the Cosmological ideas and Social values of African Peoples</u> (Oxford: Oxford University Press, 1954), xvii.

[93] Parrinder, <u>African Traditional Religion</u>, 11.

religion has less to do with the ideas themselves than with their expression by means of dissimilar elements linked to the occupations and the flora and fauna of the area. As anywhere else, here man partially expresses his ideas in terms of the geographical milieu in which he lives. It is impossible, for example, to prevent oneself from establishing a relationship between the "geometric" cosmogony of the Dogon and their environment overflowing with masses of the most varied shapes.[94]

Zahan's point that ATR is geographically conditioned deserves serious consideration. That, in fact, is why we have variations in religious symbols and officials. In regions of Africa, for example, where there is scarcity of rainfall, the office of "Rain Maker" as a significant religious priest cannot be overestimated. However, when one moves to the equatorial forest zone of West-Central Africa, where the average annual rainfall, accompanied by terrible thunderstorms, sometimes exceeds 300" in some places, the role of a similar priest slightly changes to that of "Thunder and Lightening Quencher." What is noteworthy here is that the general conception of certain religious officials in the community as having power over natural forces is the same everywhere, but their role or names vary according to the geography of the region. Examples can be multiplied in this respect.

In short, it is credible to speak of African traditional religion, in spite of the apparent cultural variations within the continent. As I shall take up in later paragraphs, the prevalence of the concept of a supreme God

---

[94] Dominique Zahan, The Religion, Spirituality and Thought of Traditional Africa (Chicago: University of Chicago Press, 1979). Original Title: Religion Spiritualite et Pensee afraicaines (Paris: Payot, 1970), trans. Kate Ezra Martin and Lawrence M. Martin.

in almost all African religious consciousness is one strong reason we can "speak usefully of African religion" and not religions.[95]

Another problem encountered in the study of ATR is the problem of terminology. That is, the question concerning the most adequate term of description for ATR. This problem partly stems from the fact that most of those who initially studied and wrote on African religious concepts were not theologians. The very first writings on ATR came primarily from anthropologists, sociologist and colonial administrators who, for want of better terms, employed mostly sociological and anthropological categories to describe theological phenomena. These inadequate, or only partially adequate terms created serious misunderstandings of what ATR truly represents. Geoffrey Parrinder puts it very succinctly in his lamentation that,

> It is probably true to say that African religion has been more misunderstood, and has suffered more at the hands of the early writers, than any other part of African life. Unhappily old misconceptions linger with us still.[96]

---

[95] Other helpful discussions relating to a suitable terminology for ATR may be gleaned from: Tite Tienou, "African Traditional Religions," in Evangelical Dictionary of World Missions, ed. Scott Moreau (Grand Rapids, Michigan: Baker Books, 2000), 46-48.; Laura Reillo, "African Religions," in Merian-Webster's Encyclopedia of World Religions (Springfield, Mass.: Merian-Webster, 1999), 17-22.; Emefie Ikenga-Metuh, African Inculturation Theology: Africanizing Christianity (Onitsha: IMICO Books, 1996); Emefie Ikenga-Metuh, Comparative Studies of African Traditional Religions (Ibadan: Claverianum, 1987); Emefie Ikenga-Metuh, God and Man in African Religion (Enugu: Snaap, 1999); Emefie Ikenga-Metuh, The Gods in Retreat: Continuity and Change in African Religion (Enugu: Fourth Dimension, 1986).; Laurenti Magesa, African Religion: The Moral Traditions of Aboundant Life (Maryknoll, N.Y.: Orbis Books, 1997).; Lois Fuller, A Missionary Handbook on African Traditional Religion (Kaduna: Baraka, 1994); O. Imasogie, African Traditional Religion (Ibadan: University Press, 1985).

[96] Parrinder, African Traditional Religion, 13. Some of such early writers cited by Professor Parrinder include; Father Merolla, William Bosman, a Dutch traveler on the Guinea Coast in the early eighteenth century, and Sir Richard Burton, to mention just a few.

What recent scholars like Parrinder, Idowu, Mbiti, Zahan and Edwin Smith, to mention just a representative few, object to in early writings on African religion is that "these earlier descriptions and studies of African religions left us with terms which are inadequate, derogatory and prejudicial."[97] Terms mostly objected to include references to African religion as; primitive, savage, native, tribal, paganism, heathenism, fetishism, juju, animism, ancestor worship, idolatry, magic and superstition.[98] The arguments put forward by those who object to these terms are not in any way suggestive of the fact that all or most of those descriptions are not applicable to certain elements of ATR. The point of contention, however, is that none of those terms by itself adequately does justice to the whole corpus of the religion.

Another point which has drawn objections from some African scholars is the attitude of condescension and racial superiority behind the labels westerners attributed to ATR. That ancient attitude not only aggravated and fueled the commerce in African slaves but also contributed to the partitioning and colonization of the entire continent by various European countries. The mentality that "civilized" Europeans were bringing their civilization to "uncivilized" African "savages;" that "Christian" Europeans were obliged to save Africans from their cultures by Christianizing them through enslavement, was one of the reasons European slave traders felt they could enslave Africans with impunity.

[97] John S. Mbiti <u>African Religions and Philosophy</u> 2d ed. (Portsmouth, N.H.: Heinemann Educational Books, 1964), 7. What Mbiti specifically objects to are tendencies in especially early German writers that African religious experiences were hardly original. The assumption, according to Mbiti, was that "African beliefs, cultural characteristic and even foods were borrowed from the outside world." He also rejects the evolutionary theory of religion which places "African religions at the bottom of the supposed line of religious evolution. Mbiti cites E. E. Evans-Pritchard's <u>Theories of Primitive Religion</u> (Oxford, 1965), E. B. Taylor's <u>Primitive Culture</u> (1871), as further readings in earlier theories.

[98] For a more thorough discussion and refutation of these labels see John S. Mbiti, <u>Introduction to African Religion</u> (London: Heinemann Educational Books, 1975); <u>African Religion and Philosophy</u> (Portsmouth, N.H.: Heinemann Educational Books, 1964); E. Bolaji Idowu, <u>African Traditional Religion: A Definition</u> (Maryknoll, N.Y.: Orbis Books, 1973); Geoffrey Parrinder, <u>African Traditional Religion</u> (Westport, Conn.: Greenwood, 1976).

Such sentiments were still present as late as the final decades of the nineteenth century. To cite an example, The Rev. Father P. Baudin, in his "account of twelve years' experience" on the Guinea coast of Africa candidly states a typical European reaction to some aspects of African culture thus:

> The European on arriving in Guinea encounters at every step in the negro villages idols of wood or clay, as grotesque as they are unclean, rudely made, and daubed with cock's blood and palm-oil by their stupid adorers. One glance suffices to fill the European with contempt for this worship; but when he soon learns that these shapeless divinities thirst for human blood, and that human victims are immolated to appease them, immediately adding indignation to contempt he execrates fetiches and fetich-worshippers, considering them thereafter unworthy of his attention.[99]

Father Baudin cannot be faulted for stating a genuine first impression of a culture radically different from his own. However, what triggers various levels of objections from some African theologians is the air of superiority, embellishments and exaggerations, normally woven into these accounts of African religion.

Having said that, I shall move on to defining ATR and discussing in outline form, its essence and structure. One striking aspect of ATR is the designation "African traditional religion" itself. Why the specificity about "African," and the additional nomenclature of "traditional" religion?

In the first place, the term "African" is most appropriate in the sense that the systems of beliefs so designated are uniquely African. As Professor John Mbiti suggests, "African religion belongs to the people."[100] Mbiti's statement properly interpreted, is that African religion evolves and revolves among Africans. It can only be practiced by Africans and

---

[99] Rev. P. Baudin, <u>Fetichism and Fetich Worshippers</u> (New York: Benziger Brothers, 1885), 5.

[100] John S. Mbiti, <u>Introduction to African Religion</u>, rev. 2d ed. (London: Heinemann Educational Books, 1975), 14.

cannot be propagated among any other group of people. In Mbiti's words:

> Because African religion developed with all other aspects of the heritage, it belongs to each people within which it has evolved. It is not preached from one people to another. Therefore a person must be born in a particular African people in order to be able to follow African religion in that group. It would be meaningless and useless to try and transplant it to an entirely different society outside of Africa, unless African peoples themselves go there with it. Even within Africa itself, religion takes on the different forms according to tribal settings. For that reason, a person from one setting cannot automatically and immediately adjust himself to or adopt the religious life of other African peoples in different settings. The peoples of Europe, America or Asia cannot be converted to African religion as it is so much removed from their geographical and cultural setting.[101]

Some of the interesting implications of Mbiti's succinct observation are that although aspects of African religious practices could be transmitted from one generation of Africans to another, there is an inherent inability of the religion to be propagated outside the African personality. This lack of propagating ability could constitute a weakness or strength.

Mbiti draws our attention to another far-reaching implication of the "African" emphasis in ATR in the following words:

> Since African Religion belongs to the people, when Africans migrate in large numbers from one part of the continent to another, or from Africa to other continents, they take religion with them. They can only know how to live within their religious context. Even if they are converted to another religion like Christianity or Islam, they do not completely abandon their traditional religion immediately; it remains

---

[101] Ibid., 14.

with them for several generations and sometimes centuries. A good example of this is the case of Afro-Americans and Afro-Caribbeans in the Americas and the West Indies.[102]

The validity of Mbiti's statement was demonstrated by the persistence of ATR among the slave population in North America, even after other aspects of the African culture had succumbed to the forces of slavery.

Also, the term "traditional" should be carefully examined. Tradition has been defined as:

> (1). The process of handing down information, opinions, beliefs and customs by word of mouth or example: transmission of knowledge and institutions through successive generations without written instructions. (2). An inherited or established way of thinking, feeling or doing: a cultural feature (as an attitude, belief, custom, institution) preserved or evolved from the past. (a custom rooted in the past). (b). a doctrine or practice or a body of doctrine and practice preserved by oral transmission. (3). Cultural continuity embodied in a massive complex of evolving social attitudes, beliefs, conventions and institutions rooted in the experience of the past and exerting an orienting and normative influence on the present.[103]

Several aspects of this definition apply to African religion. It is considered to be an indigenous and aboriginal religion, consisting of "information, opinions, beliefs and customs" transmitted by "word of mouth or example."

The practices and institutions of African religion have passed through several successive generations without any written instructions. They have been preserved from the past and are deeply rooted in the past. It can rightly be said that ATR is a "cultural continuity embodied in a massive complex of evolving social attitudes, beliefs, conventions and

---

[102] Ibid., 14-15.

[103] Philip Babcock Gove, ed. <u>Webster's Third New International Dictionary</u> (Merriam-Webster: Springfield, Mass., 1993).

institutions rooted in the past and exerting an orienting and normative influence on the present."

For example, the religious institutions of secret initiation rites, found in almost every African culture, use secret signs or languages that have passed through several generations and known only to members. The moral norms upheld by some of those institutions are so old that hardly anyone remembers their origin. But their influences are just as binding today as they were several centuries ago.[104]

Mbiti has suggested a simple but useful framework through which one could view the concept of religion, especially in Africa. In his Introduction to African Religion,[105] he provides a pentagonal model of religion consisting of "Beliefs, Practices (ceremonies and festivals), Religious Objects and places, Values and Morals," and fifthly, "Religious officials or leaders." These five parts must be taken together to constitute a religious phenomenon. Any one part by itself is an inadequate picture of religion, Mbiti stresses. Our discussion of ATR will basically include some of Mbiti's parameters. But first, some general comments about the study of ATR.

It has been stated that enough unifying factors exist in ATR to justify our use of the singular term "African Traditional Religion." However, variations and local adaptations of the same religion are so numerous that no single study can claim to cover every one of them. Hence throughout this study we shall refer to those characteristics which have direct implications for slave Christianization, rather than attempt to discuss every local brand of ATR. Having said that, we shall begin with a broad outline of the essential elements of ATR, followed by a look at its structure.

---

[104] See for example, Kenneth Little's comments on the Institutions of *Poro* and *Humoi* among the Mende of Sierra Leone, African Worlds: Studies in the Cosmological Ideas and Social Values of African Peoples, ed. Daryll Forde (Oxford: Oxford University Press, 1954).

[105] Mbiti, African Traditional Religion, 11-12.

African Traditional Religion: Its Essential Elements

We shall treat these under four main headings: Beliefs, Practice, General characteristics, and finally, Revelation and soteriology in ATR.

Beliefs

At the core of ATR are belief in the Supreme God, belief in intermediaries between God and mankind, including the divinities or nature gods, the ancestors, and belief in spirits. We shall discuss some of these beliefs only as they relate to the slave Christianization process.

Belief in the Supreme God

By far the most widely encountered concept in ATR is the belief in a Supreme God. While this fact is indisputable, some writers, nevertheless, have given much time and space to the discussion of the genesis of this belief.[106] Acknowledging none of the variant theories to be conclusive, Parrinder wisely cautions that more attention be paid to practice than theory. Thus to Parrinder what takes preeminence is "the fact that most African peoples have clear beliefs in a Supreme God, and others while less clear, at least have some spiritual beliefs."[107] In a pivotal work titled <u>Concepts of God in Africa</u>, Mbiti has demonstrated beyond any reasonable doubt, that almost every tribe in Africa has some concept of a Supreme Being.[108] Such a Being is called by various names and myths explaining his origin may differ from tribe to tribe, but the prevalence of the concept is undeniable.

It suffices to mention in passing that the issue of God's revelation is a matter of serious debate among African Theologians. Is the general

---

[106] See Geoffrey Parrinder, <u>African Traditional Religion</u>, 31, for a thorough discussion of the various theories concerning the origins of belief in the supreme God in ATR.

[107] Ibid., 32.

[108] John S. Mbiti, <u>Concepts of God in Africa</u> (New York: Praeger, 1970). A very interesting feature of Mbiti's book is the listing in the appendix, of about 267 names of tribes in African with their corresponding names or concepts of God. Included with these, are interpretations of the names into English.

revelation of God found in ATR sufficient for the salvation of Africans or do they still need a special revelation in Jesus Christ?

This last question should be noted carefully, for it is pivotal to any evangelistic enterprise geared towards Africans. And to a large extent, it was also one of the deciding factors in the evangelization or Christianization of African slaves in America. Hence one of our proposals in this study is that even though most of the African slaves brought into America had some knowledge of God through His general revelation, introducing them to the special revelation of God in Jesus Christ produced the most enduring influence on their lives.

Diedrich Westermann also compares religious views of Africans to what existed in the ancient Roman Empire:

> Namely, the belief in a Supreme being or a personified power who, in a general sense, rules the world, maintains its order, and to whom man owes the essential institutions of his life as well as his cultural achievements, but who is too vaguely conceived, or according to the native creed, too great, and too far removed, to be concerned about the personal fate of the individual.[109]

The accuracy of the writer's basic understanding of the essence of African religious beliefs is beyond dispute, but it is a little far-fetched to think that Africans can conceive God to be so removed that he has no concerns about "the personal fate of the individual." Otherwise, Westermann himself could not have admitted in another part of his book that,

> "He died the death of God" is said of a person whose death cannot be attributed to a known cause. The Duala have a form of conventional greeting: "What is troubling?" to which the reply is "Nyambe," i.e. God. Similarly the Shilluk say: "God is upon me," meaning, "he is suffering". The Safwa in Tanganyika Territory assert that the sun, that is God, brings epidemic diseases. The kuanyama explain the origin

---

[109] Ibid., 65.

of ulcers on the body by saying: *osa Kalunga*, "they came from God". Here the term translated by God really means an oppressive power from which man is not able to rid himself, or simply an inevitable fate.[110]

The concept of God's dealings with man as an inevitable fate is, in fact, so strong among Africans that for the Mende of Sierra Leone, for example, a very common utterance in times of a calamity is: *"hinda gbi lor le Ngewor le,"* meaning, every incidence in life is attributable to "Ngewor"--God. In a sense, whatever befalls you in life, good or bad, is your allotment from God. The implication being that it should be accepted without complaints.

One of the most succinct observations Westermann makes about African religiosity is the fact that there are

> manifold views regarding God, which may exist side by side in one tribe, and are transmitted in a number of proverbial maxims which originally were the result of personal experience and thought.[111]

And that these views are not mere representations of "intellectual knowledge,"

> But also very definitely convey emotion, and the emotional side of the belief is most impressively expressed in short invocations and exclamations, even in prayers and songs, and in proper names given to children. In these sayings the qualities and activities of God are described in vivid and picturesque language, sometimes with a feeling of human attachment and gratitude. God is the one who created and who maintains the world and everything therein.[112]

---

[110] Ibid., 69.
[111] Ibid.
[112] Ibid.

Thankfully, Mbiti has provided a list of such maxims and proverbial sayings as one of the appendices to his book, Introduction to African Religion.[113]

Another indication of the pervasiveness of the concept of god in Africa is its incorporation into the common names of people. For example, typical and common proper names of children among the Ibo of Eastern Nigeria include: *"UcheChukwu,"* meaning, "god's thought," *"IfeanyiChukwu,"* which means, "There is nothing beyond god," and also *Ngozichukwaka*, translated, "god's gift." Note the common suffice *Chukwu* or god, in the names.

The idea of god is also prevalent in the common everyday speech of some African tribes. A typical greeting among the Mende of Sierra Leone is just one example. It always includes the phrase; *gbe vaa bi garhun?* Which means, "What is the state of your strength?" or "how are you?" to which the almost invariable response is: *Kayi ii Ngewor ma!* Meaning; "God cannot be faulted!" or simply put, "I am grateful to God, in spite of how I feel!" The consciousness of a Supreme Being among Africans is also strongly reflected in African creation mythologies.

In his monumental and pioneering work titled "Schopfung und Urzeit des Menchen im Mythus der Afrikanischen Volker," Hermann Baumann discusses creation mythologies among several African tribes and comes to the insightful conclusion that, at the core of African myth is the idea of a "creative force" or principle, mostly identical with the "high-god."[114] It was this creative power that called forth man in creation. Baumann observes, in addition, that such a high-god is not necessarily the object of any religious cult and of no practical significance in religion. There is a general feeling of awe and reverence towards the high-god, but according to Baumann, Africans do not normally love, fear, or serve him. The debate concerning degrees of

---

[113] Mbiti, Introduction to African Religion, appendix C: Nearly two hundred proverbs and sayings have been recorded by Mbiti. It must be noted, however, that while a majority of the sayings have direct bearings on the concept of God, some are merely "wise sayings" accumulated over the years with no reference to God per se.

[114] Ibid.

worship or love Africans attribute to God is worth pursuing on its own merits. But for our purposes, however, it suffices to say that from the foregone discussion, a general idea of a Supreme Being could be safely assumed as part of the religious package African slaves brought into their captivity in America. The next issue I want to consider is the belief in spirits.

Belief in Spirits

Bolaji Idowu captures the concept of spirits in African religion very concisely in the following words:

> Spirits, according to African belief, are ubiquitous; there is no area of the earth, no object or creature, which has not a spirit of its own or which cannot be inhabited by a spirit. Thus, there are spirits of trees, that is, spirits which inhabit trees. These are special trees which are considered sacred by Africans and these are believed to be the residences of spirits.[115]

The tendency to attribute spirits to especially awe-inspiring objects like an exceptionally huge tree, or a large body of water or river, or certain lonesome places, is very common in African communities. Thus a strong belief in spirit possession exists in many African traditional practices. A fuller discussion of pertinent practices in ATR follows.

African Traditional Religion in Practice

Because of its inherent flexibility and decentralized nature, a standard practice in ATR that covers the whole continent may be hard to come by. Local variations, with geographically conditioned modifications, are common in the practice of African religion. Nevertheless, there are certain activities and rituals that tend to be integral parts of the practice of ATR wherever it is encountered. One example is the pivotal role of dance and music in ATR practices everywhere.

---

[115] Idowu, African Traditional Religion, 174.

Initiation rites into secret cults or societies are also wide spread. These are normally part of several rites of passage and mechanisms for the preservation of the moral integrity of the society.

Worship rituals and sacrificial systems may also have local variations, but core practices, such as initiation oaths and blood covenants, or sacrifices seem to be widely practiced.

To cover every facet of African religious practice falls beyond the scope of this present venture. Hence in this section of my dissertation, as in previous ones, we shall only touch on key practices which carry serious implications and direct or indirect effects on the interaction between ATR and Christianity in the experience of African slaves in North America. We shall begin with dance and music.

Dance and Music in African Traditional Religion

The liturgy in ATR tend to be entrenched in music and dance, which constitute vital ingredients, especially in communal worship. Locally made or improvised musical instruments are found in abundance. The drum is the most common. Certain drums and music are considered sacred and used only during appropriate festivals. Some songs with special significance, have been preserved over the centuries. This is especially true in secret society rituals. In most cases, the songs are known and sung only by members of a particular society.

Interestingly, music and dance were among the slaves' African culture and religious heritage that remained untouched by the adversities of slavery. In fact there is ample evidence that music and dance played key roles in the slaves' transition from African traditional beliefs to Christianity. We shall elaborate on this point in another chapter. But for now, let us take a closer look at the place of secret societies in African religious experience.

Secret Societies in African Traditional Religion

Secret societies are prevalent in many parts of Africa, most especially in West African religious practices. The initiation process is probably one of the most significant turning points in the life of a West African youth. Some form of physical mutilation has been associated with the initiation rites. For example, circumcision for boys and clitoridectomy for girls would normally be among some of the common practices. Initiation rites for boys and girls are normally separate, but the same core themes run through the processes.

In addition, characteristic marks associated with each particular society may be cut into the skin. The frequency of initiation varies from place to place, but in most cases it is usually an annual affair.

Secret societies have been known to serve several functions, such as marking rites of passage from adolescence to adulthood, as schools for both religious and general instructions in the ways of a tribe, as custodian of the moral integrity of the people, and a cohesive force binding the tribe together. Through these societies, moral values and other tribal customs are passed from one generation to the other. Secret societies also served as training ground for young warriors in preparation for the frequent tribal wars, which at some point, were fueled and intensified by the demand for captives to be sold as slaves.

Mbiti captures the general essence of an initiation ceremony in the following words:

> It is also very much a community and public affair. Therefore the whole community makes a great occasion out of it. All the necessary preparations are carried out, the boys and girls due for initiation are told in good time, everyone talks about it and waits for it with joy. The actual cutting of the skin is performed by qualified operators, and normally this is done to boys or girls in batches. Female operators do it on girls, and male operators on boys. Some details vary from people to people, such as the age when initiation is done, who carries out the operation, at what time of the year it is best done, where it is carried out, the type of preparation necessary for the boys and girls concerned, and the feasting which follows the great event. In many parts of Africa, the initiated youths are taken into seclusion in the woods for

periods lasting from few days to several months, or even longer in some cases.[116]

One specific example of a typical African secret society will suffice here. The Poro society is one on which a reasonable amount of documentation is available, including the following sketch by Geoffrey Parrinder:

> The noted Poro society of Sierra Leone is a male organization, with a corresponding Sande society for girls. The Poro is highly developed, ostensibly under the control of spirits who are represented by masked figures, behind whom is a staff of hereditary officials. Every male must belong to the Poro, and in his initiation he is equipped for his part in community life. Initiates are said to be swallowed by the Poro spirit when they enter, being separated from their families as by death, and at the end of the training they are "delivered" by the spirit and "born again". This idea of rebirth is characteristic of many of these initiation rites, and is seen also in the training of priests. The youths withdraw from the world, live a communal life, endure hardships, undergo rites which initiate them to adult mysteries, are directed by masked spirits, are given new names, sometimes even learn ritual dialects, and eventually emerge in new clothing and are restored to their families as born again to adult life. The new names and new personalities may be paralleled by the rites of other religions. In some places, particularly East Africa, Christians have experimented with purified forms of initiation ceremonies for their converts. The analogy to baptism and confirmation is too clear to be missed.[117]

---

[116] Mbiti, <u>Introduction to African Traditional Religion</u>, 97.

[117] Geoffrey Parrinder, <u>African Traditional Religion</u>, 96. For a more detailed discussion of Poro and other secret societies among the Mende of Sierra Leone, see Kenneth L. Little, <u>The Mende of Sierra Leone</u> (Routeledge & Kegan Paul, 1951).

The analogies between some of the philosophies of the African secret societies and some Christian rites should be noted carefully, for they constitute some of the continuities between Christianity and the native religions of the slaves that enhanced their conversion. This is an integral part of our thesis. We shall argue this point more thoroughly at appropriate times in our discussion.

Another useful analogy between a Christian doctrine and doctrines of African secret societies include emphasis on blood sacrifice. As Mbiti points out,

> The blood which is shed during the physical operation binds the person to the land and consequently to the departed members of his society. It says that the individual is alive, and that he or she now wishes to be tied to the community and people, among whom he or she has been born as a child. This circumcision blood is like making a covenant, or solemn agreement, between the individual and his people.[118]

In addition to the blood of each individual shed during the process, initiation rites are sealed by animal blood, such as that of a goat or chicken. Every initiate or his family provides a mandatory sacrificial animal. This is ceremoniously and sacrificially slaughtered on behalf of each initiate. The blood is sprinkled on the society's idol or "spirit," with accompanying prayers and invocations to the ancestors for protection and safety of the initiates and the tribal community at large. The flesh of the animal is cooked with ritual herbs and a portion ceremoniously fed to each individual by the Head of the society. As each person partakes of the common meal, an oath of secrecy, promising to keep the rites of the society an everlasting secret, is administered and sworn to.

Sometimes breaking such oaths is at the cost of the individual's life. The ceremony is performed in an atmosphere of great feasting, singing and dancing. The jubilation may go on for several days and nights.

The theme of death and resurrection in African secret societies and the prevalence of blood sacrifice in the same will be argued later as

---

[118] Mbiti, Introduction to African Religion, 98.

one of the continuities between ATR and Christianity which attracted the African slaves to the evangelical revivals. But before that we shall consider some general characteristic of ATR.

General Characteristics of African Traditional Religion

There are certain characteristics found in ATR that set it apart from other religious systems. The value in mentioning them lies in the fact that some of those distinctive traits are determinant factors in the survival or extinction of the African religious system when it encounters other world religions like Christianity. Also, a study of these characteristics could shed some light on the response patterns of African slaves to Christianity in North America.

The first of such distinguishing marks is the pragmatic nature of ATR. Unlike Christianity or Islam which followers can trace their origins to a specific founder, ATR enjoys no such luxury. It seems to have grown out of human necessity through reflections on the environment of its practitioners. As Mbiti suggests,

> Many factors must have played a part in its development. These include the geographical environment - mountains, rivers, deserts and forests - the change of seasons, the powers of Nature (such as earthquakes, thunderstorms and volcanoes), calamities, epidemics, diseases, birth and death, major historical events like wars, locust invasions, famines, migrations and so on. To these must be added man's reflection on the universe, the questions about its origin, the earth and the sky, the problems of evil and suffering, the phenomena of nature, and many others. Religious ideas and practices arose and took shape in the process of man's search for answers to these questions, and as ways of making human life safer and better. They are influenced by human experience and reflection.[119]

---

[119] Mbiti, <u>Introduction to African Religion</u>, 16.

The pragmatic nature of ATR naturally results in its flexibility and simplicity. In other words, although communal or public worship is definitely practiced in ATR, in most cases individuals have the liberty to experiment with various aspects of the religion. For example, certain objects or animals that are sacred to some families may not necessarily carry the same value for the whole community. Many aspects of ATR, like place, time and objects of worship can be adapted to meet individual needs without causing a huge theological controversy.

It should also be mentioned that ATR is an oral religion. Most of what survives today of African religion was transmitted by word of mouth and practice from one generation to the next.

In addition, ATR has no sacred Scripture, written history or some ancient authority to fall back on in times of confusion. There are also no systematized creeds or written dogma. Apparently, every individual practitioner is free to do whatever they prefer, even "changing whatever is necessary in order to suit their circumstances of life."[120]

In one sense, this lack of formal systematization could be due to the absence of major theological controversies in the history of ATR. In another sense, such flexibility and looseness could be a possible reason why African religion tend to be vulnerable when impacted by new religions like Christianity. Again, an elaboration on this crucial point will be done in other sections of this paper. But before leaving this area of our dissertation, we want to discuss briefly the concepts of revelation and soteriology in ATR.

Revelation and Soteriology in African Traditional Religion

Judging from the characteristics outlined above, it is probably safe to suggest that ATR is basically a human invention. It is a religion, no doubt, with elements of a general revelation of God, but ATR lays no claims to any special revelation in Jesus Christ.

This point has generated a lot of heated debate among scholars of African religion. The debate hinges on the question of whether general

---

[120] Ibid.

revelation in ATR is sufficient for the salvation of Africans. That is, in addition to the general revelation of God in ATR, do Africans still need a special revelation in Jesus Christ in order to be saved?[121] The importance of this point will be highlighted again when we discuss the result of the encounter between Christianity and African Religion.

In particular, the Christianization of African slaves in North America affords us a unique opportunity to assess the extent to which Africans could need a special revelation of God in the person of Jesus Christ, even though they might have a general knowledge of God through their native religion. Let us move on to examine other aspects of ATR, such as its structure.

The Structure of African Traditional Religion

Perhaps, the most striking and glaring differences between Christianity and ATR are encountered in their structures. As Dominique Zahan has wisely remarked:

> The entire apparatus which serves as a framework or support for these different forms of religion - places of worship, liturgy, celebrants, offerings and so on - testifies to structures so different that it is impossible for the careful observer to penetrate the profound value of African religion without totally ignoring the fundamental ideas we call "civilized."[122]

While Christianity generally tends towards complexity in organization and worship, ATR takes the opposite route. It is significant

---

[121] Some prominent African theologians like Bolaji Idowu, might argue that God, as revealed in African Traditional Religion, is all Africans need to be saved, see his <u>Oludumare: God in Yoruba Belief</u> (London: Longmans, 1962) On the other hand there are some who contend that in addition to the general revelation of God, Africans still need a special revelation in Jesus Christ for their salvation. I have discussed this issue to a great length in my M.A. thesis, titled "<u>Mahei Ngewor</u>": God in Mende Belief, unpublished (Wheaton Graduate School, Wheaton, Illinois, 1990). Here I tried to argue for the latter position, using the Mende of Sierra Leone as a case study.

[122] Zahan, <u>The Religion, Spirituality and Thought of Traditional Africa</u>, 18.

to remember this, because when we look at the way African slaves were Christianized in North America, it is evident that they were mainly attracted to the brand of Christianity that tended towards simplicity in both structure and worship. A detailed structural analysis of the two religious systems is not our primary goal in this paper. We intend, however, to highlight a few structural distinctions between ATR and Christianity. With that at the back of our minds, it becomes easier to understand why African slaves in North America could respond differently to various versions of Christianity presented to them. Part of our thesis is that the type of Christianity in which the structures had more affinities with structures of ATR is what tended to have more attraction for the Africans.

Let us take for example, the places of worship. The history of Christianity points to communal and corporate worship taking stronger and stronger precedence over individual piety. This naturally led to the erection of great edifices for the purposes of worship. Thus Gothic cathedrals, churches with stained glass windows and shelters of various kinds and shapes, have almost become synonymous with Christianity. "Contrary to this," observes Zahan, "traditional African religion is characterized by an almost complete absence of temples erected for the express purpose of providing shelter for the officiants and faithful."[123] The author suggests several reasons for the "scarcity or absence of cult buildings in Africa."[124] I shall briefly reiterate them here.

Zahan attributes the first reason to the fact that in the past, Africans had contented themselves with building imposing defensive structures rather than edifices for worship. Some of these may be found in the ruins of Zimbabwe, for example. Also, building materials and techniques in tropical Africa could not be easily adapted into producing huge monuments. It has to be noted, however, that this holds true only for the equatorial region of Africa. For the pyramids of Egypt not only served religious purpose for the Egyptians, but were also among some of the greatest architectural marvels of the world.

---

[123] Ibid.

[124] Ibid., 18.

Also, climate and the need for secrecy in some African religious worship partly account for the absence of elaborate edifices of worship in ATR. The intense heat and humidity on the Guinea Coast and the rest of equatorial Africa naturally discourage meetings in enclosed buildings or "congregational religious structures." To preserve the mysteries and secrets of many religious institutions in Africa, very few people are normally permitted into the "holy of holies" during religious gatherings. The rest of the worshippers are generally content to observe from the courtyard or open space by the shrine or temple. This is usually a tiny hut, big enough for only the priest and a few others.

The crucial role of nature in African religion could be another reason why worshippers might prefer open-air congregations to meetings in enclosed buildings. As Zahan succinctly observes: "As regulators of liturgical cycles, the sun, moon, stars, earth, animals, and plants directly influence people in 'prayer'"[125] This explains why "the idea of a temple as a place of worship is foreign to the African "believer," concludes Zahan.

In effect, geography plays a more crucial role in the African's choice of a place of worship than any other factor. This was clearly articulated by Zahan in his statement that as far as Tropical Africa is concerned,

> The specific characteristic of places of worship is in large part determined by the geographical milieu. Thus it is not so much the being to whom the cult is addressed that varies from one people to another, or one region to another, but rather the various "means" of communicating with God and their expression, the latter being necessarily related to the former. So the African, being in almost constant communion with nature, will seek in nature to achieve harmony with the divine; it is there that he will establish his place of worship.[126]

The author classifies African "natural temples" into "Water, earth, air and fire."[127] In many African communities, tremendous use is usually

---

[125] Ibid.
[126] Ibid.
[127] Ibid.

made of "springs, streams, rivers, lakes and ponds" as "aquatic temples"[128] This, in part, is based on the belief that water is the source of all life. It is thus not uncommon in many African societies to consider bodies of water as residences of ancestral and other spirits.[129] For example, among the Mende of Sierra Leone, the banks of rivers are common sites for communal or individual worship. Father P. Baudin also makes reference to similar practices among the Yoruba of Nigeria.[130]

Another prominent place of worship in African religion is that associated with "sacred trees" and groves. Almost every village has its sacred grove, normally inaccessible to non-initiates. Father Baudin describes such a place of worship among the Yoruba communities thus:

> Besides the temples in their beautiful shady squares, the blacks also dedicate to the worship of the false gods charming groves outside the city. Thither they all go in procession and revel in the dance in the open air under the cool shade of magnificent trees, the thick foliage of which shelters them from the burning rays of the tropical sun.[131]

The significance of the sacred grove and other places of worship in ATR will become clearer when we discuss the role of the revival worship atmosphere in the conversion of the slaves. For now we shall briefly discuss the sacrificial systems in ATR.

Sacrifice in African Traditional Religion

Because ATR is basically an oral religion, the importance of speech, oral invocations and formulae in worship can never be overestimated. Offerings and sacrifices, which abound in ATR are often preceded by long oral invocations. As we observed earlier, blood sacrifices are

---

[128] Ibid.
[129] Ibid.
[130] See P. Baudin, <u>Fetichism and Fetich Worshippers</u>, 18.
[131] Baudin, <u>Fetichism and Fetich Worshippers</u>, 83.

common occurrences in African religious systems. Zahan has offered a helpful description of the African sacrificial systems.[132]

Among conclusions that could be drawn from an examination of the African traditional religious system is the incurably religious nature of Africans. Every facet of the lives of individuals and society seem totally preoccupied with one religious significance or the other.

Parrinder underscores this in his book, African Traditional Religion, where he states:

> The belief in, prayers to, names of and myths about God show clearly that nearly all Africans, "untutored" though some may be, do conceive of God.[133]

Thus we can assume that probably every slave brought to North America had some idea of a Supreme Being. The names by which such a God was known to the individuals could have differed according to their tribal affiliations, but the general revelation of God was part of the religious equipment of every slave brought into the American colonies. This brings us back to some of the fundamental questions this book attempts to answer. For example, if the slaves already had some form of religion on arrival in North America, what actually happened to that heritage? What effect, if any, did the proto-religious background of the slaves have on the process of their Christianization?.

---

[132] Ibid., 33.

[133] Parrinder, African Traditional Religion, 42.

CHAPTER 3

THE PROCESS, PERSONNEL, AND PROBLEMS IN SLAVE CHRISTIANIZATION

In many concrete ways the African past and the behavior of Afro-Americans under slavery were linked. The slaves used whatever they brought with them from Africa in their memories, nerve endings, and speech to help them adapt to the new environment and to build for themselves a new life.[134]

In the last chapter, I proposed that the bulk of African slaves transported to North America in the course of the transatlantic slave trade originated from the equatorial forest region of Africa. This region is commonly referred to as the Guinea coast. I also suggested that the predominant religion of this area was ATR, with a wide spread conception of a Supreme Being, among its other characteristics. Hence our conclusion that the African slaves arrived in their new environment with a rich religious culture. Various labels, such as "pagan," "primitive," "fetish," to mention just a handful, have been used to describe the Africans' religion.

---

[134] George P. Rawick, <u>The American Slave: A Composite Autobiography</u> (Westport, Conn.: Greenwood, 1972), 30.

But whatever the designation, scholars generally agree that the knowledge of a Supreme Being formed the core of the religious heritage of the slaves.

Thus one of the basic but key concerns in the study of African-American Christianity has been the fate of the original African culture, most especially the religion of the slaves. This, without doubt, is partially my concern in this chapter. From all indications and for good or bad, the original African religion seems to have been largely replaced by Christianity. How did it happen? What was the relationship between slavery and slave Christianization? Who were the key players in the process and to what degree would their efforts be deemed successful? What, if any, were some of the problems encountered in the process of the slaves becoming Christian?

Answers to these and related questions are crucial to the formulation of an interpretive theory as to why the slaves were apparently more responsive to certain methods of Christianization than others. But before that, the question of the retention or non-retention of the slaves' original culture, including of course, his religion, must be addressed.

The Fate of the African Religious Culture of the Slaves

The issues of retention or non-retention of African traits and the extent of cross-fertilization between African and European cultures in the course of North American slavery have been among some of the most strongly contested areas in the discussion of African-American Christianity.

For example, in The Myth of the Negro Past,[135] which is a product of extensive field studies spanning the slaves' original home of West Africa, Dutch Guiana, Brazil, Haiti and Trinidad, Herskovits argues strongly for the retention of African cultural traits.

For all the regions studied, including North America, the author suggests that the strongest common denominator in terms of retained African culture is in the realm of religion. Religion in African-Americans, like in Africans everywhere, is so deeply rooted that it cannot simply be "explained as compensatory devices to meet the social and economic frustration experienced by the Negroes during slavery and after emancipation."[136] "Religion is vital, meaningful and understandable to the Negro of this country, because as in the West Indies and West Africa, it is not removed from life, but has been deeply integrated into the daily round." Thus, "it must therefore be assumed," he continues, "that not only in particular aspects of Negro religious life. but in the very foundations of Negro religion, the African past plays full part."[137]

In contrast to Herskovits' anthropological approach, Frazier enters the debate from a sociological angle. Thus he makes the bold assertion that

> in studying any phase of the character and the development
> of the social and cultural life of the Negro in the United
> States, one must recognize from the beginning that because
> of the manner in which the Negroes were captured in Africa

---

[135] Melville J. Herskovits, The Myth of the Negro Past (Bacon Hill, Boston: Beacon, 1941). In this highly controversial work, Herskovits attempts to debunk the belief that African-Americans were people without a past except for an ugly, primitive and debased existence in African savagery before their deliverance, which came through enslavement and contact with European civilization in North America. Other related writings of Melville J. Herskovits include: "Social History of the Negro," in A Handbook of Psychology, ed. Carl Murchinson (Worcester, Mass.: Clark University Press, 1935), 207-67. "The significance of West Africa for Negro Research," Journal of Negro History 21, no. 1: 15.

[136] Ibid., 207.

[137] Ibid.

and enslaved, they were practically stripped of their social heritage[138].

Frazier seems to agree with Herskovits, however, that "the area in West Africa from which the slaves were drawn exhibits a high degree of cultural homogeneity.[139] But that notwithstanding, he argues

> the capture of many of the slaves in intertribal wars and their selection for the slave markets tended to reduce to the minimum, the possibility of the retention and the transmission of African culture.[140]

Getting into specifics, Frazier argues that the demands of the slave market, which preferred young and energetic males to females, is one of the contributing factors to the slaves' non-retention of their African culture. "Young males," according to Frazier, being "poor bearers of the cultural heritage of a people."[141] In addition, Frazier contends that the dehumanizing state in which slaves were held in baracoons, under concentration camp-like conditions before shipment, and the rigors of the "middle passage," destroyed their African culture.[142] This dehumanization process, with its subsequent elimination of the African culture, reached its climax on the American plantation.

Only in matters of religious retention does Frazier appear to make some concessions. In his own words:

> There was one element in their African heritage that was able to survive capture in Africa and the "middle passage"- dancing, the most primitive form of religious expression. The slaves were encouraged to dance during the "middle passage" and in the West Indies slaves were forced to dance

---

[138] E. Franklin Frazier, <u>The Negro Church in America</u> (New York: Schocken Books 1974), 9.

[139] Ibid.

[140] Ibid.

[141] Ibid.

[142] Ibid., 10.

as part of the breaking-in process. In the "Shout-songs" on
the Sea Islands off the coast of South Carolina and Georgia,
one may discover remnants of the African religious heritage.
However, no African religious cults became established on
the American soil. The Whites did everything possible to
suppress these "heathenish practices."[143]

There is ample evidence in favor of Frazier's observation that
calculated and concerted efforts were made by some whites to eradicate
all traces of Africanism in the slaves, but whether this succeeded in
preventing the establishment of African religious cults in North America
is still debatable. Significantly, the survival of the dancing instinct as a
form of African religious retention could partly account for the slaves'
attraction to the revival movements. This point will be revisited and
elaborated on later.

Frazier and Herskovits are by no means the only participants in this
debate. Other contributors on either side shall be mentioned briefly.
Jon Butler, for example, takes Frazier's ideas to a much higher degree of
radicalism. Butler proposes that Christianity collaborated with slavery
to produce "the single most important religious transformation to occur
in the American colonies before 1776." And that this transformation was
nothing less than "an African spiritual holocaust that forever destroyed
traditional African religious systems as *systems* in North America and
that left slaves remarkably bereft of traditional collective religious
practice before 1760."[144] "The supreme irony of this holocaust," Butler
continues, "was that it paved the way for the remarkable post-1760 slave
Christianization..."[145] Incidentally, there are other plausible explanations
for the causes of the "remarkable post-1760 slave Christianization,"
other than Butler's African Spiritual holocaust theory. And one of the
goals of this study is to highlight some of those factors that precipitated

---

[143] Ibid. 86-87. The first Chapter of <u>The Negro in the United States</u> (Toronto: Macmillan, 1957), by the same author, contains another clear statement of his views on African cultural retention in America.

[144] Jon Butler, <u>Awash in a Sea of Faith</u> (Cambridge, Mass.: Harvard University Press, 1970), 130.

[145] Ibid.

slave Christianization, probably even before 1760. We shall touch on those factors later.

Robert Park[146] was another early proponent of the non-retention theory of African traits in the slaves. He was probably one of the architects of some of the myths of the Negro past Melville Herskovits tried to debunk later. Not only did Park believe in the insignificance of the "African tradition which the Negro brought to the United States," but went on to state that

> in fact, there is every reason to believe, it seems to me, that the Negro, when he landed in the United States, left behind him almost everything but his dark complexion and his tropical temperament. It is very difficult to find in the South today anything that can be traced directly back to Africa.[147]

As predecessor of Frazier's, Park attributes the causes of the loss of the African culture to the manner of slave capture and shipment of the slaves. And also to the fact that, "coming from all over Africa and having no common language and common tradition, the memories of Africa which they brought with them were soon lost."[148] Of course, Herskovits later argued quite strongly to the contrary.

Robert Park is tentative about the actual conditions under which the slaves were converted, but concedes that the only distinctive institution African-Americans developed in the United States was the church. "It is in connection with his religion that we may expect to find, if anywhere, the indications of a distinctive Afro-American culture."[149] He offers very little explanation for this phenomenon other than stating that in spite of early efforts to introduce the slaves to Christianity,

> it was not until the coming of the new, free and evangelistic types of Christianity, the Baptists and the Methodists, that

---

[146] See his article; "The Conflict and Fusion of Cultures with Special Reference to the Negro," <u>The Journal of Negro History</u> 4, no. 2 (April 1919): 116
[147] Ibid., 116.
[148] Ibid., 117.
[149] Ibid., 118.

the masses of black people, that is, the plantation Negroes, found a form of Christianity that they could make their own.[150]

Like many other scholars of African-American Christianity, Park seems to see some connection between the Great American revivals and the innate religious affinities of the slaves but provides hardly any explanation for his observations.

It is noteworthy that several years before Herskovits' attempt to debunk the myth of the Negro past, W.E.B DuBois had already blazed the trail. DuBois stressed that "each Negro slave brought to America during the four centuries of the African slave trade was taken from definite and long formed habits of social, political and religious life."[151] And that in as much as every other social institution of the African was probably destroyed by slavery, one realm that remained untouched was that of the power of the African priest. This is best expressed in the words of DuBois himself as follows:

> At first sight it would seem that slavery completely destroyed every vestige of spontaneous social movement among the Negroes; the home had deteriorated; political authority and economic initiative was in the hands of the masters, property, as a social institution, did not exist on the plantation, and, indeed, it is usually assumed by historians and sociologists that every vestige of internal development disappeared leaving the slaves no means of expression for their common life, thought and striving. This is not strictly true; the vast power of the Priest in the African State has already been noted; his realm alone - the province of religion and medicine - remained largely unaffected by the plantation system in many important particulars. The Negro Priest, therefore, early became an important figure on the plantation and found his function as the interpreter of the supernatural,

---

[150] Ibid., 119.
[151] W. E. B. DuBois, <u>The Negro Church</u> (Atlanta Ga.: The Atlanta University Press, 1903) 2.

the comforter of the sorrowing, and the one who expressed, rudely, but picturesquely, the longing and disappointment and resentment of a stolen people.[152]

I do not necessarily agree with DuBois' extrapolation that the African-American church is a direct product of this plantation priestly system. The value in his observation, however, lies in the assertion that the religious core of the African slave remained untouched by the tragedy of slavery. And as George Rawick succinctly puts it, "In many ways, the African past and the behavior of African-Americans under slavery were linked."[153] Hence contrary to suggestions that slavery totally destroyed all African traits in the slaves, Rawick believes that "the slaves used what they brought with them from Africa in their memories, nerve endings, and speech to help them adapt to the new environment and to build for themselves a new life.[154] It must be admitted, as Rawick in fact does, that,

> Afro-American societies are not bundles of African traits but products of the interactions of people whose ancestors had come from West Africa and who used African forms in order to create new behaviors that enabled them to survive in the new world.[155]

In our opinion, nowhere else is this statement more relevant in its application than in the process of slave Christianization. It also needs to be stated that perhaps one positive outcome of the heated debate over African retention is a powerful consensus on both sides of the issue that the African religious make-up of the slaves was the most enduring trait under the slave regime. It remained untouched by the brutalities of slavery, probably because it was anchored so deeply in the slaves' "memories, nerve endings and language."

---

[152] Ibid., 5.
[153] George P. Rawick, <u>The American Slave</u>, 30.
[154] Ibid.
[155] Ibid.

Demonstrating how parallel forms and images used in the revival movements ignited these residual religious longings in the slaves, thereby enabling them to embrace Christianity, is one of our tasks in this volume. We shall elaborate on this in due course. In the mean time let us focus our attention on factors that contributed to or inhibited slave Christianization.

Factors Stimulating or Inhibiting
Slave Christianization

It is generally believed that nearly two hundred years elapsed before African Slaves in North America could fully embrace Christianity. Several factors can be cited as stimulants or inhibitors in this process: One of these was early to fairly late tendencies of using Christianization as a rationale for slavery. Humanitarian sentiments were also among some of the stimulants. Political and ecclesiastical expansionist motives, as well as a genuine sense of Christian obligation, were sometimes behind slave Christianization efforts. Planter resistance and resentments to Christianity presented some of the most formidable barriers to the process. Legal and physical impediments also tended to stifle missionary efforts among the slaves. A detailed examination of these and other factors follows.

Christianization as Rationale for Slavery:
Roman Catholic Expansionism

As early as the fifteenth century the expansion of Christendom and the Christianization of Africans had been among the many reasons advanced in favor of their enslavement. A typical example was the efforts of the Roman Catholic Prince Henry of Portugal to extend the influence of Christianity in Northwestern Africa, beginning with his Ceuta expedition of 1415. Prince Henry's African adventures have been characterized by early chroniclers as endeavors "of which the 'heavens felt the glory and earth the benefit.'[156] And some of the benefits from

---

[156] See C. R. Beazley, "Prince Henry of Portugal and the African Crusade," The American Historical Review 16, (October 1910 to July 1911): 13.

his crusades included "Moorish prizes captured by his ships at various times..."[157] Understandably, as the material benefits increased, so did the crusading spirit. From Beazley's observation,

> Prince Henry appeals directly to the whole body of Christian sovereigns for aid in this "discovery and conquest."[158]

By Beazley's account, Prince Henry apparently did not receive much help from other political leaders but Papal endorsements were easily obtained for his exploits. Thus "in 1452," for example, "Pope Nicholas V., by the bull *Dum diversas* authorizes the King of Portugal to make war upon the infidels, to conquer their lands, and enslave their persons."[159] As a result, Lancarote de Freitas, one of the leaders of Prince Henry's many forays on the West African coast, led a band of Portuguese sailors in their first raid on unsuspecting Africans, capturing as many as 235.[160] And the exploiters "were all very joyful, praising loudly the Lord God for that he had deigned to give such help to such a handful of his Christian people."[161]

Once in Europe the African captives were shared among their captors in a heart-wrenching process, which, according to eyewitness accounts of the Royal Chronicler Gomes Azurara, could move many to tears. He expresses his feelings in the following very vivid narrative:

> But what heart could be so hard as not to be pierced with piteous feeling to see that company? And though we could not understand the words of their language, the sound of it right well accorded with the measure of their sadness. But to increase their sufferings still more, there now arrived

---

[157] Ibid.

[158] Ibid.

[159] Ibid.

[160] See Gomes Eannes de Azurara, "The Discovery and Conquest of Guinea," in <u>Documents Illustrative of the History of the Slave Trade in America</u> by Elizabeth Donnan (New York: Octagon Books, 1969) Donnan describes Azurara as the royal librarian, chronicler and keeper of the archives of Portugal.

[161] Ibid., 26-27.

those who had charge of the divisions of the captives, and who began to separate one from another, in order to make an equal partition of the fifths; and then it was needful to part Fathers from sons, husbands from wives, brothers from brothers. No respect was shewn [Sic.] either to friends or relations, but each fell where his lot took him. . . . And who could finish that partition without very great toil?[162]

Notwithstanding his deep sorrow and contrition over the condition of the Africans, the Chronicler still believed that as long as they eventually received baptism

their lot was now quite contrary of what it had been since before they had lived in perdition of soul and body; of their souls, in that they were yet pagans, without the clearness and the light of the Holy Faith,.[163]

Further more, if their conditions became so unbearable that some "were not able to endure it and died" they were still better off, for they would die "as Christians,"[164] concludes Azurara.

Nearly two Centuries later, similar sentiments were expressed by the slave trader, John Barbot. Barbot was apparently disturbed by the fact that slaves were "severely and barbarously treated by their [African], italics mine, masters, who subsist them poorly, and beat them inhumanly, as may be seen by the scabs and wounds on the bodies of many of them ..."[165] Thus enslavement in America was to the advantage of the Africans, argues Barbot, because

this barbarous usage of those unfortunate wretches, make it appear that the fate of such as are bought, and transported

---

162 Ibid., 28
163 Ibid.
164 Ibid.
165 John Barbot, "Description of Guinea," in <u>Documents Illustrative of the History of the Slave Trade in America</u>, Vol. 2, ed. Elizabeth Donnan (New York: Octagon 1969), 288.

from the coast to America, or other parts of the world,
by Europeans, is less deplorable, than that of those who
end their days in their native country; for aboard ships all
possible care is taken to preserve and subsist them for the
interest of the owner, and when sold in America, the same
motive ought to prevail with their masters to use them well,
that they may live longer, and do them more service. Not
to mention the inestimable advantage they may reap, of
becoming Christians and saving their souls, if they make a
true use of their condition.[166]

Interestingly, arguments advanced by some pro-slavery writers, even
as late as the mid-nineteenth century were no different. One example,
is the 1853 publication by Robert Collins, Essay on the Treatment and
Management of Slaves, which was quoted earlier.

No doubt, these sentiments were part of the entire baggage of
pro-slavery apologetics, perpetuated especially by slave traders. What
makes such statements instructive, nevertheless, is the early connections
established between Christianity, the transatlantic slave trade, and the
future of the slaves.

As far as the Africans becoming Christians as a result of their
enslavement, evidence suggests that it took nearly two centuries of
various Christianization attempts before any substantial number of the
Africans finally embraced the faith of their masters. Why it took so long
for the slaves to accept Christianity in any appreciable numbers, in spite
of serious efforts by various denominations, and individual Christians
will become clearer in the course of our discussion. But first, we shall
examine some other factors related to the slave Christianization process.

Christianization as Part of Western Colonial Expansion Strategy

Very early in their scramble for overseas colonies, many European
nations like England, France, Spain, Portugal, and the Netherlands,
appended a missionary motive to their acquisition efforts. In particular,

---

[166] Ibid. 288.

policies towards the New World, frequently included an agenda for the Christianization of the Indians as well as African slaves. For example, Royal instructions given to the Council for Foreign Plantations in December of 1660 contained the following distinct lines:

> And you are to consider how such of the Natives or such as are purchased by you from other parts to be servants or slaves may be best invited to the Christian faith and be made capable of being baptized thereunto, it being to the honor of our Crowne [sic.] and of the Protestant religion that all persons in any of our Dominion should be taught the knowledge of God, and be made acquainted with the misteries [sic.] of salvation.[167]

Some Colonial governors as well, received similar prompting from the King to "use their efforts to have slaves Christianized."[168] Specifically, Governor Culpepper of Virginia (1682), and Governor Dougan of New York (1686), were among the recipients of such instructions. Consequently, "some of the Governors urged the assemblies to pass bills for this purpose, and used their efforts to promote conversion in other ways."[169] According to Marcus W. Jernegan, some bills even discouraged masters from assigning work to their slaves on Sundays or preventing them from Sunday Church Services.[170]

Back in England strong sentiments were expressed by His Majesty's Attorney and Solicitor General that failure of the British settlers to Christianize the slaves was giving opportunities to other nations to step into the vacuum, thereby obtaining an edge over Britain in the race for territorial expansion, and also hindering the Protestant cause. In a letter circulated in all the plantations, the Attorney General wrote:

---

[167] From Documents relating to the Colonial History of New York, 36, cited by Marcus W. Jernegan, "Slavery and Conversion in the American Colonies," American Historical Review 21, no. 3 (April 1916): 504-27.
[168] Jernegan, "Slavery and Conversion," 508.
[169] Ibid. Cited by Jernegan.
[170] Ibid., 509.

> It must be owned our reformed planters with respect to the
> natives and the slaves, might learn from the Church of Rome
> how it is their interest and duty to behave. Both French and
> Spaniards, take care to instruct both them and their Negroes
> in the popish religion, to the reproach of those who profess
> a better.[171]

Apart from political motivations, there were those who were genuinely moved by humanitarian concerns to Christianize the Africans.

Christianization as By-Product
of Humanitarian Concerns

The French Code Noir or Black Code, proclaimed by Louis XIV in 1685, "stated clearly that all slaves who were transported to the French American Colonies should first be baptized."[172] Though political in essence, this law had very strong religious and humanitarian undercurrents. For example, 1685 being the year of the revocation of the edict of Nantes, the law laid special emphasis on baptism in the Roman Catholic tradition.

Also, while some used the law as a balm to soothe their seared political consciences, the Church saw it in a more humanitarian light. Pro-slavery advocates, for example, saw themselves vindicated by the Code Noir, arguing that in as much as baptism gave the pagan Africans, "doomed to eternal hell,...the chance to go to Paradise, they were therefore the greatest beneficiaries of the operation."[173] The Church, on the other hand, saw the law as an affirmation of the humanity of the slave. The French Roman Catholic Church had always insisted on the humanity of the slave with full canonical rights. Thus the Church argued that the possibility of baptism also created for the slaves, the possibility to be married voluntarily and be buried in holy ground. In

---

[171] Ibid.

[172] Philippe Hesse, "Le Code Noir: De L'homme et de L'esclave," in <u>De la Traite' 'a L'esclavage</u>, Tome II: XVIII - XIX siecles, ed. Serge Daget (Paris: L'Harmattan, 1988), 185.

[173] Ibid., 186.

other words, from the standpoint of the Church, "Baptism meant the slave was a man because the sacrament of baptism can never be given to an animal or a thing, it is the quality of humans."[174]

Also, from a sociological point of view, the Black Code clarified, once and for all, a serious ambiguity in the seventeenth and eighteenth century French judiciary system. According to the French legal statutes, it was perceived that there were two aspects to the slave: "he is certainly human in certain cases, but he is sometimes a thing in a judicial sense, placed outside of all the rights of a personality."[175] With the proclamation of the Code Noir, the ambiguity was erased and the slaves' humanity affirmed.

Ripples of this proclamation reached far beyond France. In his Historical Dictionary of Sierra Leone,[176] for example, the West African historian Cyril Patrick Foray, alludes to the fact that at some point in the seventeenth century, it was mandatory to baptize all slaves bought from Sierra Leone before taking them to Europe. Although not specifically mentioned in his book, Foray was more than likely, referring to the practical implementations of the Code Noir.

The case of the French Black Code seems to have been an isolated one in which a Royal decree mandated slave baptisms. In the British situation, royal families offered their support and encouragement but did not make slave Christianization a requirement for their subjects. For the most part, British efforts were spearheaded by individual Christians, Churches, and para-church organizations, out of a genuine sense of Christian obligation. Here we shall focus on slave Christianization attempts by the Church of England and other denominations in more detail.

---

[174] Ibid.

[175] Ibid.

[176] Cyril Patrick Foray, Historical Dictionary of Sierra Leone (Metuchen, N.J.: Scarecrow, 1977).

Christianization from a Sense of Christian Obligation

Of all the churches and agencies that took active interest in slave Christianization, the Church of England tops the list. Through pastoral letters from English bishops, efforts of individual clergy and church-based organizations, the Anglicans took an early lead in attempts to Christianize African slaves in North America. It has to be noted, however, that slave Christianization was more or less incidental to the general concern that existed in the English Mother-church over the moral decadence and spiritual decay among her sons in the New World.

There are credible indications that by mid-seventeenth to early eighteenth century, many in England became concerned not only about the colonists' negligence of their own spiritual condition but also about their callousness to the spiritual welfare of their slaves.

Thus some of the earliest documents advocating the need for slave Christianization date back to the mid-seventeenth century. A chapter in Richard Baxter's Christian Directory, published in 1673, contained "Directions to those Masters in Foreign Plantations who have Negroes and other slaves; being a solution of several cases about them."[177] This was probably one of the most logical and thoroughly Christian-based arguments in favor of slave Christianization. Baxter emphasized that Christian profession and the equality of all men before God obligated masters to share their faith with their slaves.

In 1680, Morgan Godwyn, a caustic critic of the moral laxity of the colonies and an avid advocate of slave Christianization wrote The Negro's & Indians' Advocate.[178]

Godwyn wrote with two crucial goals in mind: to "tender to the public this plea for both the Christianizing of our Negro's and other Heathen in those Plantations, and for settling (or rather reviving) of

---

[177] Cited by Charles C. Jones, The Religious Instruction of the Negroes in the United States, 6-7. In a series of directions, Baxter presents very convincing reasons why Masters needed to introduce their slaves to Christianity. The text of the directions is reproduced in Jones.

[178] Morgan Godwyn, The Negro's & Indians' Advocate, Suing for their admission into the Church: or A Persuasive to the Instructing and baptizing of the Negro's and Indians in our Plantations (London: Printed for the Author by J. D., 1860).

Religion amongst our own people there."[179] One of the Chief concerns of the writer was that the gospel had "become stale News" to the Planters, "and those glad Tidings sounding but as some Anile Fable or Dream." Thus "the necessity of this needless and troublesome charge about Religion" could not thrive among such people, "who for the most part know no other God but Money, nor Religion but Profit."[180] Godwyn seemed to be even more perturbed by the fact that while

> the most opposite Parties do compass Sea and land to make Proselytes, we only are charged with Neglect; I shall not add the opposing of it; that being the crime of such degenerated English, who with that air, have imbibed the Barbarity and Heathenism of the Countries they live in: And with whom through the want of Discipline, Christianity doth seem to be wholly lost, and nothing but Infidelity to have come in its place.[181]

It is noteworthy that although Godwyn wrote with mainly plantation owners of Southern states in mind, even Northern Puritan states, like New England seemed to have done no better in the treatment of their slaves. Thus in his early eighteenth century publication, <u>Magnalia</u>

---

[179] Ibid. See Godwyn's preface.

[180] Ibid.

[181] Ibid. In the rest of the book Morgan Godwyn starts with an identification of three basic oppositions to slave Christianization, such as the difficulty and trouble involved, the fact that it was looked upon as an unnecessary "favouring of *Popish Supererrogation*," and that it was destructive to the interest of the Planters or even life threatening. He counters these with the following three general affirmations:

1. "That the Negro's (both slaves and others) have naturally an equal right with other men to the exercise and Privileges of Religion; of which 'tis most unjust any part to deprive them.

2. "that the profession of Christianity absolutely obliging to the promotion of it, no Difficulties nor Inconveniences, how great so ever, can excuse the Neglect, much less the hindering or opposing of it, which is in effect no better than a renunciation of that profession.

3. "that the Inconveniences here pretended for this Neglect, being examined, will be found nothing such, but rather contrary."

<u>Christi Americana or The Ecclesiastical History of New England</u>, Cotton Mather describes John Eliot's reaction to planter treatment of their slaves as a lamentation,

> with a bleeding and burning passion, that the English used their *negroes* but as their *horses* or their *oxen*, and that so little care was taken about their immortal souls; he looked upon it as a prodigy that any wearing the *name of Christians*, should so much have *the heart of devils* in them, as to prevent and hinder the instruction of the poor blackmores, and confine the souls of their miserable slaves to a destroying ignorance, meerly [sic.] for the fear of thereby losing the benefit of their vassalage.[182]

Mather not only urged fellow New-Englanders to prosecute, "first the *civilizing*, and then the *Christianizing* of the barbarians in their neighborhood,"[183] but also prayed that

> the several plantations, that live on the labours of their negroes, no more be guilty of such prodigious wickedness as to deride, neglect, and oppose all due means of bringing their poor negroes unto our Lord; but may the *masters* (of whom God will one day require the souls of the slaves committed unto them) see to it that, like Abraham, they have "catechised servants;" and not imagine that the Almighty God made so many thousands of reasonable creatures for nothing, but only to serve the lusts of Epicures, or the gains of Mammonists; lest the God of Heaven, out of meer [sic.] *pity*, if not *justice*, unto these unhappy blacks, be provoked unto a vengeance which may not without horrour [sic.] be thought upon.[184]

---

[182] Cotton Mather, <u>Magnalia Christi Americana or The Ecclesiastical History of New-England</u>, first published in 1702, and reproduced from the 1852 edition and published by (New York: Russel & Russel, 1967), 576.

[183] Ibid., 581.

[184] Ibid.

Perhaps in answer to the prayers of men like Cotton Mather, David Humphreys reports that,

> In this dark state of things, the providence of God raised up several eminent persons, who observing this great calamity, became zealous to redress it; strove to awaken the people into a sense of their wants, and contributed their assistance towards recovering their country-men from this irreligion and darkness.[185]

Consequently, a deep sense of missionary awareness was kindled in England "out of which arose what may be called the *Religious Society* movement of the seventeenth century."[186] This movement was characterized by both individual and corporate zeal for foreign missions, leading to the formation of numerous societies for that purpose.

In 1685, for example, Sir Leolyne Jenkins made provision in his will for two fellowships at Jesus College, in Oxford. The fellowships covered the cost of training for those willing to obey the call of the Lord Bishop of London "to go into any of his majesty's foreign plantations, there to take upon them the cure of souls."[187] Before this, King Charles II had appointed the Honorable Robert Boyle first Governor of the company For the propagation of the Gospel amongst the heathen natives of New England, and the parts adjacent.

The King incorporated the company in 1661, but due to its confinement to only New England and its immediate environs, the venture was hardly capable of addressing the vast needs of all the colonies. In spite of its limitations, however, the company in part, created the incentive for the formation of the Society for the Propagation of the Gospel in Foreign Parts, herein referred to as SPG, some years later.

As a demonstration of his commitment to this venture, the Honorable Boyle, "did by codicil to his last Will," not only "settle an

---

[185] Ibid., 4.

[186] C. F. Pascoe, <u>Two Hundred Years of the S.P.G.: An Historical Account of the Society for the Propagation of the Gospel in foreign Parts</u>, 1701-1900 (London: The Society's office, 1901), Microfilm: BR 515, R43, 1976 Reel 33.

[187] Ibid., 5.

Annual salary, for some learned Divine or preaching Minister for ever, to preach Eight sermons in the year, for proving Christian religion against notorious infidels," but also required such preachers to assist "all Companies, and encourage them in any undertaking for propagating the Christian Religion in Foreign parts"[188]

Also, in 1679, the Bishop of London, Dr. Compton secured approval from King Charles II to build a Church in Boston "for the exercise of religion according to the church of England."[189] This came about as a result of several petitions by the inhabitants of that town. The petitions also acted as a stimulus to Dr. Compton's launching a general enquiry into the state of religion on the plantations and how ministers were provided for the colonies. To his dismay, the Bishop found, "upon search there were not above four Ministers of the Church of England in that vast Tract of North America, and only one or two of them regularly sent over."[190] To remedy the situation, he appointed Ecclesiastical Commissaries to the Colonies: the Rev. James Blair for the colony of Virginia in 1689 and the Rev. Thomas Bray for Maryland in 1696.

From his experiences in the American colonies, the Rev. Thomas Bray became instrumental in securing a royal charter for the establishment of the single most important Christian agency in the Christianization efforts of slaves in America: the Society for the Propagation of the Gospel in Foreign Parts. (SPG).

Preceded by Dr. Bray's Society for the Promotion of Christian Knowledge, herein referred to as SPCK, and as a brainchild of the Anglican Church, the SPG was founded in 1701.[191] Although the

---

[188] Ibid., 6.

[189] Ibid., 7.

[190] Humphreys, An Historical Account, 8.

[191] The Earliest and most comprehensive account of the Society is found in David Humphreys, An Historical Account. Other helpful studies on the same topic can be found in: C. F. Pascoe, Two Hundred Years of the S.P.G., Marcus W. Jernegan, "Religious Instruction;" Charles C. Jones, Religious Instructions. Also see Faith Vibert, "The Society for the Propagation of the Gospel in Foreign Parts: Its work for the Negroes in North America Before 1783." Both Humphreys and Pascoe were secretaries to the society at respective times.

society came into existence primarily to meet the sacramental needs of English settlers in North America and to combat the spread of atheism, indifference and dissent to the Anglican establishment, its attention soon became largely occupied by the Christianization of African slaves in the colonies. This change of focus resulted from reports filed by the Society's missionaries like James Blair, Elias Naeu and Thomas Bray, concerning the plight of the Africans and Indians in the North American colonies.

As one of its strategies, the society felt that "the most effectual way to convert the Negroes, was by engaging their masters, to countenance and promote their conversion."[192] At this stage, prominent ecclesiastical authorities in England also became involved in bringing slave Christianization to the front burner of Anglican concerns.

A typical example was Bishop Fleetwood. He preached a sermon before the society in 1711, in which the Bishop clearly outlined "the duty of instructing the Negroes in the Christian religion."[193] The Bishop of London also became a strong advocate of slave Christianization. In 1727 the Bishop wrote three pastoral letters, one of which was addressed to "Masters and Mistresses of families in the English plantations abroad, exhorting them to encourage and promote the instruction of their Negroes in the Christian faith."[194] The Society hoped that such an authoritative letter "from the See of London, would have the strongest influence." Hence "they printed ten Thousand copies of the letter to the Masters and Mistresses."[195] Thus to a large extent, Anglican participation in slave Christianization was carried out through the SPG.

The methodology employed to Christianize the slaves included instructions by catechists and school masters. Sermons, catechisms, and pamphlets were also used to reach the slaves. With the help of another group called, Associates of Dr. Bray, schools were established for slaves at New York, Philadelphia, New Port, Rhode Island, and

---

[192] David Humphreys, <u>An Historical Account</u>, 248.
[193] Ibid.
[194] Ibid.
[195] Copies of the letters are printed in David Humphreys, <u>An Historical Account</u>, 249.

Williamsburg. In some instances, itinerant catechists were also used to bring the Christian knowledge to the slaves.

In addition, there was a general expectation among sponsors of the Society that masters and mistresses of the slaves would take active interests in their Christianization. This did not prove as easy as hoped for. Since some slave owners were hardly committed Christians themselves, it was difficult for them to take any active interest in the Christianization of their slaves. Moreover, the fears that Christianization could change the status of the slaves prevented many masters from doing or even allowing it.

Another hindrance to slave Christianization was the fact that while parishioners saw it as the job of the preacher, the already over-committed clergyman expected the planters to be the ones instructing their slaves.

The individual strategies of Anglican missionaries varied slightly but the general philosophy and approach was the same. Dr. Le Jeau, for example, carried out his instruction mainly in his home, after divine service on Sundays. The Collect was recited first, then the slaves were taught the Lord's prayer, the creed and commandments. This was followed by explanations of the catechism and the slaves were encouraged to ask questions. Dr. Le Jeau's meetings usually lasted for about thirty minutes.[196]

Elias Naeu, on the other hand, moved from house to house, encouraging and persuading the masters to send their slaves for instruction three times a week: Mondays, Wednesdays and Fridays. He started with memorization of the Lord's prayer in English, gradually leading to the Creeds. After the Creeds, the catechism was memorized. With time the slaves learned some Bible stories by rote and could repeat them verbally.[197]

---

[196] Faith Vibert, "The Society for the Propagation of the Gospel in Foreign Parts: Its Work for the Negroes in North America Before 1783," Journal of Negro History 18, no. 2. (April 1933): 174. Also see: David Humphreys, An Historical Account of the Incorporated Society for the Propagation of the Gospel in Foreign Parts (London: Joseph Downing, 1728), 82-83.

[197] Ibid. David Humphreys, An Historical Account, 236-39. Also see Faith Vibert, "The Society for the Propagation of the Gospel in Foreign Parts," 173-76.

The lay catechist, Joseph Ottolenghe, started with prayers which he usually composed himself. After instructions in Reading, the slaves would be asked to repeat the Lord's prayer, the Creed and Catechism. This would be followed by explanations from the Catechist. The meetings usually ended with discussions on the being of God, the life and death of Jesus.[198]

Generally, Anglican, and to some extent Presbyterian methods of slave Christianization involved what Carter Woodson has succinctly termed "Religion with Letters."[199] The essence of this scheme was the hard-and-fast connection between slave literacy and Christianization.

As a working philosophy of the SPG and Anglican missionaries in general, baptism must be preceded by careful instruction. The missionaries saw it as their first duty "to educate these crude elements to enable them not only to read the truth for themselves, but also to appreciate the supremacy of the Christian religion."[200] In many cases, baptism was postponed for as long as two years until there was "a good testimony and proof" of the slaves' "life and conversation"[201] before they were baptized. One of the positive sides to such an approach was that the missionaries' reluctance to separate Christianization from literacy led to the establishment of schools for the slaves. On the other hand, the long and tedious processes of instruction proved to be counter-productive, as far as genuine conversions were concerned. In fact, the religious instructions seemed to be more of preparatory rituals for baptism than a means to real Christian conversions. For as long as a slave could memorize and recite the Creeds, the Lord's Prayer and Catechism, he

---

[198] Detailed discussions of slave Christianization methods can be found in Carter G. Woodson, The History of the Negro Church (Washington D.C.: The Associated Publishers, 1945); Carter G. Woodson, The Education of the Negro Prior to 1861 (New York: Arno Press and the New York Times, 1968); Luther P. Jackson, "The Religious Instruction of the Negroes;" Marcus Jarnegan, "Slavery and Conversion." Also see John C. Van Horne, Religious Philanthropy and Colonial Slavery (Urbana and Chicago: University of Illinois Press, 1985), 104-106.

[199] Carter Woodson, The Education of the Negro, 18.

[200] Ibid., 18.

[201] From the testimony of a missionary called Le Jeau, cited by Raboteau, Slave Religion, 115.

or she was pronounced fit for baptism. Thereafter the slave was assumed Christianized.

It should be noted at this point that beside the Anglican agenda, and to varying degrees, other denominations were also interested in the spiritual lives of the slaves.

The Quakers or Friends are one of the first of such groups that easily come to mind. Not only are the Quakers on record as the first among the denominations "for registering in 1688 the first protest against slavery in Protestant America," but by 1679 George Fox was already speaking out and "boldly entreating his sect to instruct and teach their Indians and Negroes."[202]

George Keith and William Penn were other prominent Quaker leaders who "protested against the slave trade" and also denounced "the policy of neglecting their moral and spiritual welfare."[203] It must be pointed out, however, that while the Quakers officially showed "strong interests in the religious welfare of the slaves, in practice many Quakers held slaves."[204] Even in religious instruction, some Quakers in Delaware are reported to have taken the position of leaving their slaves to "the natural light."[205] Also, due to their intense persecution by other denominations, Quaker influence in religious instruction of the slaves was severely limited.

Unlike the Quakers, the Puritans and Congregationalists do not have early impressive records in terms of an attack on the institution of slavery. This could be explained by the comparatively smaller numbers of slaves they held, and also by the lack of general assemblies or representative bodies to articulate their views. "New England divines," however, are said to have been "among the first to devote attention to the mental, moral and spiritual development of the Negroes"[206] The efforts of John Eliot and Cotton Mather mentioned earlier, are typical examples.

---

[202] Carter Woodson, The Education of the Negro, 44.
[203] Ibid.
[204] Marcus Jarnegan, "Slavery and Conversion," 512.
[205] Ibid., 513.
[206] Carter Woodson, Education of the Negro, 38.

The Presbyterians were officially silent on the rights of members to hold slaves and did nothing concrete towards the "emancipation or conversion of slaves before 1774."[207] Their interest in slave Christianization was aroused by the Great Awakenings.

The Methodists were hardly involved in slave Christianization "prior to the middle of the eighteenth century."[208] While individual clergymen like Freeborn Garrettson are on record as being against slavery,[209] an official record of action opposing slavery before mid 1700s is hard to come by. George Whitefield has been "regarded by the Negro race as its enemy for having favored the introduction of slavery."[210] Woodson believes, however, that in spite of the fact that "he advocated the importation of slaves into Georgia," Whitefield was "primarily interested in the conversion of the colored people."[211] On the whole, it is in place to suggest that Wesleyan Methodists did not take serious interest in the slaves until after the Great Awakening.

The Baptist population in the South was very small prior to 1774. Those among them who held slaves by that time were even fewer, compared to other denominations.[212] Marcus Jernegan suggests that between 1758 and 1759 a Baptist Church in Virginia probably had black members,[213] but there is no indication of any active interest of Baptists in the religious instruction of the slaves prior to the evangelical revivals.

By 1738 Lutheran Settlers in Georgia tended to oppose slavery, but due to the need for slave labor, "their Pastor Boltzius, yielded on the ground that the Negro might be given moral and spiritual

---

[207] Marcus Jernegan, "Slavery and Conversion," 514. It is suggested in this article that Presbyterian interest in slave Christianization was aroused by the Great Awakenings.
[208] Woodson, Education of the Negro, 48.
[209] Jernegan, "Slavery and Conversion," 514.
[210] Woodson, The Education of the Negro, 49.
[211] Ibid.
[212] Marcus Jernegan, "Slavery and Conversion," 515.
[213] Ibid.

advantages."[214] Records are mute on active Lutheran participation in slave Christianization.

It is clearly observable by now that prior to the mid-eighteenth century, many denominations, led by the Anglican establishment, invested tremendous efforts in slave Christianization. And thus far our discussion has revolved around factors that tended to stimulate that process. The other side to the story, however, is that in equal proportions to the stimulants, there were also many inhibitory problems in the process of the slaves becoming Christian. We shall outline some of those obstacles to slave Christianization in the following paragraphs.

Obstacles to Slave Christianization

As Raboteau has noted, "despite the widely held justification of slavery as a means of spreading the gospel,"[215] and despite ecclesiastical and royal proclamations urging Christians among the settlers to Christianize the heathen, the process of bringing the Christian message to the slaves was embroiled with many obstacles.

The first of these problems was planter opposition to slave Christianization. There was probably a handful of benevolent masters who included their house slaves in family devotions and some who took their slaves to Church, but those instances easily tend to be submerged under the fact that the most powerful and direct opposition to slave Christianization came from planters.

Perhaps, one of the best documents that articulates the Planters' position on slave Christianization and the philosophy behind their fears is Whitemarsh Seabrook's essay, read before the Agricultural Society of

---

[214] Jacobs, History of the Evangelical Lutheran Church in the United States, cited by Marcus Jernegan in "Slavery and Conversion," 51.

[215] Albert Raboteau, Slave Religion, 98.

St. John's Colleton, South Carolina, in 1834.[216] Among other things, Seabrook urged his fellow Slave Holders at that meeting to teach their slaves the "cardinal principle" that they were bound to their masters "by the laws of God and man, and that no human authority can sever the link which unites them." "The great aim, then, of the slaveholder," Seabrook continues, "should be to keep his people in strict subordination."[217] This aim, argues Seabrook, could be undermined by slave Christianization, which ran the risk of breeding "habits of irremediable insubordination" in the slaves.

He also saw another danger in the behavior and teachings of the clergymen, which was "the incorporation into their pastoral government of what emphatically is - the levelling system."[218] The fear of this levelling system or egalitarianism on which Christianity is built was probably one of the biggest stumbling blocks planters faced in allowing their slaves to be Christianized.

Some settlers feared what was, perhaps, an unwritten code in English law that Christians were not supposed to enslave other Christians. Thus if the slaves became Christians their freedom should be guaranteed. Hence the trepidation among slave owners that Christian instructions and baptism could lead to emancipation.

Another problem was that the very thought of spiritual equality with slaves was abhorrent to some masters. Some considered it a shame to have "a spiritual brother or sister among so despicable a people."[219] Christianization could also lead to sauciness in the slaves, some argued.

---

[216] See Whitemarsh Seabrook, <u>An Essay on the Management of Slaves, and Especially Their Religious Instruction</u> (Charleston: A.E. Milles, 1834). It must be pointed out that this address was given at a time when the Southern states were contemplating the adoption of religious instruction of slaves to counteract abolitionist accusations form the North that Southerners were neglectful of instructing their slaves. The speech contains a summary of essential elements of the fears and sentiments that existed among planters against slave Christianization in the South.

[217] Ibid., 7.

[218] Ibid., 14.

[219] See Peter Kalm, <u>Travels in North America</u>, 2d ed., vol. 13, cited by Albert Raboteau, <u>Slave Religion</u>, 102.

If the slaves saw themselves on the same level with their masters in spiritual matters, the next step would be laying claim to equality with white folk. This was seen as a terrible disruption in the status quo. Some settlers refused to partake of the Holy Communion at the same table as their slaves. Others even expressed the belief that slaves were very close to beasts and thus would not go to heaven.[220]

In order to persuade the planters into allowing their slaves to be instructed, Anglican clergymen who became "apologists" for slave Christianization "felt obliged to prove that Christianity would actually make better slaves."[221]

Thus in many instances, through sermons and pastoral letters, Bishops and "missionaries labored to build a stout wall between spiritual and temporal equality;"[222] between spiritual freedom and natural freedom, so to speak. One typical example was Bishop Edmund Gibson's letter to masters and mistresses of English Plantations abroad in 1727. To refute one of the Planters' arguments that Christianization would destroy or undermine the institution of slavery, the Bishop was obliged to reply that

> Christianity, and the embracing of the Gospel, does not make the least alteration in Civil property, or in any of the Duties which belong to Civil relations; but in all these Respects, it continues Persons just in the same state as it found them. The Freedom which Christianity gives, is a Freedom from the Bondage of Sin and Satan, and from the Dominion of Mens Lusts and Passions and inordinate Desires; but as to their *outward* condition, whatever that was before, whether bond or free, their being baptized, and becoming Christians, makes no manner of change in it.[223]

---

[220] See Winthrop Jordan, <u>White Over Black: American Attitudes towards the Negro, 1550-1812</u> (Chapel Hill, N.C. University of North Carolina 1968), 180-86, cited by Jon Butler, <u>Awash in a Sea of Faith</u>, 134.

[221] Raboteau, <u>Slave Religion</u>, 103.

[222] Ibid.

[223] Ibid. The full text of Bishop Gibson's letter is found in David Humphreys, <u>An Historical Account</u>, 250.

Bishop Gibson reinforces his point by appealing to Saint Paul's classic statement in I Corinthians 7:20 and 24:

> As St. Paul has expressly told us, I cor.vii.20 where he is speaking directly to this very point, Let every Man abide in the same calling wherein he was called; and at the 24th. Verse, let every Man wherein he is called, therein abide with God.[224]

On these grounds, the Bishop contends that instead of liberating men "from the duties of the station and condition in which it found them," Christianity only "lays them under stronger Obligations to perform those duties with the greatest diligence and fidelity, not only from the fear of men, but from a sense of duty to God, and the belief and expectation of a future Account."[225]

Such attitudes of the Anglican Clergy partly explain why their efforts apparently yielded very little spiritual fruit among the slaves.

Apart from their fear of Christian egalitarianism, planter resistance to slave Christianization was also based on economics. As far as the average planter was concerned the economic profitability of the slaves took precedence over their religious welfare. One can easily glean this attitude from Morgan Godwyn's frustration that planters knew "no other God but money, nor religion but profit."[226] And besides, the actions, if not words of the Planter, tended to convey the sad message that he expected the body of one slave to earn him at least twenty pounds, "but the souls of an hundred of them would not yield him one farthing."[227]

Also, planters regarded time spent in instructions, away from labor as an economic disadvantage. In many instances the only time available

---

[224] Ibid.
[225] Ibid.
[226] Morgan Godwyn, preface to The Negro's Advocate.
[227] A quotation from the Athenian Oracle, vol. 2, 460-63 (1705), cited by Jernegan, "Slavery and Conversion," 516.

for religious instruction was on the Sabbath. But this was also the only time some masters allowed the slaves to take care of their own personal needs. Of course, many slaves preferred spending whatever "free" time they had on the leisure of visiting relatives, dancing and other forms of recreation.[228] Furthermore, the clergy largely depended on the local Vestry for financial sustenance. Thus the minister's job became even more complicated by the fact that the communicants were mostly planters, who were opposed to slave Christianization.

Political considerations also made planters resistant to their slaves being Christianized. Like many others, Whitemarsh Seabrook believed that religion could create "a spirit of discontent"[229] in the slave population. "The notion was widespread that the converted negro[sic] became intractable and ungovernable, because of increased knowledge through religious instruction.[230] This, to some Planters, "increased the danger of insurrections."[231]

Social prejudice, to the extent of some planters questioning the humanity of the slaves was another hindrance to slave Christianization. Jernegan captures the kernel of it in the following words:

> The belief was common that imported Africans were hardly above beasts, and the appearance of many negroes must have given ground for such a notion. Savages of the lowest types were quite different in appearance and character from the negro of the present generation, so much changed by infusion of White blood and contact with a Christian civilization. From a social standpoint, association with the imported negro was extremely objectionable.[232]

---

[228] Ibid.

[229] Ibid. Whitemarsh Seabrook, An Essay on the Management of Slaves, 15.

[230] Hugh Jones, Present State of Virginia, cited by Jernegan, "Slavery and Conversion," 517.

[231] Jernegan, "Slavery and Conversion," 517.

[232] Ibid.

Some cited the language barriers and the heathen background of the slaves as insurmountable obstacles that could render useless any attempts at Christianizing them.

There were also other very practical problems in the process of slave Christianization. The general lack of religious fervor among the settlers, which we have already alluded to, all but guaranteed their carelessness about the religious state of their slaves. Moreover, the acute shortage of clergymen, coupled with the vast distances between the plantations rendered the job of slave Christianization almost impossible. Thus it is reported by Humphreys, for example, that on arrival in North Carolina in 1703, the itinerant missionary, the Reverend Mr. Blair

> entered upon the Duties of his Mission with great Diligence and Pains. The people were settled in such distant Plantations on several Rivers sides, that he was obliged to be continually travelling from place to place, which could not possibly be done without a Guide, both on account of the badness of the roads, and the difficulty to find them if once lost, as also by reason of the desarts [sic.] between several Plantations, some extending 40 miles in length, without any inhabitants. Besides, there was another exceeding inconvenience in travelling this Country; it was watered with seven great Rivers, all without any Bridges over them.[233]

Like many of his contemporaries, Reverend James Blair labored tirelessly and braved unbelievable physical hazards to bring the gospel to the slaves, but the missionaries found their efforts aborted by potent legislation and codes not only against slave Christianization, but their general education also.

In order to allay the fears of planters that Christianization could lead to the emancipation of the slaves, some colonial legislative bodies enacted laws "positively denying that conversion or baptism was a sufficient reason for enfranchisement and insisting that all slaves must

---

[233] Humphreys, <u>An Historical Account</u>, 129.

serve for life."[234] Jernegan indicates that "between 1664 and 1706 at least six of the colonies passed acts affirming this principle.[235]

Moreover, to safeguard planter interests in case slaves pretending to be Christians invoked English law to assert their freedom, the Maryland legislature declared in 1664 that all slaves must serve *durante vita*. The State of Virginia's legislature insisted that "the conversion or baptism of negroes or other slaves before or after importation should not be a cause for manumission."[236] The same legislature declared in 1667 that those who were slaves by birth remained so even after baptism.[237] Similar acts in the states of North Carolina, South Carolina, New York, and New Jersey also denied "that freedom resulted from baptism."[238] Thus in the words of A. Leon Higginbotham, "the law that guaranteed liberty to English men and women became the seal of slavery for Africans."[239] Laws against the assembling together of slaves were also common in this period.

What we have tried to demonstrate partly in this chapter is the long association between the enslavement of Africans and their Christianization in the course of the transatlantic slave trade. It has also been an account of only the first of approximately two centuries it took to Christianize the slaves.

From August 1620, when a Dutch man-of-war "landed twenty Negroes for sale in the colony of Virginia on the James River"[240] to approximately 1760, tremendous efforts were put into slave Christianization by almost every denomination present in the American colonies, but with minimal spiritual results.

In contrast to the first century of slave Christianization efforts, however, a fruitful turning point in the process is reported to have begun

---

[234] Jernegan, "Slavery and Conversion," 506.
[235] Ibid.
[236] Ibid.
[237] Ibid.
[238] Ibid.
[239] A. Leon Higginbotham, Jr., In the Matter of Color: Race and the American Legal Process, the Colonial Period (New York: 1978), cited by John Butler, Awash in a Sea of Faith, 138.
[240] Charles C. Jones, Religious Instruction of the Negroes, 2-3.

with the Edwardsian Great Awakenings and climaxed in the frontier Camp meetings of the late 1700s to early 1800s. This constitutes the second half of the slave Christianization process. The following chapter attempts to analyze and evaluate the effectiveness of the process before 1760.

CHAPTER 4

THE PROGRESS OF SLAVE CHRISTIANIZATION: EARLY ANGLICAN EFFORTS

To underestimate the Africanity of African-American Christianity is to rob the slaves of their heritage. But to overestimate the Africanity of African-American Christianity is to rob the slaves of their creativity. Africans were creative in Africa; they did not cease to be creative as involuntary settlers in America. The African-American Christianity that developed was neither a dark version of the Christianity preached by slaveholders nor a continuation of African religion disguised as Christianity. The story of the emergence of African-American Christianity is a story of an emergent African-American culture as well as of residual African cultures, a story of innovation as well as of tradition, a story of change as well as continuity.[241]

After examining some of the key factors that enhanced or retarded slave Christianization, the tremendous efforts and energy expended in

---

[241] Charles Joyner, "Believer I Know," in <u>African-American Christianity: Essays in History</u>, ed. Paul E. Johnson, 19.

the process, by so many individuals and organizations, an assessment of the net impact on the slaves only becomes the next logical step.

In this chapter, I intend to specifically discuss the effects of early Anglican Christianization campaigns among the African slaves in North America. The Anglicans have particularly caught our attention because they stand out in the records as one of the most, if not the most active organization in the process of slave Christianization.

A very insightful commentary on the Anglican efforts was given by Carter Woodson that, in spite of their very good intentions, "the accomplishment of the task of more thoroughly proselytizing the Negroes....belongs to the record of other sects than the Anglican Church."[242] A number of other eminent Scholars of African-American history, including David Humphreys and John C. Van Horne, tend to agree with Woodson.

In an exhaustive historical account of the SPG David Humphreys, a past Secretary of the society, concluded that the efforts of the Organization amounted to "nothing, with regard to what a true Christian would hope to see effected."[243] The full text of Humphreys' comment reads:

> It is a matter of commendation to the Clergy, that they have done thus much in so great and difficult a work. But alas! What is the instruction of a few Hundreds, in several years, with respect to the many Thousands uninstructed, unconverted, living, dying, utter Pagans. It must be

---

[242] Carter G. Woodson, The Negro Church, 21. Note that Woodson uses the term sect with reference to the Methodists and Baptists. He suggests that the Baptists and the Methodists, working together with the Scotish-Irish Presbyterians were more successful in converting the slaves to Christianity than the Anglicans. Woodson refers to "organizational and philosophical foundations of the doctrines, controversial atmosphere in which they lived, and conflict of creeds" of the Anglicans and Catholics as possible setbacks to their early efforts in slave Christianization.

[243] David Humphreys, An Historical Account, 234.

confessed, what has been done is nothing, with regard to what a true Christian would hope for.[244]

If anything can be gained from Humphreys' comment, it is his insightful observation that in spite of their huge and laudable efforts, Anglican Clergy not only failed to produce true Christian conversions among the slaves, but also showed very meager returns for their overall investment in the slave Christianization campaign.

Van Horne came to a very similar conclusion in his assessment of the contributions of Dr. Bray and Associates to slave Christianization efforts. His evaluation reads:

> How, then, can we assess the work of the Associates in the American Colonies? Certainly the numbers do not impress. Over the years the beneficence of the Associates reached, through Negro Schools, Catechists, and books, perhaps two or three thousand of colonial America's blacks. In the light of the fact that there were close to half a million blacks in the colonies on the eve of the American Revolution, the number pales into insignificance. And even those few whom the Associates did reach probably did not achieve a lasting conversion or a useful degree of literacy. Hindered by many great obstacles, the Associates' enterprise failed to establish a permanent and effective means of carrying the gospel to and fostering education among America's blacks. Yet fortified by a deep sense of right and duty, the Associates pressed on in their endeavor despite the meager results and discouraging reports.[245]

An interesting fact emerging from Van Horne's assessment is that in terms of the number of blacks reached and the quality of conversion

---

[244] Ibid.

[245] John C. Van Horne, <u>Religious Philanthropy and Colonial Slavery: The American Correspondence of the Associates of Dr. Bray, 1717-1777</u> (Urbana and Chicago: University of Illinois) 38.

among those presumably affected, early Anglican Christianization efforts were nearly a complete failure.

The failure of the Anglican Church and her appendages like the SPCK, SPG and Dr. Bray and Associates, in making a lasting spiritual impact on the slaves could be partly attributed to the many negative forces arrayed against them. Some of the hindrances, outlined in the last chapter, were but only the tip of the iceberg. For in addition to those obstacles, there were other inherent problems within the Anglican establishment that militated against their success. Some of these include the Soteriology of the denomination, the general Anglican ideology or attitude to the institution of slavery, Anglican methodology of slave Christianization and strategies employed to reach the slaves. The lifestyle of Colonists was also another factor that led to a century of almost fruitless attempts to reach the slaves with the gospel. Colonial demographics and other social changes also contributed to the feeble spiritual impact on the slaves in the first century of their existence in the United States.

For information on the progress of slave Christianization from approximately 1670 to 1770, and a critical evaluation of the efforts of that period, we have heavily relied on the testimonies and correspondences of missionaries who served on the field. Also, records of missionary Organizations, like the SPG and Dr. Bray's Associates, who were major participants in the Christianization Process, prove to be valuable sources of information pertaining to the successes or failures in that period. Testimonies of Ex-slaves also provide useful insights into the effectiveness of Anglican Christianization efforts.[246] A comment or two on the Anglican understanding of salvation is probably a reasonable place to begin.

Anglican Soteriology and Slave Christianization

One of the factors that probably rendered Anglican efforts at Christianizing the slaves impotent was their equation of baptism with spiritual regeneration. This was especially evident in their baptismal formula for infants. Joseph Tracy describes the process in the following words:

> In the "office for baptism" prescribed by the Church of England, the Priest, after application of water to the infant, is required to say:--"Seeing now that this child is regenerate, and grafted into the body of Christ's Church, let us give thanks;--." and giving thanks after the Lord's Prayer, he must say:-- "We yield thee hearty thanks, most merciful Father, that it hath pleased thee to regenerate this infant with thy Holy Spirit, to receive him for thine own child by adoption, and to incorporate him into thy holy Church." When this child dies, if he has neither been excommunicated nor committed suicide, the priest must say at his funeral:-- "For as much as it hath pleased Almighty God, of his great mercy, to take unto himself the soul of our dear brother here

---

[246] See John C. Van Horne, <u>Religious Philanthropy and Colonial Slavery</u>. This is a publication of nearly two Hundred letters exchanged between missionaries in the American colonies and the Associates of Dr. Bray; David Humphreys, <u>An Historical Account</u>, contains "Foundation, Proceedings, and successes of their missionaries in the British Colonies, to the year 1728." Other helpful accounts of the S.P.G can be found in C. F. Pascoe, <u>Two Hundred Years of the S.P.G</u>,; Charles C. Jones, <u>Religious Instruction of the Negroes</u>, Faith Vibert, "The Society for the Propagation of the Gospel in Foreign Parts." Another helpful Source include Slave narratives: Interviews with Ex-Slaves by the Federal Work Project (FWD) in 1936-38, edited and published in 19 Volumes by George P. Rawick, under the title <u>The American Slave: A Composite Biography</u>. Also see John Blassingame, <u>Slave Testimony: Two Centuries of Letters, Speeches, Interviews, and Auto Biographies</u> (Baton Rouge: Louisiana State University Press, 1977).

departed, therefore we commit his body to the ground; earth
to earth, ashes to ashes, dust to dust; in sure and certain
hope of the resurrection to eternal life, through Jesus Christ
our Lord."[247]

The implications of this formula were deep and far-reaching, not
only for the general Anglican Church membership, but also for the
ministry of their priests and missionaries. As Joseph Tracy rightly points
out, such a formula taught the members of the Church of England that
they became Children of God and heirs to heaven through the sacrament
of baptism. And that no matter what else they did or happened, if they
could avoid excommunication and suicide, their place in Heaven was
guaranteed.

Thus an "immense majority" of members of the Church of England
"actually suppose that all who die in the communion of their Church,
are saved of course, and never suspect that any regeneration can be
needed, except that which they received in baptism."[248] This point must
be carefully noted as one of the foundational issues, which in many ways
determined the level of success the Anglicans or evangelical revivalists
achieved in their ministries to the slaves. We shall come back to it when
we discuss the impact of the revival movements on the slaves.

What needs to be stressed at this point is that in general, Anglican
missionaries who engaged in slave Christianization were diehard
adherents to this doctrine of salvation. The paramount emphasis laid
on baptism by Anglican missionaries in the American colonies confirms
their commitment to such doctrine. And of course, the great length to
which the missionaries went to instruct the slaves before baptism reflects
the importance they attached to the ceremony. For example, at the very
beginning of its operations, the Proprietors of the S.P.G

---

[247] Joseph Tracy, <u>The Great Awakening: A History of the Revival of Religion in the
Time of Edwards and Whitefield</u> (Boston: Tappan & Dennet, New York: Dayton
& Newman, Philadelphia: Henry Perkins, 1842), 35-36.

[248] Ibid.

wrote...to all their Missionaries, that they should use their best endeavours, at proper times, to instruct the Negroes, and should especially take occasion to recommend it zealously to the Masters, to order their slaves, at convenient times, to come to them that they might be instructed.[249]

David Humphreys comments further that, "these Directions had a good effect, and some hundreds of Negroes have been instructed, received baptism, and been admitted to the communion."[250]

The terms of employment and job description of Anglican missionaries also contained the strict mandate that

> they should carefully instruct the people concerning the nature and use of the Sacraments of Baptism and the Lord's Supper, as being the peculiar Institutions of Christ, Pledges of communion with him, and means instituted of deriving grace from him: That they should duly consider the Qualifications of such grown persons to whom they shall administer Baptism, as also of those whom they admit to the Lord's Supper, according to the Directions of the Rubrick [sic] in our Liturgy.[251]

Anglican missionary reports and correspondence abound with indications that these directives were strictly obeyed by most of them. In his magnificent accounts of the activities of the SPG from 1701 to 1728, David Humphreys' assessment of the success of the missionaries seem to be based on the number of people they instructed and baptized. For example, a typical entry on the Reverend Samuel Thomas, who served at the Gooscreek Parish, in South Carolina, from 1702 to 1706 reads:

> Mr. Thomas discharged his ministerial office with very good success, he acquainted the Society, that tho' his communicants at first were but 5, they soon increased to

---

[249] David Humphreys, <u>An Historical Account</u>, 233.
[250] Ibid.
[251] Ibid., 70

32; that he had taken much pains also in instructing the
Negroes and learned 20 of them to read.[252]

It is reported of Rev. Thomas' successor, Dr. Francis Le Jeau, who
served the same Parish from 1706 to 1717, that "he performed all
parts of his ministerial duty with great diligence," baptizing twenty-one
Children in his first year and nineteen in the second. Dr. Le Jeau is also
credited with an increase in the number of communicants to thirty-five
under his ministry. The report further indicates that he "instructed and
baptized many Negroes and Indian Slaves." Dr. Le Jeau also earned
the reputation of sometimes keeping "catechumens on trial" for as
long as "two years."[253] An indication of how meticulous some Anglican
missionaries were in admitting slaves to baptism. By the time of his
death, in 1717, Dr. Le Jeau's congregation had grown to seventy English
and eight Negroes.[254]

Another faithful laborer among the slaves in South Carolina was the
Reverend Mr. Ludlam. He is said to have taught and baptized several
Negroes; "in one year, eleven, besides some Mulattoes."[255]

John C. Van Horne has also edited and published over one Hundred
and Eighty original letters from missionaries serving in the American
Colonies. The letters were written to the Associates of Dr. Bray, another
society that promoted not only Christianity among the slaves, but was
also involved in providing Schools and books for their education.[256] In a
letter written from New York, on October 7, 1761, the Reverend Samuel
Auchmuty informed the Secretary to the Organization, the Rev John
Warring, that in the period of his service, he had baptized no less that

[252] Ibid., 81.
[253] Albert J Raboteau, Slave Religion, 115.
[254] Ibid., 86-87.
[255] David Humphreys, An Historical Account. Fairly detailed reports on over twenty
other Missionaries who served in South Carolina, and several others who served
in North Carolina, New York, Pennsylvania, and New Jersey are recorded in Mr.
Humphreys' Historical Account, 81-200.
[256] John C. Van Horne, ed. Religious Philanthropy and Colonial Slavery: The
Correspondence of the Associates of Dr. Bray, 1717-1777 (Urbana and Chicago:
University of Illinois Press, 1985)

80 or 90 Negro Children, "and often upwards of 100, besides several adults."[257] In a single year, the Reverend John Thompson reported from Orange County, Virginia that he had baptized 13 Negroes.[258]

It is apparent in his correspondence from Savannah, Georgia, dated November 19, 1753, that Joseph Ottolenghe evaluated his success in slave Christianization by how much catechism the slaves could recite and how much knowledge they had of Anglican religion. A portion of his letters reads:

> I bless my God that I have all the success with these Poor Creatures that their Circumstances & Station in life, can well admit of. I have a good many that can say the Catechism perfectly well, & as I take all the care imaginable to explain to them in as familiar a manner as I can adapt to their low capacity; I find upon Examining them, which I do once a week, that by the blessing of God they daily improve in the knowledge of our Holy Religion.[259]

It must be pointed out that baptism and the Lord's Supper constitute some of the most important rites of the Church and highly commendable to Christians in all ages. The Anglican emphasis on education and instruction before baptism also had its place. In fact, the establishment of Schools by the Associates of Dr. Bray for the education of the slaves is probably one of the most valuable services rendered them in their miserable history.

What we see as an impediment to slave Christianization, however, was the Anglican tendency to equate baptism with salvation. From the correspondence and conversations of the Anglican missionaries, it is clear that the only requirement slaves needed to become Christians was baptism. In other words, for the Anglicans, profession of Christianity seem to have been measured solely in terms of memorization and recitation of the Creeds and Catechisms of the Church. It was more of

---

[257] Ibid., 167.

[258] Ibid., 95.

[259] Ibid., 112.

an intellectual exercise than a spiritual one. The emphasis on mental cognition, rather than an inward conversion provided the slaves with a rudimentary knowledge of Christianity without making them Christians.

In addition, the very long process of learning a new language and apparently meaningless Creeds, before the actual ritual of baptism, was partly responsible for the meager fruit Anglican efforts bore among the slaves. The Anglicans presented the slaves with intellectual challenges without addressing their real spiritual needs. There was no provision in the Anglican system for teaching the slaves how to be free from sin. Apparently, repentance was never presented to the slaves as a prerequisite to Salvation. From the Anglican point of view, as long as the slaves' behavior did not merit excommunication and they avoided death by suicide, baptism guaranteed them a place in heaven.

Thus it comes as no surprise that after many years of tireless efforts, Anglican missionaries still reported "disinclination to accept a new religion in place of their heathen rites" as one of the hindrances "to religious instruction of many slaves."[260] The new religion of the Anglicans failed to appeal to the slaves because it did not meet their deepest spiritual longings. It did not answer the fundamental question of every human heart: What must I do to be saved? Apart from their inadequate perception of salvation, the Anglican ideology of slavery also played a part in rendering their attempts at Christianization essentially abortive.

Anglican Ideology of Slavery and Slave Christianization

Another source of Anglican failure to have a deep spiritual impact on the Slaves lies in their general ideology of the institution of slavery. No doubt, Anglican policy makers and missionaries were keenly aware of the evils of slavery. Some individuals within the denomination were probably grieved by the inhuman and grossly unchristian traits that pervaded the conduct of the transatlantic slave trade, but the Church of England as an institution, never questioned "the right of members to hold slaves." In fact, they "denied that there was any inconsistency

---

[260] Marcus W. Jernegan, "Slavery and Conversion," 518-19.

between Christianity and slavery, and made no efforts to emancipate negroes because of religious scruples."[261] In a sense, Anglicans seemed interested in the soul of the slave but not his body.

This ambivalent attitude of the Church of England not only entrenched and abetted the institution of slavery, but also proved counter-productive to Anglican efforts in slave Christianization. While commending the Anglican Church and her missionary Agencies for their leading role in the pioneering century of slave Christianization, they also share some blame for the apparent lack of Christian impact on the slaves in that period. In their position as one of the most influential religious bodies in the heydays of North American slavery, their attitude became very vital in shaping the conduct of the peculiar institution.

As Jon Butler has aptly put it, "the unique Anglican domination of Christian institutional life in the late seventeenth-century southern colonies dictated Anglican dominance of public comment on slavery."[262] Consequently, Butler charges Anglican Christianization tactics with partial, if not total responsibility for the deplorable social conditions of the slaves. Professor Butler suggests, for example, that

> the Anglican ministers who were flocking to Maryland, Virginia, and the Carolinas at the same time that slaveholding escalated after 1680 rationalized, deepened, and thereby extended the doctrines emerging in the slave codes of the early eighteenth-century southern colonies. One major means was the Anglican promotion of slave Christianization.[263]

Another charge Butler lays on the account of the Anglicans is that

> the doctrine of absolute obedience articulated in the Anglicans' colonial pulpits was important in its own right. But it also became the foundation of the distinct planter

---

[261] Ibid., 511.

[262] Jon Butler, <u>Awash in a Sea of Faith</u>, 135.

[263] Ibid., 139.

paternalism that gradually characterized American slavery in the colonial and antebellum periods.[264]

And this "emphasis on absolute obedience had crucial implications for slave punishment."[265] Butler observes. We do not necessarily subscribe to Butler's conclusion that Anglican Christianization programs not only negatively shaped the institution of slavery, but also resulted in an African spiritual holocaust.[266] Our point is that Anglican ideology of slavery, which governed their activities in colonial America, played a major role in shaping the character of slavery in the antebellum South, and was partly responsible for their failure in slave Christianization.

Their dominant presence in the slave States also meant the Anglicans were caught in the quagmire of "conflicting interests, in the colonies and at home, of the British trader, the White settler, the imported Negro, and the endangered Indian."[267]

This created for them the formidable problem of reconciling "Christian idealism, imperial interests, and business profits."[268] To overcome this huddle, many Anglican Bishops and missionaries redefined the basis of North American slavery. The result was the development of "racial slavery" as opposed to "religious slavery" in

---

[264] Ibid., 143.

[265] Ibid., 145.

[266] Ibid., 129.

[267] Frank J. Klingberg, <u>Anglican Humanitarianism in Colonial New York</u> (Philadelphia: The Church Historical Society, 1940), 8.

[268] Ibid.

the American colonies.[269] In other words, to preserve British imperial influence and economic interests of the Planters, who feared that Christianization could destroy the property value of their slaves, the Anglican humanitarian organizations promoted an ideology of slavery based on the supposition that Spiritual freedom had nothing to do with physical freedom. And that "...the slave's religious condition had no relevance to his status as a slave (the only one possible if an already valuable economic institution was to be retained)..."[270]

Following the Anglican proposition to its logical conclusion, it becomes clear that the most probable reason some colonial Legislature frequently ruled in favor of keeping the black man in perpetual bondage was his complexion or race. Unfortunately, this unhealthy attitude towards the black race was present among the rank and file of the very Agencies of the Anglican Church, which played such a visible role in slave Christianization.

It has been suggested, for example, that even the Rev. Dr. Thomas Bray, who "was the Chief architect of and prime mover behind all three missionary and philanthropic organizations"--the SPCK, the SPG and later, the Associates of the late Rev. Dr. Bray--was not immune from degrading attitudes towards the African slaves.[271]

According to Van Horne, Dr. Bray had unequivocal ideas about black people. "He considered them barbarous and heathen, and he accepted the institution of slavery. His concern was for the

---

[269] Winthrop Jordan, <u>White Over Black: American Attitudes Towards the Negro, 1550-1812</u> (North Carolina: University of North Carolina Press, 1968.) In the history of the institution of slavery, religious inferiority was one of the frequent reasons for which people were enslaved. It was perfectly legal in many civilizations, including the British Empire, to enslave heathens of non-Christians. That led to the unwritten law that Christians cannot enslave other Christians. This was the basic reason why many Planters seemed to have resisted Anglican attempts to Christianize their slaves. The fear being that if the slaves became Christians they could become automatically free. The Anglicans tried to allay the fear of the planters by promoting the idea that baptism or Christianization only provided freedom from the bondage of sin and not from the bondage of slavery.

[270] Ibid., 93.

[271] John C. Van Horne, <u>Religious Philanthropy</u>, 1.

black's immortal souls, not their temporal condition."[272] Thus, at some point he even advocated slave labor as a means of supporting missionaries.[273] Van Horne provides further insights into Dr. Bray's attitude to slavery in the following words: "In April 1701, in sending Gabriel D'Emilian to Maryland as a missionary, Bray granted him 133.12.10 (pounds sterling), italics mine, "for his own Subsistence & to purchase 2 Negroes to stock his Glebe he having a family."[274] And in February 1701/2, in A memorial shewing [sic.] the necessity of one to Superintend the Church and Clergy in Mary Land, "Bray proposed to raise an adequate stipend for a commissary by purchasing 500 acres of good land to be worked by twenty slaves in order to raise tobacco and other commodities."[275]

Apparently, subsidizing their meager allowances through the use of slave labor was a common practice among Dr. Bray's missionaries. For example, in a letter addressed to the Rev. Samuel Smith on October 20, 1735, the Rev. Anthony Gavin of Williamsburg reports the expected delay of over a year in receiving his allowance from the Herinco's Parish on the James River. Thus he felt "obliged to buy slaves & other necessaries to work and get help from the land."[276] Several years before the formation of the Associates of the late Dr. Bray, the SPG had clearly and consistently demarcated a general Anglican ideology of slavery.

This ideology was formulated by some of the best brains in the Anglican leadership and delivered through the Society's annual sermons. The ideas then became a blueprint for the missionaries on the field.

Before commenting on the contents of some of the SPG sermons, it is in place to highlight the tremendous power and significance of sermons in general, in the seventeenth and eighteenth century English

---

[272] Ibid., 6.
[273] Ibid.
[274] Bray's Accounts, pt. 2, folder 66, U.S.P.G. Archives, cited by John C. Van Horne, Religious Philanthropy, 6.
[275] Bray's MSS., Sion College Library, fols. 209 - 12, cited by John C. Van Horne, Religious Philanthropy, 6.
[276] John C. Van Horne, Religious Philanthropy, 83.

society. Frank Klingberg provides a very astute summary of the situation in the following words:

> The sermon had great political significance during the bitter constitutional conflicts and civil wars of the seventeenth century; and, as one of the chief, if not indeed most important, means of communication, it was inevitably a weapon which political and religious antagonists attempted to seize and control. In fact, during the religious and political revolutions of the Tudor and Stuart times, "turning the pulpits" became the rule. Attendance at Church services was compulsory until 1688, and the sermon served not only for the announcement of extra-parochial events, but it often gave the only authoritative information as to the policy of the national governments.[277]

As a matter of fact, Elizabethan England has been dubbed "the golden age of the pulpit,"[278] reflecting the tremendous use that was made of sermons to promote various political and religious agendas. The SPG utilized the sermon tool effectively to disseminate the Anglican policy on slavery, as it related to slave Christianization. As early as its second meeting in the first year of its constitution, the SPG resolved "That there be a sermon preacht [sic.] before the society on the third Friday in every February, and that a preacher and place be appointed by the president."[279] It has been estimated that approximately Seventy-five sermons were preached in the life span of the Society, the contents of which have been described as "a mine of information about the intellectual and philosophical conceptions of the time."[280]

It must be quickly pointed out that the sermons did not always address the issue of slavery but themes varied from year to year.[281]

---

[277] Frank J. Klingberg, <u>Anglican Humanitarianism</u>, 11.

[278] Ibid.

[279] Cited by Frank Klingberg, <u>Anglican Humanitarianism</u>, 11. From the S.P.G.'s minutes of July 8, 1701.

[280] Ibid., 8.

[281] Ibid., 13.

Of those that took up slavery as a theme, three sermons have been unforgettable: They include sermons by Bishop William Fleetwood on Friday, February 16, 1710; Bishop Thomas Secker, preached on Friday, February 20, 1740-1; and Bishop William Warburton, on Friday, February 21, 1766.[282] It is worth mentioning at this point that the backdrop to the ideology propounded through the sermons and other statements by prominent Anglican clergymen was the resistance and objections of Planters to slave Christianization.[283] As mentioned earlier, the fear of the Planters also rested on the egalitarian character or leveling tendency in Christianity. There seemed to be some awareness among the Settlers, of an unwritten code in English law that would not allow Christians to be held as slaves. Hence as more reports of Planter antagonism to slave Christianization reached the SPG Directors, it became pertinent that the issue be addressed in the annual sermons.

As early as 1706, Dr. Williams, Bishop of Chichester, preached a sermon in which he laid the foundation for what later became an official Anglican policy towards Christianization, as it relates to the bondage of slaves. In his analysis of problems requiring the attention of the society at that time, Bishop Williams focussed his address on two issues: Deism and "the problems of the depth and fixity of native cultures and therefore the difficulties of the Christianization of the Indians

---

[282] The full texts of these sermons are printed in Frank J. Klingberg, Anglican Humanitarianism, 191.

[283] Charles C. Jones, Religious Instructions of the Negroes in the United States, 10. Jones has summarized the objections of the Planters under five headings as follows:

1. "If we suffer our Negroes to be instructed, the tendency will be to change the civil relations of society as now constituted."
2. "The way will be opened for men from abroad to enter in and inculcate doctrines subversive of our interests and safety."
3. "The religious instruction of the Negro will lead to neglect of duty and insubordination."
4. "The Negroes will embrace seasons of religious worship for originating and executing plans of insubordination and villainy."
5. "Religious instruction will do no good; it will only make the Negroes worse men and worse hypocrites"

and slaves."[284] With regard to slave Christianization, the Bishop briefly alluded to his disapproval of slavery, but nevertheless, proceeded to plant the seeds of two potentially destructive ideas that later characterized Anglican attitudes to the African slaves:

First, he stated unequivocally "that Christianization, the goal of all the society's efforts, did not mean emancipation, documenting his thesis from the Bible."[285] Second, he stressed "that the master had it in his own power to Christianize his slaves," citing the development of mutual confidence and security between slave and master as the rationale behind his proposal.[286] These themes were revisited and refined by subsequent speakers like Bishop William Fleetwood of St. Asaph's Parish.

Though ambivalent to a considerable degree, the sermon that "became a blueprint for the process of Christianization and education of the Negro"[287] was preached by Bishop William Fleetwood in 1711. On the one hand, Bishop Fleetwood recognized the worth of the black man by insisting that the slaves were as "equally the Workmanship of God"[288] as the Planters. He even made the bold and unusual declaration that Europeans were endowed with the same intellectual capacity as the blacks. On the other hand, he could find no legal basis, divine or worldly, that allowed the slaves to be set free as a result of Christianization.

The Bishop outlined three basic Planter "pretences," which he tried to diffuse in his sermon:

> The First is, that were their Slaves Christians, they would immediately, upon baptism, become free. The second is, that were their slaves Christians, and still continue Slaves, yet they should be oblig'ed [sic.] to treat them with more humanity and mercy, than nature and necessity of their service would admit of, to make their Masters Gainers. And the Third is much of the same kind, that were their Slaves

---

[284] Frank J. Kilngberg, <u>Anglican Humanitarianism</u>, 15.

[285] Ibid.

[286] Ibid.

[287] Ibid., 19.

[288] Ibid., 22.

Christians, they could not sell them, it being Unlawful, they say, to sell Christians.[289]

He chided these Planter apprehensions as baseless, insisting that they were "neither prohibited by the Laws of God, nor those of the land, from keeping Christian Slaves." And that "their Slaves are no more at Liberty after they are Baptized, than they were before."[290] Citing St. Paul as his authority, Bishop Fleetwood defines Christian Liberty as:

> The Liberty wherewith Christ had made them Free, was freedom from their Sins, Freedom from the Fears of Death, and everlasting Misery, and not from any State of Life in which they had either voluntarily engaged themselves or fallen into through their Misfortune.[291]

Thus describing the liberty of Christianity as "entirely Spiritual," the worthy Bishop called on all mankind to an understanding of the fact, "that his being called to the Faith of Christ, does not exempt him from continuing in the same State of Life he was before."[292]

In fact, Bishop Fleetwood stated categorically that it was a person's nationality that determined his freedom or bondage, not Christianity. In his words, "whatever Liberties the Laws indulged" to Bishop Fleetwood and his kind, they did "it to them as Englishmen and not as Christians."[293]

In essence, Bishop Fleetwood was primarily concerned about the national and economic interests of the English Race. For him, this took priority over the status of Slaves after their baptism. Thus, he was determined not to endorse "any Liberties or Privileges, than what are reconcilable with trade, and the Nation's interest..."[294] This was clearly stated thus:

---

[289] Ibid., 205.
[290] Ibid.
[291] Ibid.
[292] Ibid., 206.
[293] Ibid.
[294] Ibid.

I would not have any one's zeal for Religion (much less my own) so far outrun their judgement in these matters, as to cause them to forget that we are a people who live and maintain ourselves by Trade; and that if trade be lost, or overmuch discouraged, we are a ruined Nation; and shall ourselves in time become as very slaves, as those I am speaking of tho' [sic.] in another kind: I would not therefore be understood, in what I have already said, or in what I am to say farther, to plead for any other Liberties or Privileges, than what are reconcilable with trade, and the Nation's Interest, tho' [sic.] a little perhaps abated.[295]

Perhaps, to underscore the society's attitude to slavery, Fleetwood proudly announced towards the end of his sermon, that "by the Munificence of a truly Honourable [sic] Gentleman [Colonel Christopher Codrington]," the society had become the "Patrons of at least three hundred slaves." And that these were going to be used "to cultivate, and be maintain'd [sic] upon the two plantations he hath left to this society, for the promoting of Learning and religion."[296] The Society felt Dr. Fleetwood's sermon was "so useful a Discourse, that they printed and dispersed abroad in the plantations, great numbers of that sermon in the same year."[297] Thus Fleetwood's statement essentially became the official Anglican position on the relationship between Christianization and emancipation. Such an ideology would strongly suggest that the Anglicans were probably more interested in creating enlightened bondsmen out of the slaves than their true conversion to Christianity.

Another Anglican divine who ardently and effectively reinforced and propagated Fleetwood's ideas was Bishop Edmund Gibson of London. In his famous pastoral letters of 1727, addressed to Masters and Mistresses of Families in the English Plantations abroad,[298] Bishop Gibson went to great lengths to assure the Planters of the lack of association between baptism and emancipation. His rationale and

---

[295] Ibid.

[296] Ibid., 210.

[297] David Humphreys, <u>An Account of the S.P.G</u>, 248.

[298] Ibid. Bishop Gibson's assertions have been treated earlier in this dissertation.

arguments for such a position were basically the same as those employed earlier by Bishop Fleetwood.

A former Secretary to the SPG provides some insight into the popularity and extensive circulation of Bishop

Gibson's letters: According to David Humphreys, "they printed ten thousand copies of the letter to the Masters and Mistresses." And the letters were sent to "all the Colonies on the Continent, and to all the Islands in the West Indies, to be distributed among the masters of families, and other Inhabitants."[299]

Three decades later, the ideologies propounded by Bishops Williams, Fleetwood, and Gibson were still recurring in SPG sermons. In his 1740 sermon, for example, Bishop Thomas Secker described the condition of the slaves in the colonies as consisting of "servitude most laborious and their Punishments most severe."[300] However, that did not move the Bishop to express any opposition to slavery, but instead buttressed the prevailing ideology that

> "The Scripture, far from making any alteration in the Civil Rights, expressly directs, that every man abide in the condition wherein he is called, with great indifference of mind concerning outward circumstances."[301]

As a protective measure for the colonies against dangers of slave indignation, Secker suggested the use of the gospel "to compose and soften their vindictive and sullen Spirits...to make their tempers milder, their lives happier." And while doing this, he cautioned, "no imagination can be suggested to them, of any worldly Exemptions or privileges arising from their profession of it."[302] From the testimonies of Anglican missionaries and slaves, it is clear that this ideology became the modus operandi for SPG missionary activities in the Colonies.

---

[299] David Humphreys, <u>An Historical Account</u>, 249.

[300] Ibid., 217.

[301] Ibid., 223.

[302] Ibid.

For example, to reinforce the fact that baptism was not a means to emancipation, the Rev. Thomas Le Jeau devised a declaration to which slaves were frequently required to swear before he could baptize them. He describes the process and rationale behind it in the following words:

> To remove all pretence from the adult slaves I shall baptise of their being free upon that account, I have thought fit to require first their consent to this following declaration: You declare in the presence of God and before this congregation that you do not ask for Holy Baptism out of any design to free yourself from the duty and obedience you owe your master while you live, but merely for the good of your soul and to partake of the graces and blessings promised to the members of the Church of Jesus Christ."[303]

Records of Slave testimonies also abound with indications that Anglican missionaries faithfully incorporated the policies of the Church of England in their ministry to the slaves. Peter Randolph records a Slave's perspective on Anglican attitudes to slavery in the following words:

White ministers taught the slaves that they did not deserve freedom, that it was God's will that they were enslaved, that the devil was creating those desires for liberty in their breasts, and that runaways would be expelled from the Church. Then followed the slave beatitudes: blessed are the patient, blessed are the faithful, blessed are the cheerful, blessed are the submissive, blessed are the hardworking, and above all, blessed are the obedient.[304]

Perhaps, contrary to both Anglican and general European assumptions about the intellectual caliber of the black captives at that time, the slaves were intelligent enough to discern from such Christianization efforts, what was Christian or not. As long as the Anglicans callously neglected the bondage and intense sufferings of

---

[303] Frank J Klingberg, <u>An Appraisal of the Negro</u>, 13.

[304] Ribinson W. H. <u>From Log Cabin to the Pulpit</u> (Eau Clare, Wisconsin: 1913), 74-79, cited by John W. Blassingame, <u>Slave Community</u>, 63.

the Africans, and contested only for their souls, all missionary efforts at Christianizing the slaves would prove as ineffective as pouring water on a duck's back.

The Anglican version of Christianity only minimally affected the slaves because they stripped the gospel of its essence as the power of God unto salvation. The Clergymen, in the words of Winthrop Jordan, "had been forced by the circumstance of racial slavery in America into propagating the gospel by presenting it as an attractive device for slave control."[305] There were, nevertheless, some who saw the plight of the Africans from a more humane and sensible perspective. William Warburton, Bishop of Gloucester, was a typical example.

In his anniversary sermon of February 21, 1766, Bishop Warburton unleashed a most vitriolic indictment against the institution of slavery. He uncharacteristically referred to the slaves as "vast multitudes yearly stolen from the opposite Continent, and sacrificed by the Colonists to their great idol, the GOD OF GAIN."[306] He also drew attention to the absurdity of talking "(as in herds of cattle) of Property in rational Creatures!"[307] William Warburton could as well have been one of the very few dissenting voices among the Anglican hierarchy at that time, when he boldly declared that, "...nothing is more certain in itself, and apparent to all, than that the infamous traffic for slaves, directly infringes both divine and human law."[308] Speaking quite out of step with the official position of his denomination, Bishop Warburton was probably one of the first people to observe the salient fact that the Anglican ideology of caring for the souls of the slaves but neglecting "their temporal interests" was a porous endeavor. He succinctly articulated his insightful remark and suggestion in the following words:

> The Savages, I say, observing in us a total disregard of their temporal interests, will with difficulty be brought to think, the other matters, pressed upon them, of much importance,

---

[305] Winthrop Jordan, <u>White over Black</u>, 191.
[306] Frank J. Klingberg, <u>Anglican Humanitarianism</u>, 246.
[307] Ibid.
[308] Ibid.

or their Teachers greatly earnest. But when they have been first of all so sensibly obliged, as by our means, to be redeemed from the miseries of a brutal life, and set at ease by the security and accommodations of society, they will naturally give a grateful and serious attention to their Benefactors, instructing them in sublimer truths, and directing them to still more substantial happiness.[309]

This was probably one of the best approaches to Slave Christianization. But unfortunately, Bishop Warburton's advice came either too late or was not heeded by his colleagues. For the Anglican slave policies were directly the opposite of Warburton's wise suggestions. And that was partly responsible for the demise of their Christianization efforts. Related to their cheap soteriology and shaky ideological foundation, as causative agents for the lack of spiritual impact on the slaves, was the strategy adopted by the Anglicans in their bid to Christianize African slaves in North America.

Anglican Strategy and Its Effects on Christianization

Very early in its inception, Proprietors of the SPG regarded dependence on the Masters and Mistresses to Christianize their own slaves as one of their most promising strategies. As soon as the Society "resolved to do their utmost" to instruct the slaves, letters were sent to all their missionaries urging them to put their best efforts into the program. They were told to "especially take occasion, to recommend it zealously to the Masters, to order their Slaves, at convenient Times, to come to them, that they might be instructed."[310]

This strategy was again recommended in one of the very early sermons of the SPG. In his sermon of 1706, Bishop Williams of Chichester, while outlining the problems and plans of the society, "took the ground that the master had it in his power to christianize his slaves, greatly to the advantage of both parties."[311] As reported by Klingberg,

---

[309] Ibid., 245.
[310] David Humphreys, An Historical Account of the S.P.G., 233.
[311] See also Frank J. Klingberg, Anglican Humanitarianism, 15.

Bishop Williams' rationale behind his suggestion was the fact that, the slaves were "wholly in the power of their masters, and are not in a condition to refuse whatever they demanded of them;...." The Bishop goes on to brilliantly elaborate on his point as follows:

> What a security will this be to their masters, when those
> that now fear more than an enemy are in one and the same
> interest, when there will be a mutual trust and confidence,
> and they that are now watched and guarded for fear of doing
> mischief will be a safeguard to their masters for preventing
> it.[312]

But as brilliant as his ideas were, their practical implementation became one of the most seriously frustrating hindrances to Anglican Christianization hopes. Because for numerous reasons, including fears that baptism could lead to emancipation,[313] the Planters proved to be the greatest opponents of slave Christianization.

And, as the Bishop himself observed in his speech, there was a tremendous amount of spiritual degeneracy among the Planters. To the degree that he characterized the white colonist as being in such "a shameful state of apostogy" [sic.] as to be "little better than infidels."[314] If the Planters did not care about their own personal spiritual lives, it hardly made any sense at all, for anyone to expect them to care for that of their slaves.

Another debilitating effect of such a strategy was the burden Anglican missionaries were under in order to win the approval of masters to instruct their slaves. To overcome Planter resistance to

---

[312] Idem. <u>Twelve Anniversary sermons preached before the Society</u>, 26-27, cited by Frank Klingberg, <u>Anglican Humanitarianism</u>, 16.

[313] Some of the reasons why Planters opposed slave Christianization have been listed in the last chapter. For more detailed treatment of Planter resistance, see: Charles C. Jones, <u>Religious Instruction of the Negroes</u>; David Humphreys, <u>An Account of the S.P.G.</u>; Morgan Godwyn, <u>The Negroes & Indians Advocate</u>; C. F. Pascoe, <u>Hundred Years of S.P.G.</u>.

[314] <u>Twelve Anniversary Sermons</u>, 29, cited by Klingberg, <u>Anglican Humanitarianism</u>, 16.

religious instructions, Anglican clergy became apologists for slave Christianization. And "almost every apologist for the evangelization of the slaves felt obliged to prove that Christianity would actually make better slaves."[315]

It also became common practice for Clergymen to appeal to the profit motive of the masters, by advocating that Christian slaves would be more profitable to their owners, "for they are taught to serve out of Christian love and duty."[316] Thus by aligning themselves with the oppressors to win the oppressed, the Anglican Clergy only ended up antagonizing many slaves against their version of Christianity.

Sadly, the method of slave Christianization does not seem to have enhanced the process in any better way than the strategy Anglicans adopted.

Anglican Methodology of Slave Christianization

Rigid ecclesiastical control and insistence on rote learning as their chief method of instruction, contributed largely to the meager returns observed from Anglican Christianization efforts. While individual circumstances of the missionaries required slight adaptations in time and place of instruction for the slaves, the general format, content and method of instruction seem to have been firmly regulated by the Anglican hierarchy.

By the second year of operation, the SPG was fairly settled, not only on the expected conduct of their missionaries, but also on the ground rules for working among the slaves. "Conformity to the Doctrine and Discipline of the Church of England"[317] was one of the non-negotiable components of their prescribed method. The Missionaries had strict orders to diligently teach the people about the essence of the Sacraments of Baptism and the Lord's Supper and

---

[315] Albert J. Raboteau, <u>Slave Religion</u>, 103.
[316] Ibid.
[317] David Humphreys, <u>An Historical Account</u>, 68.

that they should duly consider the Qualifications of such grown persons to whom they shall administer baptism, as also of those whom they admit to the Lord's Supper, according to the Directions of the Rubrick in our Liturgy.[318]

There was nothing wrong with the Church's emphasis on careful instruction and consideration of a candidate's qualifications before the administration of the sacraments. What proved a hindrance to slave Christianization, though, was that in the case of the slaves, the qualifications sought after were more of outward behavioral changes than an inner transformation.

It was quite evident in the methodology of the Anglican missionaries that "civilizing" the slaves through western education took precedence over their inward spiritual regeneration, as qualifications for baptism. Some missionaries are on record for taking as much as two years to instruct the slaves before baptizing them.[319] The very tedious process of instructions, including the formidable tasks of learning a new Language, and adjusting to a completely new culture and environment, possibly took all fun out of religious instruction classes for the slaves. Besides, the rigors and demands of chattel slavery must have left the slaves with little or no energy for the stiff regiment of Anglican religious instructions.

The use of sermons was also highly recommended to the missionaries by the Society. As David Humphreys recalls, "the Society advise [sic.] their Missionaries not to decline any fair opportunity of preaching to any number of people as may be occasionally met together from remote and distant parts, tho' it may not be a Sunday or Holyday [sic.]."[320] The value of sermons as evangelistic tools can hardly be doubted, but Anglican missionary sermons failed to impress the slaves because they were often pregnant with double standards in their contents and applications to slaves and masters. The contents of Anglican sermons to Slave Owners were radically different from what the slaves received.

---

[318] Ibid., 70.
[319] The classic example of Francis Le Jau's, mentioned in our last chapter will suffice here.
[320] Ibid., 70.

For the Planters, the sermons probably revolved around "the fundamental Doctrines of Christianity, and the Duties of a Sober, righteous, and godly Life, as resulting from such Doctrines."[321] This was strictly according to the SPG stipulations.

In the case of the slaves it was different. A typical and favorite sermon of White ministers to slaves read thus:

> Servants, obey your masters. Do not steal or lie, for this is very wrong. Such conduct is sinning against the Holy Ghost, and *in base ingratitude to your kind and loving masters, who feed, clothe, and protect you.*[322]

One of the commonest texts on which missionaries preached to slaves was: "He that knoweth his master's will and doeth it not shall be beaten with many stripes." In elaborating on such a text, many preachers would develop and interpret it to the slaves as a basis for their unconditional acceptance of any form of punishment the masters mete out to them, just or unjust.[323] As John Blassingame has observed, many Anglican clergymen preached a truncated gospel to the slaves in order to avoid "incurring the planter's wrath." As a result, "most masters saw religion more as a way of preventing rebellion than as a way of saving the slave's soul."[324]

The slaves' perception was probably not very different from that of their masters. This was, indeed, a sad indictment against Christianization methods of many clergymen in the antebellum South. The crucial effect of slave demographics on Christianization is also worth mentioning at this point.

---

[321] David Humphreys, <u>An Historical Account</u>, 70.

[322] Ibid. Peter Randolph, <u>Sketches of Slave Life</u> (Boston, 1855), 62, cited by John W. Blassingame, <u>The slave Community</u>, 63.

[323] William Wells Brown, <u>My Southern Home</u> (Boston: A.G. Brown & Co. 1880), 15-16.

[324] Ibid. John W. Blassingame, <u>The Slave Community</u>, 61-62.

Slave Demographics and Its Effects on
Slave Christianization

It has been suggested that changes in Southern slave demographics, beginning in the early decades of the eighteenth century, contributed to Anglican failure in Christianizing the slaves. According to John Boles, the huge numbers of African slaves brought directly into North America, without undergoing the usual "acculturation (and "seasoning") in the English or even Spanish Sugar Islands,"[325] presented added problems to the job of an already over-stretched Anglican clergy. This is expressed much more clearly in the Author's own words as follows:

> For whites, rapidly increasing numbers of slaves who spoke African languages, worshiped African deities, and simply seemed strange in an uncomfortable way (African-born slaves came to be called "outlandish" to distinguish them from culturally more familiar American-born blacks) represented a threat to the stability of the southern slave societies. Soaring slave populations meant that these "alien" blacks often outnumbered the Whites, a situation deemed dangerous by English Planters living on isolated plantations.[326]

In this context, it is understandable that security reasons were also largely responsible for Planter opposition to slave Christianization, rendering Anglican efforts even more tedious. And in addition, the ignorance, apparent stubbornness, and the residual African traditional religions in the Newcomers tended to pose some of the greatest threats to the Anglican Clergy efforts. In his S.P.G. sermon of 1740, Bishop Secker referred to this as one of the reasons for the slow progress of their missionaries. After outlining some of the stumbling blocks to Anglican efforts in Christianizing the slaves, he made the suggestion that:

---

[325] John B. Boles, <u>Masters And Slaves in the House of the Lord</u>, 3.
[326] Ibid., 3-4.

When these obstacles are added to the fondness they have for their old Heathenish Rites, and the strong Prejudices they must have against Teachers from among those, whom they serve so unwillingly; it cannot be wondered, if the Progress made in their Conversion prove but slow.[327]

This was not an isolated opinion expressed by Bishop Secker, but an apparently persistent problem, which Bishop Edmund Gibson had attempted to address in his pastoral letter to Masters and Mistresses in 1727. In that letter Bishop Gibson described the number of slaves ... "employ'd [sic.] within the several governments" of the colonies as "prodigiously great" and was "not a little troubled, to observe how small a progress" was being made "in a Christian country, towards delivering those poor creatures from Pagan Darkness and Superstition in which they were bred."[328] Making reference to some of the difficulties in the process, the Bishop cited the fact

that the Negroes are *grown persons* when they come over, and that having been accustomed to the Pagan rites and Idolatries of their own Country, they are prejudiced against all other Religions, and more particularly against the Christian.[329]

To overcome these difficulties, Bishop Gibson came up with the brilliant suggestion of concentrating their Christianization energies on the Children of the slaves, "who were born and bred in our Plantations, who have never been accustomed to Pagan Rites and Superstitions...."[330] The accuracy of the Bishop Gibson's observation is beyond dispute, but one wonders whether his categorical statement about the absence of African rites and superstitions among American-born African slaves was not a little naïve.

---

[327] Frank J. Klingberg, Anglican Humanitarianism, 217. The full text of Bishop Secker's and other S. P. G. sermons are printed in this outstanding book by Frank Klingberg.
[328] David Humphreys, An Historical Account of the S.P.G., 257-58.
[329] Ibid., 258.
[330] Ibid., 260.

For John Boles has, in fact, suggested the opposite. According to Boles, the sharp rise in slaveholding towards the beginning of the second quarter of the eighteenth century led to an improved southern economy, and subsequent improvement in slave family life. And that as soon as "the emerging Creole (native-born) slave population" attained an annual growth rate higher than that of the imported Africans, and

> with slaves now normatively housed in family groupings, with little ones afoot, slave parents rediscovered the importance of cultural values and rituals. So long as the slave population had been overwhelmingly young and male, African cultural forms were forgotten or repressed. But now slave men and women, united as spouses and parents, had youngsters growing up whose transitional life moments- birth, puberty, marriage - needed to be marked with those symbol-rich ceremonies scholars call "rites of passage." Slaves therefore became increasingly receptive in the mid-eighteenth century to rituals that gave supernatural validation to aspects of their this-world existence.[331]

Clearly, it was not the absence of African rites and superstitions among American-born slaves that attracted them to Christianity, but rather, the continuities between those rites and evangelical Christianity.

In a very insightful statement, Boles suggests that the slaves easily identified such rituals in the evangelical revival movements, which began in the third decade of the eighteenth century. According to Boles, the revivals provided another aspect of Christianity, with close enough parallels to ATR, as to attract the attention of the slaves, who had previously shown little interest in their masters' religion. The following direct quotation from Boles probably renders more justice to his salient observation that:

> Several aspects of African traditional religion bore close enough parallels to Christianity that bondspeople who were initially disinterested in the White man's religion could--once

---

[331] John B. Boles, <u>Masters and Slaves</u>, 6.

they glimpsed another side to it--see sufficient common ground between the Whites' Christianity and their own folk religions to merit close examination. That willingness, that openness, on the part of blacks to the claims of Christianity was all the entree White evangelicals needed.[332]

One of the examples the Author cites as a common denominator for ATR and Christianity is the parallel between the "tripartite hierarchy of deities--nature gods, ancestral gods, and an omnipotent creator god who was more remote though more powerful than the others," and the Christian Trinity. The concept of spirit possession in African traditional religion, as a "sure sign of contact with the divine," was also suggested as another point of contact between the two religions.

A one to one correlation between the African pantheon and the Christian Trinity is probably not as easily observable as John Boles suggests. Otherwise, his observations are almost indisputable. Moreover, just as one can observe in the works of many scholars before him, there is more to the story than Boles has stated. For example, the parallels between the evangelical revivals and ATR, have received only casual treatment in literature on Slave Christianity thus far.

Thus part of my thesis in this research is that the parallels or continuities between evangelical Christianity and ATR were some of the major factors that attracted the slaves to the revivals, and subsequently, to Christianity. As a corollary, the absence of such rituals and symbols in the Anglican version of Christianity, largely accounted for its failure to significantly impact the slaves. These points will be elaborated on in the following sections.

---

[332] Ibid.

CHAPTER 5

THE PROGRESS OF SLAVE CHRISTIANIZATION: EFFECTS OF EVANGELICAL REVIVALISM

There is a fair amount of consensus among scholars of African-American Christian history that "the Great Awakening represented "the dawning of a new day" in the history of the conversion of slaves to Christianity."[333] However, what seems to be woefully lacking from most of the literature is a plausible or substantial explanation as to why the slaves were apparently more responsive to Christianity during the evangelical revivals than in the previous century, despite the tremendous efforts of various missions and organizations. One of our goals in this chapter is to investigate this interesting phenomenon through a careful study and analysis of the effects of the evangelical revivals on the slaves.

It is probably a little farfetched, and certainly unreasonable to assume that every African slave in North America fully embraced Christianity at one point or the other. John Boles has suggested that

---

[333] Carter G. Woodson, The History of the Negro Church (Washington, D.C.: Associated Publishers, 1992), 20. Albert Raboteau echoes Woodson's sentiments in his book, Slave Religion, 128. Other Authors who share this view include, W. E. B. Dubois, Charles C. Jones, Jon Butler, J. Franklin Frazier, Melville J. Herskovits and George P. Rawick, to mention just a handful.

"Blacks worshipped in a variety of ways, and some did not participate in any Christian worship, for, especially in the colonial period, a smattering of blacks practiced Islam and others clung tenaciously to traditional African religions."[334] However, it is also equally true that by the time of emancipation, "the doctrines, symbols, and vision of life preached by Christianity were familiar to most."[335] In fact, "by the eve of the civil war, Christianity had pervaded the slave community,"[336] and an unprecedented numbers of blacks were already either firmly established in mixed congregations or in separate Churches of their own.

It has been estimated, for example, that the Southern Baptists had a black membership of about 200,000 in 1845 and this grew to 400,000 in 1860[337]--a hundred percent increase in fifteen years. Notwithstanding persistent restrictions on their religious life, DuBois indicates that "in 1859 there were 468,000 Negro Church members reported in the South, of whom 215,000 were Methodists and 175,000 Baptists."[338] Sydney Alhstrom records astronomical increases in these figures in the years immediately before and following the emancipation proclamation in 1863. He estimates that by the end of the nineteenth century, "there were 2.7 million Church members in a black population of 8.3 million."[339] The depths to which Christianity had taken root among African slaves between the mid-eighteenth century and the end of the nineteenth century was also evident in their commitment to preaching and foreign missions.

Instances of converted slaves enduring unbelievable pain or even expressing willingness to die for their faith abound in slave testimonies and in the history of African-American Christianity. Andrew Bryan is a typical example. In narrating the history of the colored Baptist Church in the city of Savannah, which was officially formed at the end

---

[334] John Boles, Masters and Slaves, 2.
[335] Raboteau, Slave Religion, 212.
[336] Ibid.
[337] Luther P. Jackson, "Religious Instruction of Negroes," 95.
[338] W. E. B. DuBois, The Negro Church, 29.
[339] Sydney Ahlstrom, A Religious History, 698.

of 1792, DuBois includes the following intriguing testimony of Bryan's commitment to preaching the word of God:

> Andrew, surnamed Bryan, a man of good sense, great zeal, and some natural elocution, began to exhort his black brethren and friends. He and his followers were reprimanded and forbidden to engage further in religious exercises. He would, however, pray, sing and encourage his fellow-worshippers to seek the Lord. Their persecution was carried to an inhuman extent. Their evening assemblies were broken up and those found present were punished with stripes! Andrew Bryan and Sampson, his brother, converted about a year after him, were twice imprisoned, and they with about fifty others were whipped. When publicly whipped, and bleeding under his wounds, Andrew declared that he rejoiced not only to be whipped, but would freely suffer death for the cause of Jesus Christ, and that while he had life and opportunity he would continue to preach Christ. He was faithful to his vow and, by patient continuance in well-doing, he put to silence and shamed his adversaries, and influential advocates and patrons were raised up for him.[340]

The testimony of James Smith[341] is another powerful example of the resilience of some Christian slaves in the face of tremendous threat to their faith and danger to their lives.

As a bondsman to a very cruel master in Virginia, James Smith became converted while still a slave. After much scrutiny by Church officials, he was accepted into the Baptist Church and baptized. "Not long after this, he felt loudly called upon to go out and labor for the salvation of souls among the slave population with whom he was identified."[342] No doubt, his master perceiving this as a distraction to the other slaves, went to great lengths to stop James, but in vain. To

---

[340] W. E. B. DuBois, The Negro Church, 19.

[341] See the interview of James Smith by Henry Bibb, "Lost and Found," in The *Voice of the Fugitive* (January 15, February 26, March 11, April 22, and June 3, 1852), reprinted in Slave Testimony, ed. John Blassingame, 276-78.

[342] Ibid., 276-78.

prevent him from the exercise of what the slave considered to be his duty to God and his brethren, his interviewer reports that, Smith

> was sometimes kept tied all day Sundays while other slaves were allowed to go just where they pleased on that day. At other times he was flogged until his blood would drip down at his feet, and yet he would not give up laboring whenever he could get the opportunity, on the Sabbath day, for the conversion of souls. God was pleased to bless his labors and many were led to embrace the Saviour [sic.] under his preaching.[343]

Frustrated by his inability to stop James Smith from preaching, his master callously separated him from his wife and little Children by selling him to a slave-trader. At the conclusion of the sale, Mr. William Wright, his former master offered a testimonial of Smith's character that there

> "was but one fault to this boy," he was trustworthy, faithful, hard to work, but he would run about at nights and on Sundays trying to preach the gospel among the slave population, which had a tendency to divert their attention from work, and made them dissatisfied also, and that he had frequently flogged him with rough hide until his back was literally bathed with blood, and yet he'd slip off and do the same thing over again.[344]

Smith apparently received nastier punishments for his faith at the hands of his new master. At his new home on a Georgia cotton plantation, rules against holding religious meetings were even stricter. Smith, nevertheless, violated the rules and soon many slaves became interested in praying. Learning about this, the Over-seer tied him up to receive one hundred lashes, unless Smith promised not to ever pray again. Smith is reported to have replied that "he could never pledge

[343] Ibid., 276-78.
[344] Ibid.

himself to refrain from praying, though his life should be taken from him."[345] And "for this expression," his biographer continues, "he was most unmercifully "bruised and mangled."[346] Even when tied to a heavy block of wood, guarded by the slave driver for the whole night, to prevent him from singing or praying, Smith would break into fervent prayers as soon as his Guard fell asleep.

Apart from the personal risks and sufferings for their faith, a strong foreign missionary zeal is also reported among some slaves and ex-slaves after the mid-seventeen hundreds. Among many that went out as missionaries, the examples of George Lisle and Lott Carey will suffice here.

DuBois reports that immediately after the war of Independence, George Lisle left the United States for Jamaica and began a Church with only four members in 1783. "By 1790 he had baptized more than 400 persons on that island." And by 1841, his congregation, which was "the first non-Episcopal chapel" in Jamaica, had grown to 3,700 members.[347]

Lott Carey, whom DuBois describes as once "very profligate and wicked," before he was converted to the Baptist faith in 1807, "organized the African Missionary Society in 1815." This was "the first missionary society in African missions."[348] To underscore his commitment to preaching and missions, DuBois testifies that Carey rejected a salary raise from $800 to $1,000 a year from his employers at a Richmond tobacco factory, in order to go to Liberia as a pioneering missionary. It is reported that "after serving a very useful and varied career in Liberia for seven years Cary died there in 1828."[349]

It is evidently clear that by mid-eighteenth century through the year of their emancipation, many African slaves in North America had developed an affinity for Christianity that neither risk of personal lives

[345] Ibid.

[346] Ibid.

[347] W. E. B. DuBois, The Negro Church, 34.

[348] Ibid.

[349] See Fisher, "Cary the Colonizing Missionary," Journal of Negro History 7, cited by Luther P. Jackson, "Religious development of the Negro in Virginia, From 1760-1860," 201.

nor the lure of money could sway. Viewed from the background of the previously feeble Anglican impact on the slaves, this amazing growth and depth of Christian influence among people of African descent, between approximately 1760 and 1860 demand an explanation.

How did the African slaves and ex-slaves finally come to embrace Christianity as their own? How and why did they develop such strong Christian faith that some were willing to lay down their very lives rather than betray their commitment? How did the slaves become not only adherents to Christianity, but also ardent propagators of a religion they had apparently rejected at first? Answers to these and related questions would seem to come from two principal sources: The influence of evangelical revivals on the slaves and the subsequent late eighteenth to nineteenth century plantation mission, which primarily targeted the black race in the Southern states of North America.

North American Evangelical Revival: A Brief Background

In the mid-eighteenth to nineteenth century North America, an evangelical revival "swept as a tidal wave of religious fervor over the colonies from New England to Georgia."[350] To both its friends and foes, to revivalist and revisionists alike, this phenomenon stands out as one of the most conspicuous landmarks in North American Christian history.

The revival, which became known in North America as the Great Awakening, was both "international and interdenominational in its scope."[351] The Great Awakening, which was already in bud by the end of the second decade of the eighteenth century and in full bloom by 1734, was preceded by a period of great spiritual and moral laxity in

---

[350] Wesley M. Gewehr, <u>The Great Awakening in Virginia, 1740-1790</u> (Gloucester, Mass.: Peter Smith, 1965), 3.
[351] Ibid.

the colonies.[352] The evangelical fervor and Puritan ideals of the first generation of Congregationalist, Presbyterians and others had declined to abysmal levels by the end of the seventeenth century.

This woeful decline in religious enthusiasm in the colonies has been broadly attributed to three crucial developments in the New England congregations: the Half-Way covenant (1662), the Decrees of reforming Synod (1679-80) and the doctrine of federal theology.[353] The Half way covenant was designed to accommodate within the Church, those who fell short of the original Puritan qualifications for full membership. The Original Church constitution required that only the regenerate would be granted full Church membership.

---

[352] Ibid. For more comprehensive accounts of the Great Awakening, the following books and Articles are very helpful: Joseph Tracy, The Great Awakening: History of the Revival of Religion (New York: Arno Press, 1969); Wesley Gewrhr, The Great Awakening in Virginia, 1740-1790 (Gloucester, Mass.: Peter Smith, 1965); Edwin Scott Gaustad, The Great Awakening in New England (New York: Harper & Brothers, 1957); Catherine C. Cleveland, The Great Revival in the West (Gloucester, Mass.: Peter Smith, 1959.); Charles A. Johnson, The Frontier Camp Meeting (Dallas, Tex.: Southern Methodist University Press, 1955); Morgan F. Davenport, Primitive Traits in Religious Revival (New York: AMS Press, 1905); Jonathan Edwards, "The Great Awakening," in Works of Jonathan Edwards, ed. C. C. Goen, 1 (New Haven & London: Yale University Press, 1972); William Warren Sweet, Revivalism in America: Its Origin, Growth and Decline (Gloucester, Mass.: Peter Smith, 1965); William Warren Sweet, Religion and the Development of American Culture, 1765-1840 (Gloucester, Mass.: Peter Smith, 1963); William Warren Sweet, The Story of Religions in America (New York & London: Harper Brothers, 1930); John Boles, The Great Revival, 1787-1805 (Lexington, Kentucky: The University of Kentucky Press, 1972); Richard M'Nemar, The Kentucky Revival (Cincinnati: John Browne, 1807), Microfilm: Religion in America, Early Books and Manuscripts, BR. 515.R43, 1976, Reel 27; Charles Chauncey, Seasonable Thoughts on the State of Religion in New England (Boston: Rogers & Fowle, 1743); Charles Chauncey, Enthusiasm Described and Cautioned Against (Boston: J. Draper, 1742) Microfilm: BR.515.R43, 1976, Reel 11; Timothy L. Smith, Revivalism and Social Reform (New York & Nashville: Abingdon, 1957) 80-128; Iain Murray, Revival and Revivalism (Edinburgh: The Bearer of Truth Trust, 1944, 225-98; Bernard Weisberger, They Gathered at the River (Boston: Little Brown, 1958.)

[353] Ibid. Jonathan Edwards, The Great Awakening, 12.

The doctrine of federal theology taught that the covenant of grace covered the progeny of the regenerate. Consequently, when the first generation of Puritans baptized their children, it was with the expectation that those children would automatically profess conversion in adulthood. Since baptism was considered "the sign and seal of the covenant."[354] But unfortunately, "many members of the second generation could not honestly testify to such an experience."[355] Not only did this create a cloud of doubt over their relationship to the visible church, but it also became even more problematic and intolerable for them to present their own children for baptism.[356]

To circumvent these problems, the Synod radically redefined the concept of "a Church of visible saints" by stripping it of the old requirement, which demanded "a profession of experimental faith."[357] In essence, the Synod accepted that unconverted parents "who were of upright life and would accept the discipline of the Church,..might present their children for baptism."[358] "The subtle tendency of these decisions was to relax anxiety about personal regeneration and raise tentative hopes of salvation by character."[359]

Thus these developments greatly weakened the Church, as her doors became wide open to worldliness and the unconverted. Wesley Gewehr summarizes the condition of the Churches in the following words:

> The Half-way Covenant which permitted morally respectable persons to enter the Church although they had not experienced conversion, opened the doors to laxity and worldliness. There also seems to have been no little defection from sound doctrine. Among the Presbyterians, too, little was known of vital experimental religion, and there was much complaint of lack of zeal and fidelity in the preaching of the gospel, to say nothing of the conviction

---

[354] Ibid.
[355] Ibid.
[356] Ibid.
[357] Ibid.
[358] Ibid.
[359] Ibid.

that many members of the Synod of Philadelphia were in an unconverted state. The Anglicans were no better off, indifference, coldness, formality and lack of spirituality characterizing both clergy and laity. Religious destitution was also great among the Lutheran and Dutch Reformed churches of New York, New Jersey and Pennsylvania. In a word, prior to the Great Awakening the evangelical doctrines were obscured by externals, the religion had become a matter of dead formality in Churches everywhere throughout the colonies.[360]

It was this state of moral and spiritual declension that engendered a sense of "remarkable religious concern"[361] in many inhabitants, especially of the New England colonies. As Gaustad has clearly expressed, "Many of the third and fourth generations, haunted by a sense of apostasy and by feelings of religious inferiority, looked back with envy and guilt to the older sterner forebears."[362] This resulted in ardent desires, expressed through fervent prayers and fiery sermons, to reach back and recapture the essence and power of the "old time religion" of their ancestors.

By 1720 the preaching of Theodore Frelinghuysen had ignited sparks of revival among the Dutch Reformed in New Jersey. While in 1726, William and Gilbert Tennet were stirring the revival spirit among the Presbyterians.[363] But by far, a greater movement of the spirit, with remarkable effects on blacks, was to result from Jonathan Edwards' ministry at Northampton, Massachusetts, starting in 1734.

---

[360] Wesley M. Gewehr, <u>The Great Awakening</u>, 2-4.

[361] Edwin Scott Gaustad, <u>The Great Awakening in New England</u> (New York: Harper & Brothers, 1957), 16.

[362] Ibid.

[363] Ibid. Wesley Gewehr, <u>The Great Awakening</u>, 4-5.

Effects of Evangelical Revivals on Blacks

In <u>A Faithful Narrative of the Surprising Work of God in the Conversion of Many Hundred Souls in Northampton</u>,[364] Edwards makes it clear "that the Northampton conversions of 1734-35, so far as they stemmed from the influence of his preaching, were produced by what he intended as a doctrinal corrective."[365] Thus the fantastic spiritual results were truly surprising. In his first report, contained in a letter to the Rev. Dr. Benjamin Coleman of the Battle street Church in Boston, Edwards describes the Great Awakening as "the present extraordinary circumstances of this town, and the neighboring towns with respect to religion."[366] Wesley Gewehr describes some of the effects of the revival in the following words:

> In the midst of spiritual deadness Edwards began to proclaim anew the evangelical doctrines. Remarkable conversions followed and Edwards soon had an entire community under the spell of his preaching. People became deeply concerned about eternal things and came in great throngs to hear him. They even met in private houses day and night to talk religion and to pray for pardon. In six months more than three hundred, or practically the entire population above sixteen years, were converted in Northampton.[367]

The awakening quickly spread to other towns in the Connecticut valley. Perhaps, one aspect of the revival that stood out most clearly in Edwards' mind was "the universality of it in affecting all sorts, high and low, rich and poor, wise and unwise, old and young, vicious and moral..."[368] No doubt, blacks were among the recipients of this "extraordinary dispensation of providence."[369]

---

[364] The full text of this memorable work of Jonathan Edwards is reproduced in <u>The Great Awakening, The Works of Jonathan Edwards</u>.

[365] Ibid., 7.

[366] Ibid., 99.

[367] Wesley Gewehr, <u>The Great Awakening</u>, 5.

[368] Jonathan Edwards, <u>The Great Awakening</u>, 107.

[369] Ibid.

In his <u>A Faithful Narrative</u>, Edwards testifies that, "there are several Negroes, that from what was seen of them then, and what is discernable in them since, appear to have been truly born again in the late remarkable season."[370] Also, in the preface to Edwards' <u>The Distinguishing marks of the Work of the Spirit of God</u>,[371] William Cooper describes the effects of the Great awakening in the following dramatic terms:

> Sprightly youth have been made to bow like willows to the Redeemer's scepter, and willingly to subscribe with their own hands to the Lord. And out of the mouths of babes, some little children, has God ordained to himself praise, to still the enemy and the avenger [Ps. 8:2; Matt. 21:16]. Of all ranks and degrees: some of the great and rich, but more of the low and poor. Of other countries and nations: Ethiopia has stretched out her hand; some poor Negroes have, I trust, been vindicated into the glorious liberty of the children of God.[372]

In an abridged form of Edwards' report on the effects of the New England revival, Benjamin Coleman records that among those converted, "several Negroes also appeared to have been born again."[373] As the revival continued to reap positive harvests among the apparently most wretched people, "and dregs of mankind, the poor Indians," Edwards adds the addendum that, "many of the poor Negroes also have been in like manner wrought upon and changed."[374]

Perhaps, the most revealing commentary on the profound effect of the awakening on blacks came from one of the most notorious critics of the evangelical revivals.

Charles Chauncy listed Exhorters among those "things of a bad and dangerous tendency" in the movement. He seemed particularly galled

---

[370] Ibid., 159.
[371] The text of this interesting discourse is also published in Jonathan Edwards, <u>The Great Awakening</u>, 214.
[372] Jonathan Edwards, <u>The Great Awakening</u>, 219-20.
[373] Ibid., 122.
[374] Ibid., 330.

by the fact that blacks were among the Exhorters in the evangelical revivals. Chauncy's vitriolic comment reads thus:

> Men of all occupations, who are vain enough to think themselves fit to be *Teachers* of others; Men who, though they have no learning, and but *small capacities*, yet imagine they are able, and without study too, to speak to the *spiritual profit* of such as are willing to hear them: Nay, there are among these Exhorters, *Babes* in *Age* as well as understanding. They are *chiefly* indeed *young persons*, sometimes *Lads*, or rather *Boys*; Nay, *Women* and *Girls*; yea, *Negroes*, have taken upon them to do the business of *Preachers*.[375]

This comment is just one of many references to black preachers during the evangelical awakening and the years immediately following.

During his ministry in North America, for example, George Whitefield is said to have witnessed the conversion of many blacks. "Leaving Philadelphia in 1740 Whitefield reported that "nearly fifty negroes came to give me thanks for what God had done for their souls."[376] A black convert through Whitefield's ministry is said to have "preached to crowded audiences."[377] Hence Raboteau's very insightful observation that "when the full tide of the Great Awakening swept over the colonies, beginning in 1740, blacks were among those lifted to new heights of religious excitement."[378] As the revival spread into the Southern states, we encounter even more remarkable conversions of blacks.

---

[375] Charles Chauncy, <u>Seasonable Thoughts on the State of Religion in New England</u> (Boston: Rogers and Fowle, 1743), 226.

[376] Quoted by Winthrop Jordan, <u>White Over Black</u>, 213

[377] Boston Gazette, April 29, 1765, cited by Winthrop Jordan, <u>White over Black</u>, 213.

[378] Raboteau, <u>Slave Religion</u>, 128.

The Spread of Evangelical Revival to Southern States

In his book, <u>The Great Awakening in Virginia, 1740-1790,</u>[379] Wesley Gewehr demonstrates that although it originated in New England, the Great Awakening was not confined to its roots. Rather, by the eve of the revolution, the revival had spread from New England into New Jersey, Virginia and North Carolina. It's rapid expansion into almost all the Southern states in this period is attested to by the phenomenal growth in black Presbyterians, Baptists and Methodists in the South.

Although Gewehr is mainly concerned with the Great awakening in Virginia, his book has also become paradigmatic for a succinct account of the spread of the revival in the South. The author describes the pre-revival spiritual conditions of Virginia as in hardly any better shape than what existed in the rest of the colonies. "In Virginia, at the beginning of the eighteenth century, not more than one in twenty were members of the Church, and a smaller proportion in the other Southern colonies."[380] The situation was even worse for the lower classes, including blacks who constituted one-half of Virginia's 300,000 inhabitants in the early decades of the eighteenth century.[381] Thus William Sweet rightly observes that "the first great religious movement which made any serious impression upon the common people of the American colonies was that known as the Great Awakening.[382]

The Great awakening, came to the Southern States in three phases:[383] The first phase started in 1740 and lasted till 1759, under the ministration of Presbyterian laymen. It became known as the Hanover revival because Hanover County served not only as the nucleus of the revival, but it also became "the mother of Southern Presbyterianism."[384] The Reverend Samuel Davies was one of the Clergymen later sent by the New Side synod of New York to consolidate the work. Upon arrival in Virginia, the African slaves immediately arrested Samuel

---

[379] Wesley Gewehr. <u>The Great Awakening in Virginia.</u>
[380] William Sweet, <u>American Historical Review</u>, 35: 887.
[381] Charles C. Jones, <u>Religious Instruction</u>, 36.
[382] William Sweet, <u>American Historical Review</u> 35: 887.
[383] See Wesley Gewehr, <u>The Great Awakening in Virginia.</u>
[384] William Sweet, <u>American Historical Review</u> 35: 887.

Davies' attention. Among his congregation of about 300 or more regular attendees, Rev. Davies describes his impressions of the black members in the following words:

> Never have I been so struck with the appearance of an assembly, as when I have glanced my eye to that part of the meeting-house where they usually sit, *adorned* (for so it had appeared to me) with so many black countenances, eagerly attentive to every word they hear and frequently bathed in tears. A considerable number of them (about a hundred) have been baptised, after a proper time for instruction, having given credible evidence, not only of their acquaintance with the important doctrines of the Christian religion, but also a deep sense of them in their minds, attested by a life of strict piety and holiness.[385]

Reverend Davies narrates his pleasure of once seeing 40 blacks at communion, "all of whom made a credible profession of Christianity, and several of them gave unusual evidence of sincerity."[386] He also indicated that "more than 1,000 Negroes attended on his ministry at different places where he officiated alternately."[387] Just when the Presbyterian revival was waning, the Baptist awakening began.

The Baptists initiated the second phase of the Southern revivals, which lasted from about 1760 to 1775. Led by Shubel Stearns and Daniel Marshall, the Baptists first settled in Sandy Creek. And through their method of aggressive evangelism, "the Sandy Creek Church grew within a short time from sixteen to over six hundred members."[388] As a result of the revivals, the Baptists saw phenomenal growths in black membership from the mid-eighteenth century to the early decades of the nineteenth.

Edwin Gaustad has suggested that "Baptist growth in the seventeenth century was exceedingly slow," with only "4 Baptist Churches in the

---

[385] Charles C. Jones, <u>Religious Instruction</u>, 36.

[386] Ibid.

[387] Ibid.

[388] William Sweet, <u>American Historical Review</u> 35: 888.

colonies in 1660."[389] Thus the unprecedented increase enjoyed by the denomination in the mid- to late decades of the eighteenth century has been rightly attributed to the effects of the evangelical revivals. "The waves of revivalism in all the colonies directly or indirectly augmented this religious body.[390]

The Third phase of the Southern revival began in 1772 and peaked in 1776. It was led by the Methodists. Through the hard work of Devereaux Jarratt and Methodist itinerants like Francis Asbury, Methodism grew at a very rapid pace, especially among the down trodden blacks of the South. Black converts were frequently mentioned in the reports of the Methodist evangelists. In a letter to John Wesley in 1770, for example, the itinerant evangelist, Mr. Pillmore included the following comment: "the number of blacks that attend the preaching affects me."[391] Charles C. Jones reports a great Methodist revival in Virginia between 1773 and 1776, where one itinerant's letter mentions that "the Chapel was full of white and black." Another letter states that; "hundreds of Negroes were among them with tears streaming down their faces."[392]

In terms of actual black Methodist membership, we shall rely heavily on only estimates. One report on the state of Methodism in the colonies, for example, indicates that by May 1777 there were "40 preachers in the different circuits and about 7000 members in the society, besides many hundreds of Negroes, who were convinced of sin, and many of them happy in the love of God."[393]

Unfortunately, progress of the evangelical revivals was inhibited by the American War of Independence. And in the words of Gewehr, "It required yet another Awakening to complete the victory of evangelical Christianity,"[394] especially among the African population. We shall refer

---

[389] Edwin Scott Gaustad <u>Historical Atlas of Religion in America</u> (New York: Harper & Row, 1962), 10.

[390] Ibid., 12.

[391] Charles C. Jones, <u>Religious Instruction</u>, 39.

[392] Ibid.

[393] Ibid., 40.

[394] Wesley Gewehr, <u>The Great Awakening</u>, 167.

to this next phase of evangelical outreach as the Post-Revolutionary Revivals.

The Post-Revolutionary Revivals and
Slave Christianization

As mentioned earlier, the momentum of the evangelical revivals was interrupted by the American Revolution, "but by 1785 to 1789 the spiritual campaign was on again in full blast."[395] By means of what has come to be known as the Camp meeting strategy, the revivals took on a new dimension and gravity, which produced even more abundant fruit among blacks than in previous years. Luther P. Jackson states it succinctly thus:

> At this time, unlike the preceding, the operations were carried on by all the denominations at the same time. All of these revivals, we must note, but more especially those following the Revolution, brought in Negro converts by the thousands as well as the whites. Christianity now becomes a thing for all classes.[396]

The precise origin and occasion of the huge outdoor revivals, which became characteristic of the American frontier after the Revolution are still a matter of debate.[397] Charles Johnson however finds some parallels between John Wesley's outdoor preaching in England, as early as 1739 and what became a common practice in the American colonies in the closing decades of the eighteenth century. In both cases, Johnson suggests "open-air preaching, emotion, and rowdy opposition by outsiders,"[398] as common traits. Desire and necessity also seem to have

---

[395] Luther P. Jackson, "Religious Development of the Negro," 171.

[396] Ibid.

[397] See Charles A. Johnson, <u>The Frontier Camp Meeting</u> (Dallas, Tex.: Southern Methodist University Press, 1955) See chapter 2 for a thorough discussion of the genesis and necessity of Camp Meetings.

[398] Ibid., 26.

played a part in stimulating out-door meetings in both England and the American colonies. Johnson makes the insightful suggestion that:

> In America also, in the decades before 1800, preaching in the wooded clearing was common. The practice stemmed from both desire and necessity. The new settlers loved the out-of-doors, where natural beauty often turned their thoughts toward spiritual concerns. Church meeting-houses in the backwoods were also frequently too small to hold the numbers that attended. In some of the border regions the problem was not lack of space but the complete absence of a Church building.[399]

Hence any number of small out-door revivals might have been held by any number of individuals prior to the last decade of the eighteenth century, but "the significant point," according to Johnson, "is that they did not achieve any universal popularity or standard form until after 1799."[400]

This was when "the first extraordinary appearances of the power of God began in Logan and Christian Counties; on the waters of Gasper and Red rivers"[401] in Kentucky. Credit for this remarkable initial outpouring has been associated with the labors of "the fiery Presbyterian minister, James McGready--and with the religious quickening he in so large a measure created, the great Revival in the West."[402] Whatever reasons and personnel that might have precipitated Camp meetings, the issue of crucial concern to us in this paper is how those revivals radically affected Africans in the American colonies.

The pervasive effect of the post-Revolutionary revivals was succinctly captured in Gewehr's statement that "all classes from the well-to-do to

---

[399] Ibid., 27.

[400] Ibid., 32.

[401] Richard M'Nemar, <u>The Kentucky Revival</u> (Cincinnati: John W. Browne, 1807), 19 Microfilm: Religion in America Part I, Early Books and manuscripts, BR. 515 R 43, 1976, Reel 27.

[402] Charles Johnson, <u>The Frontier Camp Meeting</u>, 32.

the Negroes were reached."[403] Some of the positive effects of the revivals on the white population were observed in their willingness to bring their slaves to revival meetings, and the slaves demonstrated remarkable fondness for camp meetings.[404]

Of course, the blacks fully shared in the tremendous emotional energy of the meetings and were subject to the same characteristically remarkable bodily exercises which accompanied the revivals, such as falling to the ground, jerking, barking, dancing and trance-like unconsciousness.[405] But perhaps, an even more profound effect on the slaves was their remarkable conversion and absorption into the various Churches.

In particular, the profound effect of the revivals on the black population before and after the Revolution, was reflected not only in the fact that "thousands were converted and baptized,"[406] resulting in large intakes into the Methodist, Presbyterian and Baptist congregations, but also in the birth of independent black Churches.

In 1792, for example, Jedidiah Morse, obviously flabbergasted by the unbelievable rate of Methodists expansion, remarked that: "Their numbers are so various in different places, at different times, that it would be a matter of no small difficulty to find out the exact amount."[407]

Perhaps, a bit more precise than Morse, DuBois estimates that black membership "in the Methodist denomination from 1791 to 1795, inclusive, were 12,884, 13,871, 16,227, 13,814, 12,179."[408] "In 1800 there were 15,688 Negro Methodists through out the country."[409] The author has also suggested that by 1793, a quarter of the total

---

[403] Wesley Gewehr, The Great Awakening in Virginia, 173.

[404] John D. Long, Pictures of Slavery in Church and State (Philadelphia: John Dixion Long, 1857) 159, cited by Charles Johnson 113.

[405] Catherine C. Cleveland, The Great Revival in the West (Gloucester, Mass.: Peter Smith, 1959) chapter 4; Richard M'Nemar, The Kentucky Revival, 61.

[406] William DuBois, The Negro Church, 18.

[407] Cited by Edwin Gaustad, Historical Atlas, 74.

[408] William DuBois, The Negro Church, 19.

[409] William Sweet, The Story of Religion in America (New York and London: Harper & Brothers, 1930), 421.

Baptist membership of 73,471 was black.[410] By 1813, the black Baptist membership had more than doubled, growing from 18,000 to about 40,000.[411] Ernest Thompson estimates that "at the outbreak of the Civil war approximately 200,000 Negroes held membership in the Methodist Churches in the South; and the Baptists were probably more numerous."[412] It is interesting to note that a vast majority of the black converts from the revivals continued to be part of the white congregations, especially in the South, until their emancipation was proclaimed in 1863. And that blacks and whites were segregated, not only at the camp meetings,[413] but also during Sunday Worship Services. Thus as soon as "the Negroes were now free and many of them, if for no other reason than to put their freedom to the test, were anxious to separate themselves from the Churches of their former masters."[414] In some cases, the white congregations encouraged and supported the formation of separate black Churches.

Dubois reports, for example, that as early as "towards the close of 1792, the first colored Baptist Church in the City of Savannah began to build a place of worship."[415] This Fellowship was served respectively by notable black preachers like George Lisle, and Andrew Bryan, who became famous for his willingness to endure extreme physical abuse rather than give up preaching. In 1793, Jesse Peter started another African Church in Augusta, Georgia.[416] Perhaps, another indicator of the firm root Christianity had taken among the Africans was the phenomenal growth of the independent African congregations. William Sweet provides valuable insights into the rate of Church growth among blacks in the following words:

---

[410] Charles C. Jones, The Religious Instruction, 53.

[411] Ibid., 58.

[412] Ernest Trice Thompson, Presbyterians in the South 1607-1861 (Richmond, Virginia, John Knox 1930).

[413] Charles Johnson, The Great Awakening, 113-21.

[414] William W. Sweet, The Story of Religion in America, 473.

[415] William E. B. DuBois, The Negro Church, 19.

[416] Ibid.

The ease with which a Baptist Church could organize largely accounts for the great number formed among negroes, though the practice of baptism by immersion likewise attracted negroes to that Church. The Independent negro Methodist Churches also grew at amazing rapidity during the years following the war. The African Methodist Episcopal Church, which had been formed in Philadelphia in 1816, and until the Civil War had existed only among northern negroes, by 1880 had nearly 400,000 members, mostly in the South. The African Methodist Episcopal Zion Church, organized in New York in 1820, in ten years during this period grew from 26,746 members to nearly 200,000.[417]

Thus, the positive effect of the American evangelical revivals on the slave population is certainly undeniable. The question that still remains to be answered, however, is why the revivals in general, and camp meetings in particular, held such a tremendous attraction for the African slaves and ex-slaves.

In its most basic and general form, the answer to this question constitutes the thesis of our dissertation: that the continuities between evangelical revivalism and ATR were largely responsible for drawing the slaves to the revivals, and subsequently their conversion to Christianity. We have identified three basic areas in which the revivals struck familiar cords with the innate religious heritage of the Africans as follows: the content of revival messages, the conduct of revival meetings, and the character of revival settings.

Before further elaboration it would be helpful to make a couple of observations and clarifications: First, that the relationship between Christianity and ATR is not entirely continuous. There are possibly as many discontinuities between the two religions as there are continuities. For example, the Written Word of God or Scripture and the incarnate Word of God or God's Special revelation in Jesus Christ, both of which are foundational to Christianity, are concepts quite foreign to ATR.

---

[417] William W. Sweet, <u>The Story of Religion in America</u>, 474.

Second, that our use of the term "continuity" does not imply one to one correlation between Christianity and ATR. The term is used more or less in the sense of easily identifiable traits in Christianity that could have appealed to the African traditional religious instincts of the slaves. By continuity we also mean terminology common to both religious systems.

Having said that, it is now in place to discuss the determinant factors in the slaves' positive response to the evangelical revivals.

The Contents of Evangelical Revival Messages

The messages of the evangelical revivals probably varied in intensity of delivery, depending on the oratory skills and personality of the Evangelist. The very vivid depictions of Heaven and Hell and other "frightening" illustrations characteristic of the revival messages were probably chosen in relation to the type of congregations addressed. It is also possible that local variations of certain aspects of the revivals did exist, but what seemed to have remained constant was the basic content of the messages: the need for a "new birth."

The doctrine of the "new birth" has been identified as the core of the revival message.[418] This was not a new invention by the preachers in the Great Awakening, but probably one of the most significant ideas in the history of religion, which dates back to the Reformers. It was strongly "held by the Orthodox Congregationalists of New England, and others who harmonize with them."[419] The "new birth" has been defined as,

> The doctrine, that in order to be saved, a man must undergo a change in his principles of moral action, which will be either accompanied or succeeded by exercises of which he is conscious, and can give an account; so that those who have been thus changed, may ordinarily be distinguished from those who have not; from which it follows, that all who exhibit no evidence of such a change, ought to be considered and treated as unregenerate, and in the road to

[418] Joseph Tracy, The Great Awakening, 9.
[419] Ibid.

perdition, and therefore not admitted to the communion of the Churches.[420]

The "new birth" was thus the culmination of a process, which began with an awakening or realization that a person was not part of the regenerate and led to self-examination. "The result of self-examination is the discovery of guilt, or, in the technical language of practical theology, conviction of sin."[421] Conviction of sin produced remorse or repentance, and consequently, the sinner's complete faith in Jesus Christ as the sacrificial Lamb of God, whose blood washes away sin and guilt through the grace and forgiveness of God. This process culminated in the salvation of the individual.

The urgency and necessity of the "new birth" was often portrayed through such vivid illustrations of the eternal suffering of the unregenerate, that it usually produced dramatic effects on the audience. For example, Jonathan Edwards describes some of the initial effects of the awakening in New England in the following words:

> This town never was so full of love, nor so full of joy, nor so full of distress as has lately been. Some persons have had those longing desires after Jesus Christ, that have been to that degree as to take away their strength and very much to weaken them, and make them faint.[422]

Indeed, the effects of Edwards' sermons produced such strong emotional reactions that Frederick Davenport felt the combination of

[420] Ibid.

[421] Ibid., 10.

[422] Jonathan Edwards, unpublished letter of his Faithful Narratives, 104-105. As the revivals spread, physical effects on audiences became so dramatic that many Critics dismissed the revivals as works of the devil. For some of the literature opposing the revivals, especially in New England, read: Charles Chauncey's writings: Seasonable Thoughts on the state of Religion in New England (Boston: Rogers & Fowle, 1743); Religious Commotions in New England Considered; An answer to the Rev. Mr. Jonathan Edwards' Sermon, entitled The Distinguishing Marks of the work of the Spirit of God (Boston: Green, Bushell, and Allen, 1743); Charles Chauncey Enthusiasm Described and Decried (Boston: J. Draper, 1742).

Edwards' personality and the gravity of his message "was psychologically if not theologically predestined to produce much mental and nervous disorder"[423] in the New England population. Interestingly, such physical and emotional manifestations were not restricted to the Edwardsian awakening, but became common phenomena through out the history of the revivals.

Through such direct and candid preaching, the revival messages offered hope to the hopeless slaves, gave them an identity in Jesus Christ, reminded them of the responsibility of personal accountability to God, and the promise of a relationship with Jesus Christ. More than that, the slaves heard in revival messages, concepts that rang a bell of familiarity with their African traditional religious background. The theology of the revival messages was one such concept that resonated with the African traditional religious conceptions of the slaves.

For example, the strong emphasis on the sovereignty and prerogative of God in saving sinners from sin coincided with the African conception of a supreme and creator god, whom ATR recognizes as the prime cause of all occurrences, good or bad. Another concept of God in the revival messages that probably appealed to the Africans was the emphasis on God's universal and personal love for mankind.

Also, the strong theme of death and resurrection in revival sermons became another point of contact with the slaves' previous religious experiences. Not only was the death and resurrection of Jesus Christ central to revival preaching, but the whole process of the "new birth" was usually presented in the imagery of dying to self and rising up as a new person in Christ. This theme, which was at the core of the revival process of conversion, contained many parallels to the West African religious process of initiation, of which most of the slaves were probably aware.

---

[423] Frederick M. Davenport, <u>Primitive Traits in Religious Revivals: A study in Mental and Social Evolution</u>. (London & New York: Macmillan, 1905), 113. In this book, Davenport attempts to offer a purely psychological and sociological explanations of the revivals. He suggests that the physical manifestations were due to psychological and mental imbalances produced by the fearful sermons of the revivalists.

As was mentioned earlier, secret societies in West Africa serve various purposes, ranging from marking rites of passage from childhood into adulthood to meeting complex religious needs of the people.[424] The importance of initiations as mysterious but pervasive practices in African culture, has been underscored by Zahan thus:

> We can...understand that while it is possible to chart the distribution of certain cultural elements which accompany initiation and its social signifiers, it is impossible to concretely locate initiation itself. It exists everywhere, asserting its authority as the spiritual base of the African soul, as background on which all religious revelations--from the most insignificant to the most imposing--are registered.[425]

One of the basic philosophies of almost every secret society in West Africa is the idea that upon initiation, the neophyte dies to his or her old self and graduates as a completely new person. The symbolic death can take place in forest groves, caves or other sacred space designated for the purposes of the society. "Among certain groups the grotto or cave is 'replaced' by an artificial excavation in the ground when the symbolic death of the initiates is performed."[426] The initiation sites have been described as part of an elaborate system of "Elementary Cathedrals"

---

[424] For more comprehensive discussions of the topic see: W. T. Harris, "The Idea of God among the Mende"; Robert T. Parsons, "The Idea of God among the Kono of Sierra Leone" in African Ideas of God: A Symposium, ed. Edwin Smith, 260-76 (London: Edinburgh House, 1950); Kenneth L. Little, "The Role of the Secret Society in Cultural Specialization"; Colin M. Turnbull, "Initiation among the Bambuti Pygmies of the Central Ituri, "in Culture and Societies of Africa, ed. Simon and Phoebe Ottenberg, 421-42 (New York: 1960); The Religion, Spirituality and Thought of Traditional Africa, ed. Dominique Zahan (Chicago, London: University of Chicago, 1979), chapter 4. We have also dealt with Secret Societies in appreciable details in chapter 2 of this dissertation.

[425] Dominique Zahan, The Religion, Spirituality and Thought, 55.

[426] Dominique Zahan, Societes d'Initiation Bambara: le Kore (Paris and the Hague: Mouton, 1963), 323-24, cited by Dominique Zahan, The Religion, Spirituality and Thought, 25.

common to ATR. Zahan vividly describes further uses of such natural temples in the following lines:

> At times, again through the intermediary of these temples, man enters the "digestive" stomach of the earth, whose role is then to "smash" the initiate, to "pulverize" his old personality in order to fashion a new one. In the past, initiation into the *Komo* society of the Bambara, which was intended to transform the individual by means of such "crushing" of the personality, often took place in a grotto. But the "rebirth" of the initiate can also be compared to the "rebirth" of vegetation when the rains return to make the earth fertile.[427]

Very similar concepts and terminology have been used by Kenneth Little to describe initiation practices among the Mende of Sierra Leone.[428] The Mende have at least four secret societies: the *Poro, Wunde, Sande, Humoi and Njayei* societies. "The above societies are not exclusive to the Mende, but are shared widely, with the exception of the Wunde, among adjacent peoples, such as the Sherbro, the Krim, the Gola, etc., whose cultural affinities with the Mende are very close."[429]

Little's comment on the initiation ritual and philosophy of the Poro is especially instructive for us: "The Poro boy is "swallowed" by the spirit when he enters the bush, and the marks made on his back signify the spirit's teeth. At the end of his time, he is delivered by the spirit and reborn."[430] To underscore the change that has taken place while the initiates were in the "stomach" of the spirit, the boys are usually "reborn" with freshly shaven heads and each of them is given a new

---

[427] Ibid.

[428] Kenneth L. Little, "The Role of the Secret Society in Cultural Specialization," in <u>Culture and Society of Africa</u>, ed. Simon and Phoebe Ottenberg, 199. Note that the feminine equivalence of the *Poro* is the *Sande*. Incidentally, the current writer is born and bred Mende and therefore personally familiar with the Secret Societies described by Kenneth Little.

[429] Ibid.

[430] Ibid.

name or assumes one. From the day of their "rebirth" and hence forth, non-initiates or *Kpoweisia*[431] can only address the *sowo hinis*[432] by their new names.

The point here is not to equate Christian conversion with African initiation rites, but to illustrate the fact that it is a parallel existing between concepts and terminology of revival sermons and those of ATR to attract the attention of the slaves.

Another point of contact between the two religions that might have appealed to the slaves is the idea of blood sacrifice. Again, this was touched upon in my discussion of ATR.[433]

The concept of the blood of Jesus being shed for the sins of the slaves, though probably heard for the first time, could be easily grasped when one considers that the most prevalent ritual in ATR is blood sacrifice. Mbiti shares the following intriguing insights on sacrificial systems in ATR:

> The practice of making sacrifices and offerings is found all over Africa. By this practice material or physical things are given to God and other spiritual beings. This marks the point where the visible and invisible worlds meet, and shows man's intention to project himself into the invisible world.

---

[431] This is the plural form of *Kpowei*, which literally means "Fool". The implications being that before one is initiated into the secret society, one has not attained true knowledge. To be without the experience of initiation is tantamount to being a fool or "unregenerate."

[432] *Sowo hini* is the Mende term for one who has successfully gone through the "death" process and met all requirements of the Poro and is "reborn" to take his place in society as a mature male, with all due privileges. Before this, the uninitiated is termed *Kpowa*, which means one without knowledge. For in Mende tradition, a man's knowledge is never complete until he adds the wisdom of the secret society to it.

[433] The point I want to make here is that the concept of sacrifice as a religious ritual or phenomenon, with which the slaves were already intuitively familiar, could have been one of the elements in evangelical Christianity that made it easily understandable to the Africans. It has to be pointed out that in the slave testimonies examined the narrators mostly speak about how and not why they were converted or attracted to revival meetings.

People make sacrifices and offerings of almost any animal or object. The distinction between sacrifices and offerings is this: sacrifices involve the shedding of the blood of human beings, animals or birds; offerings do not involve blood but concern the giving of all other things, such as foodstuffs, water, milk, honey or money. In African societies, life is closely associated with blood. When blood is shed in making a sacrifice, it means that human or animal life is being given back to God who is in fact the ultimate source of all life. Therefore the purpose of such a sacrifice must be a very serious one.[434]

Another helpful commentary on the crucial place of blood sacrifice in African religion comes from Zahan. He suggests that:

African spiritual life is so impregnated with the idea of immolation that it is practically impossible to find a people on that continent whose religious practices do not include the slaughter of the most diverse victims. It can even be said that sacrifice is the keystone of this religion. It constitutes the supreme "prayer," that which could not be renounced without seriously compromising the relationship between man and the Invisible. By sacrifice we mean the flowing blood of slaughtered animals. And it is from the actual blood of animals and human beings who have fallen on innumerable altars that its entire value in Africa derives.[435]

Thus coming from a religious background steeped in blood sacrifice, the African slaves were not only attracted to the euphoria of the revivals, but the idea of Jesus Christ being the sacrificial lamb for their sins must have also had a tremendous impact on them.[436] The conduct of the meetings also played a role in the massive conversion of the slaves.

---

[434] John S. Mbiti, Introduction to African Religion, 63.

[435] Dominique Zahan, The Religion, Spirituality and Thought, 33.

[436] See my comments on page 256.

The Conduct of Evangelical Revival Meetings and Slave Christianization

There many interpretations of the phenomena of the Great awakening.[437] But whatever their interpretive position or bias, revisionists and revivalist alike, tend to agree that the conduct of the evangelical revivals could be described, among other caricatures, by three main words: emotionalism, flexibility, and egalitarianism. By and large, it was these three ingredients in the conduct of the revivals that touched the nerve-cords of the slaves and thereby facilitated their conversion. We shall briefly examine them one at a time.

Emotionalism is perhaps, the most distinct imagery many contemporary critics and supporters seem to have of the revivals. For example, Frederick Davenport presents the Great Awakening as "essentially a form of impulsive social action."[438] The basic assumption of his book being that "the typical religious revival is characterized by the dominance of emotion in mass and in control."[439] Using a purely sociological framework of interpretation, based on the doctrine of mental and social evolution, the author attributes the emotional fervor of the revivals to primitive traits in humans, which are developmentally speaking, only one stage above animals on the evolutionary scale.

In the frame of mind, and with the assumption that Africans are the most primitive of all races, Davenport offers the following commentary on their involvement in the revival movements:

> Thoroughly religious animal as he is by nature, with extraordinary emotional endowment added thereto, he would find it very difficult to withstand the almost constant tide of revival that sweeps over his community.[440]

---

[437] See Frank Lambert, <u>Inventing the Great Awakening</u> (Princeton, N.J.: Princeton University Press, 1999).

[438] Frederick Davenport, <u>Primitive Traits in Religious Revival</u>, chapter 1.

[439] Ibid., viii.

[440] Ibid., 48-49.

Davenport's assessment of the African slaves' religious affinities and unusual emotional endowments can hardly be disputed. It has to be noted, however, that in most of the revival meetings whites were just as emotional as blacks. Also, blacks were not passively swept away in emotional tides of revival, as Davenport tends to portray, but the similarities between revival worship and religious celebrations in ATR were probably some of the main attractions for the Africans. For example, the singing and dancing characteristic of revival meetings were not a strange phenomena to the Africans, because essentially, "African Religion is found in music and dance."[441] It has already been mentioned in this study that music, dance and singing are an integral part of every African community and religion.

> "Music is used in all activities of African life: in cultivating the fields, fishing, herding, performing ceremonies, praising rulers and warriors, hushing babies to sleep and so on."[442]

In relation to African religious practices, Mbiti reveals that

> the religious rituals, ceremonies and festivals are always accompanied by music, singing and sometimes dancing. Music gives outlet to the emotional expression of the religious life, and it is a powerful means of communication in African traditional life. It helps to unite the singing and dancing group and to express its fellowship and participation in life.[443]

After several years of field studies in West Africa, Melville Herskovits' findings are very similar to that of Mbiti. He makes the interesting observation that "one striking similarity between the cultures of the continent is the method of Worship." Herskovits also asserts that "it is not too much to say that the essence of African ceremonialism is the

---

[441] John Mbiti, <u>Introduction to African Religion</u>, 25.
[442] Ibid., 9.
[443] Ibid., 27.

dance; further, that religious dancing is invariably accompanied by singing and, among most African folk, by drum-rhythms."[444]

This is probably one of the very strong reasons why the African slaves looked forward to the seasons of revival with such great anticipation. The opportunity of uninhibited emotional expression and participation in Camp meetings through singing, music, dancing and other physical activities, were definitely great attractions for the black participants.

And of course, that naturally paved the way for the profound spiritual fruit revivalist reaped from among the slaves. John Long describes the slaves' fondness of camp meetings as follows:

> By no class is a camp meeting hailed with more unmixed delight than the poor slaves. It comes at a season of the year they most need rest. It gives them all the advantages of the ordinary holiday, without its accompaniments of drunkenness and profanity.. they can jump to their hearts' content.[445]

During camp meetings, the phenomena of falling, fainting, barking, jerking, and trances, supposedly induced by the influence of the Holy Spirit, were rampant. This is more than likely to have awakened in the slaves, the latent African religious practice of spirit possession. The phenomenon of spirit possession as an indication of contact with the divine, is a common occurrence in ATR. It is found at the core of African mysticism and spirituality.

In his study of the religion, spirituality, and thought of traditional Africa, Dominique Zahan comes to the following conclusion:

> We can confidently affirm that throughout all of Africa the techniques for acquiring the state of "ecstasy" contain a common denominator, the temporary alienation of the very being of the person concerned. Participation in

---

[444] Melville Herskovits, "Social History of the Negro," in A Handbook of Psychology, ed. Carl Murchinson, (Worchester, Mass.: Clark University Press, 1935), 207-67.

[445] John D. Long, Pictures of Slavery in Church and State (Philadelphia: John Dixion Long, 1857) 159, cited by Charles Johnson, The Great Awakening, 114.

mystical life through ecstasy is "leaving" in order to "return," "abandoning" one's kinsmen in order to "find" them afterwards, and especially letting go of oneself totally in order to "recover" oneself anew. Mystical ecstasy is a "death" followed by resurrection.[446]

Zahan further suggests that spirit possessions seem to be particularly common in Western Africa, the region from which most of the slaves were obtained, and where the author's study was largely carried out. One vivid example described by the author is the case among the Ashanti of Ghana. According to Zahan's testimony:

In recent years "possession" by the divinity has been particularly well-studied in several West African peoples. It is thus to this geographical area that our remarks will be limited. Among the Ashanti mystical life takes on a character more individual than social. The "call" is, so to speak, spontaneous and generally occurs at the time of celebrations and customary religious ceremonies. The person affected by divine favor abruptly changes the rhythm of his dance by accelerating it and giving evident signs of a rupture in communication between him and others. He can also fall into convulsions and, with wild eyes, start to tremble all over his body. Both of these symptoms are generally interpreted by the officiating priest as the surest index of divine solicitation.[447]

Amazingly, eyewitness accounts of the Logan and Christian County revivals, on the banks of the Gasper and Red rivers in Kentucky, in the Spring of 1801, indicate very similar phenomena to what Zahan describes among the Ashanti. The effect of revival preaching on the audience is described by Richard M'Nemar in the following words:

---

[446] Dominique Zahan, <u>The Religion, Spirituality and Thought of Traditional Africa</u>, 128.

[447] Ibid., 129.

And under such an overpowering weight of divine goodness, as tongue could not express, they were constrained to cry out, with tears and trembling, and testify to full and free salvation in Christ, for all that would come; and to warn their fellow-creatures of the danger of continuing in sin; and entreating them in the most tender and affectionate manner; to turn from it; and seek the Lord, in sure and certain hope that he would be found. Under such exhortations, the people began to be affected in a very strange manner. At first they were taken with an inward throbbing of heart; then with weeping and trembling: from that to crying out in apparent agony of soul; falling down and swooning away; till every appearance of animal life was suspended; and the person appeared to be in a trance. From this state they would recover under different sensations which will be more particularly noticed hereafter.[448]

As the revivals rapidly spread to other areas, the ecstatic and emotional behaviors of black participants seemed to have reached such high levels that

at another encampment a camp official tried vainly on two successive days to convince a group of slaves that their "convulsive outbursts [were] wrong, and disturbing to both themselves and others." Irrepressible as they were in their expression of their religious feelings, the Negroes never seemed to feel entirely free to work in their own way until the white people closed their services and went to their tents.[449]

It must be mentioned that convulsive outbursts were not peculiar to blacks. Almost every participant in the revivals, including at times, white scoffers who only came to disrupt the meetings, were affected by the unusual physical manifestations.

---

[448] Richard M'Nemar, The Kentucky Revival, 20.
[449] Charles Johnson, Frontier Camp Meetings, 114-15.

The suggestion has also been made that in the African context, a person could be "possessed" by spirits other than God."[450] And interestingly, while Revivalists attributed spirit "possessions" in the Great awakenings to the Holy Spirit, critics tended to think that it was the work of Satan or spirits other than God.[451]

Be it as it may, our proposition is that the ecstatic and emotional aspects of the revivals were partly responsible for the massive black participation, because in them, the slaves saw rituals they could easily identify with, given their previous religious background and practice.

Conversion experiences during the revivals normally started from the anxious or mourners bench, and usually led to very strong convictions that sometimes left the penitent in a state of trance-like coma for several hours. Upon recovery from this state, the converts sometimes narrated extra-terrestrial experiences, confirming that they had indeed become changed and new persons. Of course, these were experiences limited exclusively to the "initiates" or those touched by the Spirit.

Thus conversion experiences involving fainting in revival meetings were common to all races, but some scholars like George Rawick have found certain elements in conversion narratives "which are unique to blacks."[452]

Black conversion narratives seem to contain predominantly detailed descriptions of trances and spirit possession that normally left converts temporarily unconscious. Also, similar phraseology and other common threads tend to run through the experiences of the slave converts. For example, in God Struck me Dead: Religious Conversion Experiences and Autobiographies of Negro Ex-slaves, researchers from Fisk University interviewed about one hundred ex-slaves in the 1920s and found out that individuals whose conversion experiences were recorded

> go through a dramatic experience-sudden sickness, blurring vision, painful pressures of the heart followed by "death"

---

[450] Zahan, The Religion, Spirituality and Thought, 128.

[451] See the writings of Charles Chauncey, for example.

[452] George P. Rawick, The American Slave: A Composite Autobiography, From Sundown to Sunup, 45.

experience in which one sees hell but is saved by the grace of God, or is shown a "big glorious city" wherein resides a man who commands him to "go tell others of your experience." Finally they are brought to life - or rebirth experience. Although each individual tells his death and rebirth in his own way and with his own artistic embellishment, there is a common thread that runs through all the documents.[453]

Some excerpts from the narratives are reproduced below to illustrate the point:

(a) One day while in the field plowing I heard a voice. I jumped because I thought it was my master coming to scold and whip me for ploughing up some more corn. I looked but saw no one. Again the voice called, "Morte! Morte!" With this I stopped, dropped the plow and started running but the voice kept on speaking to me saying, "Fear not, my little one, for behold! I come to bring you a message of truth."

Everything went dark and I was unable to stand any longer. I began to feel sick and there was a great roaring. I tried to cry and move but was unable to do either. I looked up and saw that I was in a New world. There were plants and animals and all. Even the water, where I stooped to drink, began to cry out, "I am blessed but you are damned! I am blessed but you are damned! With this I began to pray and a voice on the inside began to cry, "Mercy! Mercy! Mercy!"

As I prayed an angel came and touched me and I looked new. I looked at my hands and they were new; I looked at my feet and they were new. I looked and saw my old body suspended over a burning pit by a small web like a spider web. I again prayed and there came a soft voice saying, "my little one, I have loved you with an everlasting love. You are

---

[453] George P. Rawick, Gen. ed., <u>God Struck Me Dead</u> (Westport, Conn.: Greenwood, 1972), 2-3.

this day made alive and freed from hell. You are a chosen vessel unto the Lord..."[454]

(b) When God struck me dead with his power I was living on 14th. Avenue. It was the year of the centennial. I was in my house alone and I declare unto you when his power struck me I died. I fell out on the floor flat on my back. I could neither speak nor move for my tongue stuck to the roof of my mouth; my jaws were locked and my limbs stiff.
In my vision I saw hell and the devil. I was crawling along a high brick wall, it seems, and it looked like I would fall into a dark roaring pit. I looked away to the east and saw Jesus. He called to me and said, "Arise and follow me."[455]

(c) One night I went to the mourner's bench - I seemed to have a weight of the house on me - and I was in darkness. And whilst I was down on my knees I looked up and I didn't see no house-top or sky. I just saw the clear heavens and it looked milkish and I said, "Lord, what is this? And He said, "It is love." Then a shower of rain came down on top of my head and went to the toes and I was just as light as any feather and I had on a long white robe and I sailed and went upwards. Then I met a band of angels, angels who were praising God and they looked at me and said, "Praise ye the Lord." The next morning I thought I didn't have any religion and I heard a voice saying, "I have chosen you out of this world. Go tell the people what I have done for you."[456]

(d) God first manifested Himself after I had been going to the mourner's bench and had been prayed for by the members of the Church for a long time.. I got very faint and started to praying. Then I died and I saw my body lying on the edge of a deep gap. A little man came up to me and said, "Arise and go." I said, "Lord, I can't get up or move else I

[454] Ibid., 3.
[455] Ibid., 20.
[456] Ibid., 53.

will fall." He reached out his hand and anointed my head and said, "Arise and follow me for I am the Way, the Truth and the Light. I will make a way where there is no way.[457]

It might be misleading to think that every black convert went through the same dramatic experiences as recorded above. There were some that probably became Christians without falling into trances or fainting. A case in point is the testimony of one of the interviewees in *God Struck Me Dead*. In stark contrast to the experiences of most of the ex-slaves interviewed, one person had this to say:

> My religion means as much to me as any one else but I have not had all of the varied experiences that most of the older people say they have had. I have not had a chance to see any kind of funny forms or anything like that to make me afraid because I think if I would have had to spend time in a cemetery or some secluded place for two or three days I would have never been converted. This is my religion and it is based on the greatest book in the world, the Holy Bible. "Repent, believe and be baptized and you shall be saved." This is my religion and I believe it will take me to heaven just as greatly as any one else's will. I have seen nothing nor heard nothing but only felt the spirit in my soul and I believe that will save me when I come to die.[458]

Indeed, our goal in reproducing the above conversion narratives is not to evaluate the quality of the experiences, but to demonstrate that although couched in Christian terminology, symbols, and to some extent meanings, the roots of the slaves' religious behavior in North America were African.[459] In embracing evangelical Christianity, the

---

[457] Ibid., 62-63.

[458] Ibid., 103.

[459] George P. Rawick has a helpful discussion on this in From Sundown to Sunup, Chapter 3. In this work, Rawick identifies some of the characters in the slave conversion narratives with similar characters in African religion or Mythology. For example, the "little man" in most of the narratives is equated with the Yoruba god *Elegba* or *Legba*, 47.

slave's previous religious experiences were not obliterated, but instead became useful to him in making sense out of what was otherwise a totally foreign concept.

Melville Herskovits refers the religious culture as one of those African retentions that persistently manifests itself in North American black Christian worship. Contrary to opinions that the institution of slavery destroyed every trace of African culture in the slaves, the author draws attention to the fact that

> negroes in the United States are Christians, yet it is possible to see among certain groups of them expressions of Christian worship that are unknown in Europe. The songs of the American Negroes - the spirituals - have long been thought of as African, though there are many today who hold that these are merely borrowings of well-known European hymns. Whether or not these represent in their imagery simple borrowings, or have taken on "accretions," the place of the song in the religious service, the accompaniment by hand-clapping, tapping the feet, and instruments of percussion such as the tambourine, do not partake of European religious cultural behavior. Spirit possession (by the Holy Ghost) manifested through dances - "shouts"- in which the motor behavior is clearly African, is found in some Negro Churches.[460]

In one way or the other, African slaves in North America could easily identify with the freedom of emotional expression in worship and the sense of personal contact with the divine in the conduct of the evangelical revivals, because these were crucial elements in their own latent religious heritage.

Another aspect of the evangelical revivals that attracted the slaves was that, by and large, the meetings were grounded in the egalitarian foundations of Christianity. Granted that at some of the revival meetings

---

[460] Melville Herskovits, "Social History of the Negro," 254-55.

whites and blacks met separately, nevertheless, a spirit of egalitarianism prevailed in most gatherings.[461]

As Johnson has observed, "Revivalism gave to the Negro a rare opportunity to express his higher life, an opportunity denied him in most other spheres. Socially and psychologically it gave him release."[462] It is probably not far fetched to suggest that it was in the revival meetings that slaves first had a taste of freedom and equality with white people. For the message of the revivalist was the same for slave and master: "All have sinned, and are therefore destined for hell, unless they repent." "No one can see the Kingdom of God unless he is born again."[463] In revival meetings all were lost sinners before God. And those who believed, whether slave or master, would be saved.

John Boles reports that "from the moment of their organization, typical Baptist or Methodist Churches included black members, who often signed (or put their "X") on the founding documents or incorporation."[464] And in Boles estimation, "it is fair to say that nowhere else in southern society were they treated so nearly as equals."[465] No doubt, such inclusiveness and egalitarianism of these two denominations partly accounts for the many blacks that affiliated with their Churches during and after the revivals.

The flexibility of some of the denominations in their polity and rituals also became an attraction for the slaves. Baptists and Methodists provided enough leadership opportunities for blacks to attract and retain them. For example, the Baptist philosophy of the autonomy of the local Church empowered blacks to lead their own congregations. It was also significant and revolutionary that among the Methodists and Baptists, black exhorters sometimes ministered even to whites. "The Baptists had Negro preachers for Negro members as early as 1773."[466] By 1800, "the Bishops of the Methodist Episcopal Church were authorized to ordain

---

[461] Charles Johnson, Frontier Camp Meeting, 114.

[462] Ibid., 115.

[463] John 3:3 (NIV).

[464] John B. Boles, Masters and Slaves in the House of God, 9.

[465] Ibid.

[466] DuBois, The Negro Church, 21.

African preachers in places where there were houses of worship for their use."[467] In the Baptist Church, academic qualifications mattered but very little; "the only requirement for preaching was a certain degree of piety and the "call to preach."[468] And, of course, for many slaves the natural thing after conversion was the "call to preach," especially to other slaves. Apart from the content of revival messages and the conduct of the meetings, the physical character of revival settings also contributed to slave conversions. We shall examine this in brief.

Character of Revival Settings and Slave Christianization

The outdoors and purely natural settings of most revival gatherings, especially after the Civil War, not only reminded the slaves of religious settings in their native West Africa, but also probably acted as one of the stimuli that brought them to the meetings.

According to descriptions provided by historians of the Great awakenings, there was hardly any difference between a typical revival atmosphere and religious celebrations in a West African jungle community. Just as Charles Johnson has recorded that "the setting of the early Kentucky camp meeting was 'nature's temple'--the forest clearing,"[469] in the same sense, and for practically the same reasons, Dominique Zahan refers to places of worship in ATR as "natural temples."[470]

In addition to clearings in the forest grove as one of the cardinal centers of religious celebrations in West Africa, Zahan has identified "the four basic elements of water, earth, air and fire," as constituting "the clearest outline" of West African nature temples.[471] Interestingly, these same elements were very much a part of the North American revival camp settings. This partly explains why the African slaves felt so much at home in revival meetings. We shall take a closer look at the physical

---

[467] Ibid., 20.

[468] Luther P. Jackson, "Religious Development of the Negro in Virginia," 175.

[469] Charles Johnson, <u>The Frontier Camp Meeting</u>, 41.

[470] Dominique Zahan, <u>Religion, Spirituality and Thought of African Tradition</u>, 20.

[471] Ibid.

characteristics of some places of worship in ATR and how similar scenery of revival settings could have attracted the African slaves.

Let us begin with the role trees or the forest played in the equation. Plant life or trees in general play a very important role in West African religion. Because of its tropical geography, West African vegetation consists mostly of very thick and impenetrable equatorial forests. Trees in this region can sometimes grow to incredibly large dimensions. Thus "the tree, of all African "sanctuaries," affirms Zahan, "is the one most directly and universally in touch with the divinity."[472]

Trees are not worshipped in ATR but they represent "the power, wealth, uprightness and everlastingness of the Invisible."[473] Worship at the bases of huge trees is a common phenomenon in West Africa, but what holds a particularly sacred place in the life of each village is the sacred grove. Henri Junod describes the role of trees and forest groves in African religion as follows:

> Placed on the path of relations between man and the spiritual powers, the tree acquires an even greater value when it forms a part of the thickets and groves in which man holds religious meetings, and by which he isolates himself from the view of the uninitiated. In fact, groves are the most preferred places of worship in African religion.[474]

Zahan underscores the importance of the forest grove in African religion in the following profound statement:

> But if the grove, sacred in its entirety, constitutes the image of knowledge, then the interior clearing represents the end of the path toward learning: the sky, the abode of pure souls, the "holy" space par excellence. This is why it is generally prohibited for anyone to enter with his shoes on; would it

---

[472] Ibid., 28.

[473] Ibid.

[474] Henri A. Junod, The Life of a South African Tribe, 2d ed. (London: Macmillan, 1927), 332-33, cited by Zahan, The Religion, Spirituality, and Thought, 28.

be proper to soil the sky with all the impurities collected by shoes on earth?[475]

As we indicated earlier, both desire and necessity made preaching in the wooded clearing a common practice in North American revivals.[476] And "these desirable locations were not hard to find in newly settled regions,"[477] Charles Johnson suggests. The reason being that, "...men with ax and sledge could quickly convert a two- to four-acre tract of forest land into an encampment."[478] Thus, according to Johnson, before camp meetings usually started

> there was a hectic activity as the prospective worshippers arrived at the spot, a week before or just prior to the meeting time. Underbrush was cleared away, trees felled, and preparations were made for a tent city.[479]

Just as the clearing in the African forest grove was regarded as "the 'holy' place par excellence," so also was the core of the camp meeting always "the open-air auditorium."[480] This sheds tremendous light on some of the reasons why blacks loved to come to camp meetings. The parallels between a North America revival Camp setting and a West African forest "sanctuary" are too obvious to miss.

Our knowledge of the African's love for outdoor religious celebrations should also help us understand why in their time of extreme oppression, African slaves would "steal off into the woods" to sing and pray.[481] And according to the testimony of an ex-slave, even physical hardships like "whipping did not stop them from having meetings. When one place

---

[475] Ibid.
[476] Charles Johnson, The Frontier Camp Meeting, 27.
[477] Ibid., 42.
[478] Ibid.
[479] Ibid.
[480] Ibid.
[481] John B. Cade, "Out of the Mouths of Ex-slaves," Journal of Negro History 20, no. 3 (1935): 329.

was located [by the Masters], italics mine, they would find another one."[482]

At the time when the blacks did not have their own churches, another ex-slaves recalls that

> on Sunday they (the slaves) would have services after the White people had theirs. Most times, however, the slaves held their meetings in the woods under (brush) arbors made by them. The preacher came from some other plantation; he preached about heaven and hell. There they were not allowed to pray for freedom, but sometimes the slaves would steal away at night and go into cane thickets and pray for deliverance; they always prayed in a prostrate position with the face close to the ground so that no sound could escape to warn the master or overseer.[483]

Mrs. Channel, an ex-slave on a plantation in Louisiana testified to similar experiences among African slaves on her plantation. She recalls that although religious services among slaves were strictly forbidden,

> the slaves would steal away into the woods at night and hold services. They would form a circle on their knees and the speaker would also be on his knees. He would bend forward and speak into or over a vessel of water, to drown the sound. If anyone became animated and cried out, the others would quickly stop the noise by placing their hands over the offender's mouth.[484]

Several reasons could be advanced for slave prayer meetings in the woods, including fear of the master, state laws prohibiting the gathering of not more than a certain number of slaves together, especially for religious meetings. But another deep-seated reason was that in spite

---

[482] Ibid.
[483] Ibid., 330.
[484] Ibid., 331.

of all the rigors of slavery, the slaves were still African in the deepest recesses of their being, where memories of their old religion hardly died.

The slaves found other symbolic links between their old religion and the evangelical revivals. One of those links was the association of camp meetings with river banks. Charles Johnson explains the expediency of conducting camp meetings close to large bodies of water as follows:

> Since frontier Churches were frequently located near waterways, it was only natural that camp sites were chosen near springs or creeks, and if possible on navigable rivers. Hence the distinctive names of the encampments of the Great Revival- "Muddy River," "Drake's Creek," "Red River," and "Cabin Creek." Aside from its aesthetic appeal, the chosen site had to provide drinking water, dry ground, shade, pasturage for the horses, timber for tentpoles and firewood.[485]

One reason this aspect of the revival meetings could have appealed to the slaves is that, as indicated earlier in our study, "Springs, streams, rivers, lakes, and ponds constitute the great aquatic "temples" of African religion."[486] Among many African tribes, like the Mende, for example, "bodies of water are sometimes considered to be the residence of "ancestral deities."[487] A water cult exists in Mende belief, under the guardianship of *Tinga*, the water Queen or "Geni." When a person is possessed by the water spirit, or *Tinga* falls in love with someone, as normally understood, he or she would desperately rush to the stream or river absolutely unconscious of his or her behavior, and unless restrained, the victim normally drowns.

The water cult is wide spread in Africa and according to Zahan, "Worship on the banks of rivers and streams is not only public. Often it is individual and personal, particularly when it involves prayers for the fecundity of women, as is seen in West Africa."[488] The point I am

---

[485] Charles Johnson, <u>Frontier Camp Meeting</u>, 42.

[486] Dominique Zahan, <u>The Religion, Spirituality and Thought</u>, 20.

[487] Ibid., 21.

[488] Ibid.

trying to make is that the African slaves already had a conceptually strong association between water and religious festivals and therefore found the revival meetings very familiar in that respect. Thus drawn by the physical situation of the camp meeting, it was easier to present the gospel to the black attendees.

Campfires also played a significant role in attracting blacks to revival meetings. Some form of illumination was always needed at Camp meetings. Thus Johnson suggests that in the early years of Camp revivals, "the lighting was provided by candles and pine knot torches affixed to preaching stands, trees, or other convenient places."[489] The use of fire to illuminate the Camps and the effect on the meetings has been well documented by Johnson. He paints the scenery in the following picturesque words:

> When campfires were located in the front of the tents, they also helped light up the worship area. Gradually, fire stands known as "fire altars" came into regular use. These stands were erected in the four corners of the auditorium and consisted of earthen covered platforms on upraised tripods some six feet high. Barks, twigs, or "pine wood fires" burned on top of the layer of earth and sod. Later, oil lamps were utilized. At night, the glare of the campfire, the flickering candles and torches, the blazing fire altars all added an eerie touch to the colorful services.[490]

While the white participants at revival meetings simply enjoyed the light provided by the campfires, those same fires served a deeper religious purpose for most of the black attendees. For it has been documented that the element of fire is "among the most profound and hidden of all the treasures of African culture."[491] There is a great deal of secrecy surrounding the cult of fire in Africa, but nevertheless, states Zahan, "Temples" related to fire are more numerous than one might think, since any hearth where an African woman prepares food can

[489] Charles Johnson, <u>Frontier Camp Meeting</u>, 48.
[490] Ibid.
[491] Zahan, <u>The Religion, Spirituality and Thought</u>, 29.

be properly considered a sacred place of worship. This is not so much because of the holiness of the food but because of the "sanctity" of fire. But hearths form only one of several types of fiery "sanctuaries"; there are the blacksmith's forge and active volcanoes besides.[492]

The importance of fire in African religion is underscored by the place of the forge in rural West African communities. According to Zahan, "After the hearth, the most important "temple" of fire is the forge."[493] In the African context, the forge is not only a place where skillful men produce weapons of iron and farming implements,

> But the forge is often a place of worship too. Its ground is sacred, and one enters barefoot in order not to communicate to the "temple" the impurity of the shoe. It is also a place of peace. No dispute is tolerated there, not because of the "spirits" which live there but because it represents a celestial space.[494]

Of course what makes the forge so sacred is the fire it contains which is used to make the iron malleable.

Among the Kpa Mende of Sierra Leone, for example, the core component of the *Wunde* society or cult is fire. No *Wunde* ritual or celebration can occur, except around a huge campfire.

Hence the presence of "fire altars" and so many campfires burning at revival meetings was a vivid reminder to most of the Africans of their own religious heritage. This raised their comfort level with the revivals to a point where they were willing to listen to the revival messages as well.

It should be noted carefully that parallels between the message, conduct, and physical setting of the revivals and ATR did not in themselves convert the slaves to Christianity. But rather, our proposition is that the continuities or parallels between the two religions engaged and attracted the slaves to revival meetings. And one of the natural

---

[492] Ibid.
[493] Ibid., 30.
[494] Ibid.

consequences of their free and willing participation in the meetings was their conversion to Christianity.

In essences, it was easier and more comfortable for the slaves to embrace Christianity at revival meetings because of the apparent familiarity of the revival atmosphere and the fact that revival presentations started with seemingly what was known to them and progressed to the unknown.

Perhaps, one of the best summations of the profound impact of the revival teachings on the black population is found in Wesley Gewehr's statement, that

> the very essence of these teachings was to place all men on a plane of exact equality in the Christian Church. Social rank counted for naught with the preachers of the Great Awakening. The Church was open to all alike - to slaves and freemen, to poor and rich, to learned and ignorant - so long as a man professed justification through faith in Jesus Christ. Thus we see in the evangelical groups a great leveling influence at work, which could not fail to have important consequences.[495]

Indeed, consequences of the evangelical revivals on the history of American Christianity are numerous. The revivals changed the course, composition and character of American Churches in profound ways. In particular, the great Awakening occupies a very special place in African-American Christian experience. We shall briefly mention some of the consequences of the revivals on the black population:

As discussed earlier, one of the immediate and most obvious results of evangelical Christianity on the slave population was not only conversions, but also increased black membership in the Churches. No doubt, some slaves attended their masters' Churches before the evangelical revivals, but voluntary associations of blacks, with especially Methodist and Baptist Churches became more common, with dramatic

---

[495] Wesley Gewehr, The Great Awakening, 187.

increases of blacks within these two denominations reaching record highs in the wake of the Awakenings.

Of course, both blacks and whites were positively affected by the revivals. Luther Jackson has described the period 1760 to 1790 as "the hey-day for the Negro in Virginia and the country at large."[496] In this period, and as a result of their own conversion, the attitudes of slave owners to slave Christianization took on a more positive outlook. According to Wesley Gewehr, "Much was done to educate the blacks and ameliorate the conditions of their bondage, while considerable numbers of them were emancipated as a direct result of the revivals."[497] As a matter of fact, in 1787-88,[498] "the Methodists manumitted upwards of a hundred slaves at a single session at the court in Sussex County."[499] Also,

> Certain Baptist leaders and laymen were likewise fully converted to this idea of emancipation on the grounds that "God created all men equal and free" and that no law, moral or divine, gives one a right to or property in the person of his fellow creatures. Among these persons were John Leland and David Barrow. The latter Churchman was so firmly opposed to slavery that he first manumitted his own slaves in 1784 and later moved to Kentucky where there was more opposition to slavery. The famous Robert Carter of Nomini Hall, Westmoreland county, owner of several hundred slaves, gradually emancipated all of them after joining the Baptists.[500]

The acts of setting slaves free as a result of the influence of the revivals were not limited to individuals. "One of the denominations of the Great Awakening placed itself officially on record as opposed

---

[496] Luther P. Jackson, "Religious Development of the Negro in Virginia from 1760 to 1860," Journal of Negro History 16, no. 2 (April 1931): 177.

[497] Wesley Gewehr, The Great Awakening, 249.

[498] Ibid.

[499] Ibid.

[500] Luther P. Jackson, "Religious Development of the Negro," 178.

to the institution of slavery and made a heroic effort to bring about its abolition."[501] Soon others would adopt a similar stance.

State Legislature in Virginia, for example, relaxed their rules to make manumission easier. "Whereas since 1691 masters were restrained in manumitting their slaves, by the act of 1792 "any person" might emancipate and set free "his or her slaves."[502] Consequently, by 1810, "the number of free Negroes in Virginia increased from less than 3,000 to 30,000. Here again we recognize the spirit of freedom and equalitarian teachings of the revivalists."[503]

Needless to say that in the North, abolitionist activities reached higher levels of intensity as a result of the revivals. Thus to allay accusations by Northern abolitionist that Southerners were neglectful of the spiritual lives of their slaves, "there was a decided increase in religious activity for the Negroes. One evidence of increased interest was the rise of a new unit of activity--the plantation mission."[504] According to Jackson,

> The plantation mission represents an effort of the Churches to go out into the remote areas, the highways, the hedges, where black men had but little contact with white men. This effort then indicates a missionary spirit, a religious zeal which in itself is indicative of a new day in Southern life.[505]

Out of such conscious efforts by Southern Christians to reach more of the slave population with the gospel message, coupled with the spirit of equality kindled by the revivalist, the need for separate black Churches naturally arose.

With the multiplication of independent black churches also came an era of powerful black preachers and evangelists. A typical example that easily comes to mind is "Uncle Jack," a converted Baptist, who

---

[501] Wesley Gewehr, The Great Awakening, 249.

[502] Luther P. Jackson, "Religious Instruction," 179.

[503] Ibid.

[504] Luther P. Jackson, "Religious Instruction of the Negroes," 73.

[505] Ibid.

was licensed as a plantation preacher in Nottoway county, Virginia, in 1792.[506] Uncle Jack is said to have "maintained a very orderly Baptist Church among his own people but his contacts were just as frequent with the whites as with blacks."[507] He was instrumental in the conversion of his Master's son "and when whites generally were under spiritual concern they would apply to no other teacher."[508] Among other good qualities about Uncle Jack was the fact that, "he was thoroughly evangelical in that his preaching made God everything and man nothing."[509]

Another black preacher called Negro Lewis preached frequently to large congregations numbering three hundred, or even four hundred on other occasions. Using the natural state of man as his theme, Lewis frequently urged his hearers "not to remain in an unconverted state but to come and accept Christ by faith that they might be reconciled to God."[510]

Among black Methodist preachers Harry Hoosier or Black Harry stands tall. The Methodist Quarterly Review carried the following testimony of Black Harry's preaching abilities:

> Aside from this testimony we have already been extravagantly informed from other sources that Black Harry was one of the greatest orators in America, that he sometimes filled the pulpit in place of one of the Methodist Bishops, and was accounted more popular than Asbury himself.[511]

It is noteworthy that while black preachers ministered mainly to black Congregations, there were some who were sought after by white churches as well. For example, William Lemon was very effective in preaching to a white Church in Gloucester county, Virginia. "He was described as not white in complexion though he had been washed

---

[506] Raboteau, Slave Religion, 135.
[507] Jackson, "Religious Instruction of the Negro," 185.
[508] Ibid.
[509] Ibid.
[510] Ibid., 176.
[511] Methodist Quarterly Review 18 (May 1782): 423, cited by Luther P. Jackson. "Religious Development of the Negro," 176.

(white) in the laver [sic] of regeneration."[512] A white Baptist Church at Portsmouth, Virginia, not only employed Josiah Jacob Bishop as their preacher, but the Church "thought so much of Bishop that it purchased his freedom and that of his family."[513]

Indeed, it has to be pointed out again that not every black slave in North America embraced Christianity as a result of the evangelical revivals. Some probably became Christians by some other means. There were others who probably never accepted Christianity. But the records, as I have surveyed, indicate that by the eve of emancipation, a vast majority of Africans in North America had been Christianized.

The story of the nurture, growth, and development of the African-American Church, which was a product of slave Christianization, has received much attention from eminent writers, such as DuBois, Woodson, and Raboteau, to mention just a handful. Much attention has also focused on positive strides in other vital areas of African-American life in North America. These include education and socio-political awareness through the agency of black church organizations.

My goal in this dissertation has not been to repeat the story of that process, but simply to draw attention to the African factor in the genesis of African-American Christianity. In doing that, I have attempted to highlight the crucial role of the continuities and discontinuities between Christianity and ATR in the conversion of African slaves to Christianity in North America. My findings are summarized in the following chapter.

---

[512] Ibid.
[513] Raboteau, Slave Religion, 134.

CHAPTER 6

CONCLUSION

Initially,...English contact with Africans did not take place primarily in a context which prejudged the Negro as a slave, at least not as a slave of Englishmen. Rather, Englishmen met Negroes merely as another sort of men. Englishmen found the natives of Africa very different from themselves. Negroes looked different; their religion was un-Christian; their manner of living was anything but English; they seemed to be a particularly libidinous sort of people. All these clusters of perceptions were related to each other, though they may be spread apart for inspection, and they were related also to circumstances of contact in Africa, to previously accumulated traditions concerning the strange and distant continent, and to certain special qualities of English society on the eve of its expansion into the New World.[514]

There is still a cloud of uncertainty over the number of Africans sold into slavery in the course of the transatlantic slave trade. A reasonable estimate stands at between ten and sixteen million.[515] Of this number,

---

[514] Winthrop Jordan, <u>White Over Black</u>, 4.
[515] See Paul Lovejoy, "The Impact of the Atlantic Slave Trade on Africa."

approximately half a million ended in North America.[516] And with the probable exception of a few, most of these slaves belonged to the African traditional religious system, but by the eve of their emancipation, a large number of them had become professing Christians.

That crucial encounter between Christianity and the original ATR of the slaves, in the context of their enslavement in North America is the subject of investigation in this study. How, when, and why did the slaves abandon their former religion to become Christians?

This chapter attempts a summary and analysis of answers to the above and related questions, as uncovered by our research. Implications of our findings for the African-American Church, evangelical missions, and evangelistic enterprises in general will be touched upon. We will also suggest areas that might be of interest to future researchers in this field of study.

Summary of Study

It is clear from the findings of this study that most of the Africans sold as slaves in North America originated from West Africa. There were Muslims among the imported Africans, and some were probably exposed to the Christian ritual of baptism before they were taken from their homeland. But comparatively, the largest number of the captives came from the background of ATR, which is the predominant religious culture of this region.

The flexibility and decentralized nature of ATR allows for many local variations but the core and most widespread of beliefs in the religion is the belief in a Supreme Being. This Being is known by various tribal names and may not necessarily enjoy direct worship, but the preponderance of references to God in day to day conversations points to a high degree of general divine-consciousness among Africans. It is a

---

[516] See Hugh Thomas, The Slave Trade: The Story of the Atlantic Slave Trade; 1440-1870 (New York: Simon & Schuster, 1997) 804. (appendix three); Charles C. Jones, Religious Instruction, 5. Both of these authorities indicate that 500,000.000 African slaves were imported into North America between 1620 and the American Revolution.

very common practice among the Ibo of Eastern Nigeria, for example, to use the divine suffix *Chukwu* (God) in naming children.

Thus the slaves entered their land of bondage with some knowledge of God. They were not totally devoid of religion or awareness of God, as some, especially Anglican missionaries presumed. It was partly ignorance of the slaves' religious background that kept westerners, including many scholars of African-American religion, totally oblivious to the continuities and discontinuities between Christianity and the slaves' native religion.

Also, the stark difference in European and African complexion, and in their manners of living, made it difficult for some to accept the full humanity of the Africans. Emil Ludwig, for example, even wondered how the untutored African could conceive of God.[517] Hence early attempts at slave Christianization were from the premise that the Africans were totally pagan or ignorant of God.

From that perception of the slaves, and as early as the fifteenth century, when the Portuguese brought their first African captives home, a link was immediately established between Christianizing the Africans and their enslavement. Some felt justified in enslaving them as long as their bondage and servitude gave the Africans the opportunity to become Christians.

Colonial expansionism, humanitarian concerns, and a sense of genuine Christian obligation were some of the other reasons behind efforts to Christianize the Africans.

For many years a heated debate festered among scholars of African-American religious history concerning the fate of the slaves' original culture in their state of bondage. One school of thought, represented by E. Franklin Frazier, is that the rigors of chattel slavery totally destroyed every trace of African culture in the slaves, with the exception of the religious culture. Another school, popularized by Melville Herskovits, suggests that the slaves retained some elements of African Culture, including the religious culture in particular.

---

[517] Statement by Emil Ludwig, quoted in Geoffrey Parrinder, <u>African Traditional Religion</u>, 9.

One of the interesting findings of this study is the unanimity of both sides of the debate on the fact that the most enduring part of the slaves' primary culture was his religion. This is contrary to earlier suggestions "that the Negro, when he landed in the United States, left behind him almost everything except his dark complexion and his tropical temperament."[518] Thus early Anglican attempts at slave Christianization found ATR to be one of the most formidable obstacles to slave conversion.

This study also reveals that the slaves' native religion encountered Christianity in two stages. The first stage consisted of predominantly Anglican efforts to bring the slaves under Christian influence. For several reasons discussed in the study, this attempt was a failure. The Anglicans were hindered not only by the persistence of the slaves' traditional religion, but also by other obstacles such as the resistance of the Planters to the Christianization of their slaves and social prejudice against the Africans.

The Anglican notion of salvation, their methodology, strategy of Christianization, and changing slave demographics were also among inherent problems which largely contributed to their failure to impact the slaves. Anglican ideology of the institution of African-American slavery in general, was also a major reason why the slaves refused to accept their brand of Christianity.

The second stage of encounter between Christianity and ATR was through the evangelical revivals or Great awakenings. The successful impact of the revivals on the slaves not only produced massive conversions, but also triggered the formation of African-American Church congregations and missionary enterprises.

Unlike the feeble results from the Anglican efforts, our study reveals that the Great Awakenings in North America, beginning with the Edwardsian revivals in 1734 and culminating in the frontier camp meetings after the civil war, were most instrumental in bringing about a fruitful spiritual harvest among the slaves. This was the genesis of

---

[518] Robert Park, "The Conflict and Fusion of Cultures," 116.

African-American Christianity and the birth of the African-American Church.

The quest for answers to the question of why the slaves were more responsive to Christianity during the evangelical revivals than during the earlier Anglican attempts was the main thrust of my study.

I suggest that several parallels or continuities between the slaves' original religion and evangelical Christianity attracted them to revival meetings. Such continuities existed in the content of the revival messages, the conduct of the revival meetings, and the character of the revival settings.

While the parallels in themselves did not convert the Africans to Christianity, they nevertheless, attracted the slaves to the meetings, thereby facilitating their conversion.

I also propose that discontinuities between the two religious systems rendered ATR vulnerable and susceptible to Christianity. By means of the revivals, the enslaved Africans encountered new ideas about the Supreme Being whom they knew in Africa, such as his love for all races and classes of mankind. They also discovered the urgency and importance of their personal responsibilities to God, that every individual sin demands God's judgement. These were concepts of God absent in ATR, where sin was not necessarily against the Supreme God but primarily against the community.

What constituted Christianity's greatest assets, such as God's incarnate Word, or special revelation in Jesus Christ, His Written Word or Scripture, and the universality or ability of Christianity to be propagated among all peoples, were the greatest weaknesses or liabilities in ATR. These discontinuities were also crucial in the slaves' transition from ATR to Christianity.

Analysis of Findings of Study

Probing shipping records related to the Atlantic slave trade, ethnolinguistic inventories, biographies of former slaves and testimonies of former slave traders confirmed that most African slaves in North America originated from the Guinea region of West Africa.

It was established that the predominant religion of West Africa, the region from which most slaves were captured, was ATR. The essential elements of ATR were found to be the belief in a Supreme Being, belief in intermediaries between God and mankind, and belief in spirits.

Music and Dance, as well as the Cult of secret societies were also established as integral practices in the African religious system. Despite its flexibility and ability of adaptation to individual needs and geography, the ritual of blood sacrifice was found to be common among practitioners of ATR.

A general revelation of God through ATR was proved to be undeniable, but this study also argues that the special revelation of God through Jesus Christ was a foreign concept to Africans before they were brought to North America.

The study also demonstrated that ATR claims no founder and lacks written authority or Scripture. The religion is passed from one generation to the other through oral traditions. It is bound within the confines of the African personality and cannot be propagated among non-Africans.

Among other possible factors, the religious background of the slaves, as our study demonstrates, made all the difference in their response to Christianity, as presented first by the Church of England and later by the evangelical revivalists. An analysis of results from both Anglican and evangelical Christianization efforts revealed that the revivals were more instrumental in the conversion of the slaves than the Church of England. We shall attempt an analysis of the possible reasons we have suggested for this phenomenon.

It should be noted, first of all, that within the context of the capture and enslavement of Africans in North America two crucial encounters took place: First, there was the encounter between two distinct anthropological divisions of mankind: the dark-skinned African Race and Caucasians. The second encounter, naturally resulting from the first, was the interaction between two worldviews or religious systems: Christianity and ATR. Perceptions formed at the first level of contact played a significant role in the success or failure of evangelistic efforts among the blacks.

For example, at the first contact between Europeans and Africans, "the most arresting characteristic of the newly discovered African was his color."[519] "Englishmen actually described Negroes as *black*--an exaggerated term which in itself suggests that the Negro's complexion had powerful impact upon their perceptions."[520] The point here being that English perceptions of Africans not only led to the enslavement of one race by the other, but also tended to influence every other relationship between blacks and whites in North America.[521] Such perceptions colored Anglican evangelistic efforts among the slaves, which partly explains their minimal impact on the Africans.

The general English perceptions of the African further explain the basis of a fundamental Anglican philosophy of slave Christianization: "that the slave's religious condition had no relevance to his status as a slave."[522] "It was racial, not religious, slavery which developed in America," Winthrop Jordan rightly concludes.[523] That the Anglicans share responsibility for such a development, was clearly demonstrated by this study.

Thus, in the hands of the Anglican establishment, Christianity became a tool of oppression, rather than liberation. By refusing to affirm

---

[519] Winthrop Jordan, White Over Black, 4.

[520] Ibid.

[521] A very thorough treatment of this point is found in Winthrop Jordan, White Over Black 3-43. Jordan makes the following very insightful observation in his book: "Long before they found that some men were black, Englishmen found in the idea of blackness a way of expressing some of their most ingrained values. No other color except white conveyed so much emotional impact. As described by The Oxford English Dictionary, the meaning of black before the sixteenth century included, "Deeply stained with dirt; soiled, dirty, foul... Having dark or deadly purposes, malignant; pertaining to or involving death, deadly; baneful, disastrous, sinister... Foul, iniquitous, atrocious, horrible, wicked...Indicating disgrace, censure, liability to punishment, etc. Black was an emotionally partisan color, the handmaid and symbol of baseness and evil, a sign of danger and repulsion. Embedded in the concept of blackness was its direct opposite - whiteness. No other colors so clearly implied opposition, 'beinge coloures utterlye contrary;' no others were so frequently used to denote polarization."

[522] Ibid.

[523] Ibid.

the full humanity of the African slave, Anglican evangelistic programs tended to be both ambivalent and contradictory. In one sense they tended to cater for the soul of the African while neglecting his body. In another sense, they seemed more interested in the intellectual development of the slaves than their salvation. Thus for the Anglican missionaries baptism took precedence over true repentance and conversion, cognition of Christian principles were placed above affection for God.

By insisting on their principle of "religion with letters," the Anglicans simply overlooked, and thus failed to meet the felt need of the Africans, which was freedom from the bondage of sin and slavery.

Hence after many years of Anglican labor among the slaves, the Africans could only be credited with fondness for their old heathenish ways, with "disinclination to accept a new religion in place of their heathen rites."[524]

A radically different picture emerged with the advent of evangelical revivalism. The evangelical revivals seem to have succeeded where the Anglicans apparently failed. An analysis of some of the reasons for this is in place.

In the first place, the revival evangelists' perception of Africans was different from what the Anglican leadership generally held. Granted that at some camp meetings, blacks met separately from whites, but the evangelicals generally accepted the slaves as God's creation, equal in importance to whites. In the revival meetings, race, color of skin and level of education were less important than the relationship of mankind to God.

Second, to the evangelical preachers, the crucial issue was that, "all have sinned and fallen short of God's glory,"[525] and that included blacks as much as whites, slaves as well as masters.

Slaves and masters were sinners before God who needed to repent or perish. At revival meetings, the egalitarian and inclusive nature of Christianity was fully expressed. It is not far fetched to say that it was in the context of the revivals that the slaves had their first taste of freedom and equality with their oppressors. The very idea of freedom from the

---

[524] See Marcus W. Jernegan, "Slavery and Conversion."

[525] Romans 3:23 NIV (paraphrased).

bondage of sin must have given hope to the slaves that their external bondage could be lifted by the same God who was able to free them from the power of sin. In the revivals, the slaves saw the promise of total liberation: From the bondage of sin and slavery.

Third, the evangelical message of the "new birth" made a huge impression on the slaves. The concept of dying to the old self and undergoing inner regeneration to be reborn as a new person in Christ was very timely for the bondsmen. There could have been nothing more uplifting for the slaves than the realization that in Christ they could shed off their old identity, which included the stigma of slavery, and start a brand new life. Of course considering their previous religious background, this concept made more sense than memorizing apparently meaningless creeds as was the case under the Anglican regime.

Fourth, and unlike the Anglicans, the evangelicals stressed affection for God and his affection for man, rather than an intellectual appreciation of Christianity. The revivals were criticized as being emotional, but as Edwards asserts in his A Treatise Concerning Religious Affection, "Man is a unitary being in whom "all acts of affection...are in some sense acts of the will, and all acts of the will are acts of the affections."[526] Therefore, continues Edwards, "True religion consists in Holy affections."[527] "The things of religion take place in men's heart no further than they are affected with them," says Edwards.[528]

Thus Edwards concludes that "the informing of the understanding is all in vain, and farther than it affects the heart; or which is the same thing, has influence on the affections."[529] Such opportunities of freely expressing and receiving affections, which were a hallmark of the Revivals, is one reason the slaves loved to participate in the meetings. For people totally cut off from their roots and as emotionally starved as the slaves, who were instead filled with bitterness against their oppressors, it was revolutionary for the Africans to be introduced to a God who loved them personally and who in turn craved their love.

[526] The Works of Jonathan Edwards, vol. 4, ed. John E. Smith, 66.
[527] Ibid.
[528] Ibid.
[529] Ibid.

Fifth, the possibility of instantly becoming a Christian, immediately following conviction, repentance and confession, without going through a tedious period of religious instruction placed the revival outreaches at an advantage over the Anglicans, as far as slave conversions went. Also, in revival meetings new converts were allowed to exhort and encourage those going through the process of conversion. Thus without any formal theological education, slaves became very effective in communicating revival messages to other slaves. In the Anglican economy, even competent lay leaders were highly restricted in what they could do until after formal ordination. This partly accounts for the larger conversions at revival meetings compared to Anglican religious instruction meetings.

Conversions at revivals could also be explained in terms of dynamics that came into play when the African Traditional religious worldview encountered Christianity. In previous sections of this study, we indicated that the continuities between the two religious systems were main attractions for the slaves who attended revival meetings. We also mentioned that as well as the continuities, discontinuities between the two worldviews equally contributed to the conversion of the Africans. Three main areas of discontinuities, such as the special revelation of God in the incarnation of Jesus Christ, Scriptural Authority, and the tendency in Christianity to be propagated universally, will be briefly touched on. These were precisely the points on which ATR collapsed when it encountered Christianity in the context of slave Christianization.

No doubt, the slaves were aware of the general revelation of God on arrival in North America, but the God they knew was distant and impersonal. They knew Him to be all-powerful, but not as a personal savior. The incarnation, death and resurrection of Jesus Christ for the remission of personal sin were new concepts of God the slaves encountered only through evangelical teachings. The discovery by the slaves that the incarnate sacrifice of Jesus Christ offered an antidote to personal sin, unlike the blood sacrifices and other rituals in ATR, helped the Africans in their transition from their former religion to Christianity.

Furthermore, without a written authority, ATR is less dogmatic than Christianity. There is therefore neither a standard practice in ATR nor a personal obligation on adherents to follow any prescribed convention. It is more or less, a religion of convenience and in situations where the religion fails to meet immediate needs, it can be easily abandoned for more pragmatic options.

In their bondage, the more authoritative Christian promises and examples inscribed in the Christian Scriptures, tended to offer more hope to the slaves than African religious concepts they could hardly remember. Thus in the context of the revivals Christianity became a more pragmatic substitute for the slaves' original religion. The written stories like the liberation of the Jews from Egyptian bondage had more relevance to the slaves' immediate need than faint memories of their African religion. Also, because such stories were in written form, the slaves could refer to them as frequently as necessary. With the passage of time and the rigors of slavery such a quick appeal to ATR became less and less practical.

The localized nature of ATR or its confinement to the African personality also meant that when that personality is in danger, the carriers of ATR become less effective. As the concerted effort by some slave owners to rid the Africans of all their previous culture weighed on them, the African personality was drastically changed. For example, as the languages and symbols in which to communicate their religious ideas were destroyed, it became more and more difficult for generations of the slaves to pass on the same qualities of their religious heritage to succeeding generations. Hence ATR became vulnerable to the most viable alternative, which was evangelical Christianity.

Another point of interest is that ATR thrives better as an African community religion. Its practices are mostly community oriented. One of the devastating effects of slavery on the Africans was the destruction of their community spirit. And the destruction of a sense of African community essentially weakened, though not obliterated the impact of ATR among the slaves. Fragmented and isolated in many instances, the hold of the ATR community spirit on the Africans became greatly lessened. Thus during the revivals, the invitation into a personal relationship with God through Jesus Christ was much easily acceptable to the Africans. They have just found a religion that not only satisfied the old incurably religious African nature, but also promised hope of physical and eternal liberation. Evangelical Christianity was that religion.

Implications of Findings of Study

The findings of this study have positive implications for the African-American Church, evangelism and cross-cultural evangelical missions in general.

Raboteau has adequately and insightfully described the importance of the Church in the life of African-Americans in the following words:

> As the one institution which freed blacks were allowed to control, the Church was the center of social, economic, educational, and political activity. It was also a source of continuity and identity for the black community. In their Churches, black worshippers continued for decades to pray, sing, preach and shout as they or their parents had done during slavery.[530]

The truism expressed by Raboteau is almost indisputable, and thus underscores the fact that the study of any aspect of African-American Christianity carries with it the tremendous potential of making significant contributions to improving the lives of many African-Americans in North America.

This study, which was aimed mainly at drawing more attention to the African roots and connections in African-American Christianity, touched on only a tiny fragment of such a worthy venture. If the findings of this study shed some light on the origins of African-American Christianity, my efforts would have been rewarded.

For an understanding of the roots of African-American Christianity is one sure way to a better understanding and appreciation of the nature

---

[530] Albert Raboteau, <u>Slave Religion</u>, 320.

of the African-American Church, and consequently her contribution to the lives of African-Americans, past and present and future.

Further more, African-American livelihood could be much better if future plans for their general welfare takes the historically positive role of Christianity in the lives of Americans of African decent into consideration.

It is also my hope that the findings of this study have reinforced some basic evangelical missionary principles. Granted, the evangelization of Africans in North America did not follow conventional missionary routes, but it was still an effort in missions and evangelism. As Raboteau has indicated:

> The history of the religious instruction of the slaves involved three parties: planters, missionaries, and slaves. The slaves' response to evangelization varied, but it was always conditioned by the circumstance of slavery. There was something peculiar about the ways African slaves were evangelized in America. Traditionally, "preaching the gospel to all nations" meant that the Christian disciple was sent *out* with the gospel *to* the pagans. In America the reverse was the case: the pagan slave was brought to a Christian disciple who was frequently reluctant to instruct him in the gospel.[531]

Indeed, both the negative and positive aspects of slave Christianization efforts in North America could be instructive for cross-cultural missions and evangelism today.

For example, my study has demonstrated that perceptions formed as a result of differences between the cultures of the missionary and that of the evangelized goes a long way in determining the success rate of the mission. Unless prayerfully guarded against, the usually stark and naked differences in the missionary's complexion, his culture, and that of the evangelized, could be a hindrance to effective ministry. This was clearly evident in the mission of the Anglican Church to the African slaves. The danger here is that the missionary might spend a lot of time and

---

[531] Ibid., 120.

efforts trying to convert the natives to his culture instead of converting them to Christianity.

Also, the failure of the Anglicans to evangelize the slaves partly stems from the fact they started from the false premise that the Africans were ignorant, pagan, and totally devoid of any religion. A much helpful approach is to recognize that there have always been other religions beside Christianity. Exploring the continuities and discontinuities between Christianity and other religious systems could prove helpful as a cross-cultural evangelistic or missionary strategy. This was demonstrated in the case of ATR and evangelical Christianity in the experience of African slaves. A sad mistake in modern missions is to emphasize the discontinuities between Christianity and other religions at the expense of looking for possible points of convergence in the two religions.

Further, a cross-cultural missionary enterprise that fails to recognize God's general revelation in other cultures, no matter how primitive they might appear, is doomed to failure. That was one of the mistakes of Anglican mission to African slaves in North America. If the possibility of a general revelation of God in the culture of the evangelized is admitted, it becomes easier to move from that to a recommendation of His Special revelation in Jesus Christ. The reality of the matter is that what is lacking in most cultures is not a general knowledge of God, but an awareness of His special revelation in the incarnation of Jesus Christ.

That leads us to the fact that in cross-cultural missions, it might be helpful to start from the known and proceed to the unknown. Had Anglican missionaries taken the care to understand the religious background of the slaves and what knowledge they might have possessed before arrival in America, their efforts might have yielded more fruit. When the slaves saw apparently familiar symbols in evangelical revivals, they became more inclined to attend the meetings and were perhaps, more willing to listen to the gospel message.

Finally, the intricate relationship between evangelism and social concern was clearly brought out in our study. To neglect the physical conditions of the evangelized and contend for their souls, could be as fruitless as simply caring for the physical needs of people at the neglect of their salvation. Anglican failure to evangelize the African slaves, which partly resulted from their policy that "the slave's religious condition had no relevance to his status as a slave," is a case in point. A cross-cultural mission that caters to the total liberation of mankind, as we saw in the American evangelical revivals, holds the best promise of success.

Recommendations for Further Research

This study is very far from being exhaustive in the exploration of the vast domain of African-American Christian experience while in bondage. At best, I have probably raised a lot of questions that might stimulate further research in this area.

It might be exciting, for an example, to investigate reasons why the religious culture of the slaves was apparently more resilient to the destructive forces of slavery than other aspects of the original African culture.

Also, the issue of the attraction of the Africans to evangelical revivals by the parallels between Christianity and ATR was observed only for African slaves in North America. Whether this theory holds for the encounter between the two religions in other places like on the continent of Africa itself is still open to further research. It is my hope that other scholars might see this as a viable case for further investigation.

As only a tiny contribution to many recent attempts at studying the religious history of African slaves in North America, it is my hope that this study will draw some attention to the challenging but long neglected field of African-American Christianity.

APPENDIX A

SOURCES OF SLAVE SUPPLIES IN THE
ATLANTIC SLAVE TRADE
ACCORDING TO SIGISMOND KOELLE'S
ETHNOLINGUISTIC
INVENTORY, PLOTTED ON THE AFRICAN MAP, PHILIP D.
CURTIN, THE ATLANTIC SLAVE TRADE: A CENSUS,
(MADISON, WISCONSIN: UNIVERSITY OF
WISCONSIN PRESS, 1990), 246.

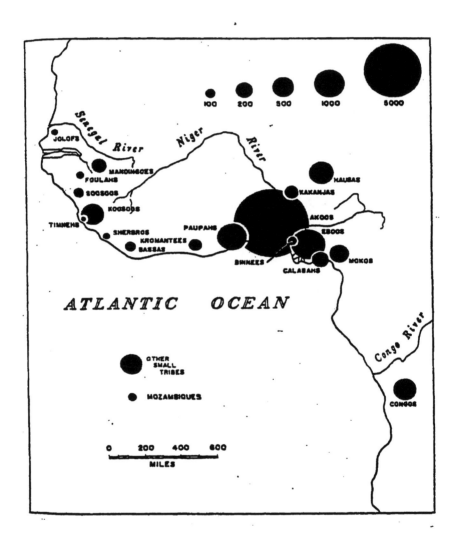

BIBLIOGRAPHY

Adamu, Mahdi. "The Delivery of Slaves from the Central Sudan to the Bight of Benin in the Eighteenth and Nineteenth Centuries." In The Uncommon Market: Essays in the Economic History of the Atlantic Slave Trade, ed. Henry A. Gemery and Jan S. Hogendorn, 163-79. New York: Academic Press, 1979.

Ahlstrom, Sydney E. A Religious History of the American People. New Haven and London: Yale University Press, 1972.

Ajayi, Ade J. F. "Samuel Ajayi Crowther of Oyo." In Africa Remembered, ed. Philip Curtin, 289-316. Madison, Milwaukee and London: The University of Wisconsin Press, 1968.

Andrews, Dee E. The Methodists and Revolutionary America, 1760-1800: The Shaping of an Evangelical Culture. Princeton: The Princeton University Press, 2000.

Andrews, William L., and Henry Louis Gates, Jr. Slave Narratives. New York: Library Classics of the United States, 2000.
Anstay, Roger. The Atlantic Slave Trade and British Abolition: 1760-1810. Atlantic Highlands, New Jersey: Humanities Press, 1975.

Austen, Ralph A. "The Trans-Saharan Slave Trade: A Tentative Census." In The Uncommon Market: Essays in the Economic History of the Atlantic Slave Trade, ed. Henry A. Gemery and Jan S. Hogendorn, 23-76. New York: Academic Press, 1979.

Bailey, David Thomas. "A Divided Prism: Two Sources of Black Testimony on Slavery." Journal of Southern History 46, no. 3 (1980): 392-404.

Bailey, Kenneth. "Protestantism and Afro-Americans in the Old South: Another Look." Journal of Southern History 41, no. 4 (1975): 451-72.

Barbot, John. "John Barbot's Description of Guinea." In Documents Illustrative of the History of the Slave Trade to America 1441-1700. Vol. 1, ed. Elizabeth Donnan, 282-301. New York: Octagon Books, 1969.

Bascom, William R., and Melville J. Herskivits. Continuity and Change in African Cultures. Chicago: University of Chicago Press, 1959.

Baudin, Pere Noel. Fetichism and Fetich Worshippers. New York: Benziger Brothers, 1885.

Baumann H., and D. Westermann. Les Peuples et Les Civilisations De L'Afrique. Paris: Payot, 1967.

_____. Schopfung und Urzeit Des Menschen im Mythus Der Afrikanischen Voker. Berlin: Andrews & Steiner, 1936.

Beazley, Charles R., and E. Prestage, eds. The Chronicles of Discovery of and Conquest of Guinea. Trans. G. E. de Azurara. 2 Vols. London: Halukyt Society, 1896.

_____. "Prince Henry of Portugal and the African Crusade of the Fifteenth Century." The American Historical Review 16 (October 1910 to July 1911). Microfilm E.171A57, Reel 5

Blassingame, John W. The Slave Community: Plantation Life in The Antebellum South. New York: Oxford University Press, 1972.

_____. "Using the Testimony of EX-Slaves: Approaches and Problems. Journal of Southern History 41, no. 4 (1975): 451-72.

_____. Slave Testimony: Two Centuries of Letters, Speeches, Interviews, and Autobiographies. Baton Rouge: Louisiana State University Press, 1977.

Boles, John B. The Great Revival, 1787-1805: The Origins of the Southern Evangelical Mind. Lexington, Kentucky: The University Press of Kentucky, 1972.

_____. Slaves & Masters in the House of the Lord: Race and Religion in the American South, 1740-1870. Lexington: The University Press of Kentucky, 1988.

Boorstein, Daniel. The Americans: The National Experience. New York: Random House, 1965.

Bosman, William. A New and Accurate Description of the Coast Of Guinea. English translation, 2d. ed. London: Cass, 1967.

Brown, John. Slave Life in Georgia. Savannah: Beehive, 1972.

Brown, William Wells. My Southern Home. Boston: A. G. Brown & Co., 1880.

Bush, Michael L. Serfdom and Slavery: Studies in Legal Bondage. New York: Longman, 1996.

Butler, Jon. Awash in a Sea of Faith. Cambridge, Mass.: Harvard University Press, 1970.

_____. "Enthusiasm Described and Decried: The Great Awakening as Interpretive Fiction." Journal of American History (Sept. 1982): 305-25.

Cade, John B. "Out of the Mouths of Ex-Slaves." Journal of Negro History 20, no. 3 (1935): 294-337.

Caron, Peter. "Of a Nation Which the Others do not Understand: Bambara Slaves and African Ethnicity in Colonial Louisiana, 1718-60." In Routes to Slavery, ed. David Eltis and David Richardson, 89-121. London: Frank Cass, 1997.

Carreta, Vincent. Unchained Voices: An Anthology of Black Authors in the English-Speaking World of the Eighteenth Century. Lexington: The University of Kentucky Press, 1996.

Chambers, Douglas B. "My Own Nation: Igbo Exiles in the Diaspora." In Routes to Slavery, ed. David Eltis and David Richardson, 72-97. London: Frank Cass, 1997.

Chauncy, Charles. Enthusiasm Described and Cautioned Against. Boston: J. Draper, 1742.

_____. Seasonable Thoughts on the State of Religion in New England. Boston: Rogers & Fowle, 1743. Microfilm: BR.515 R43, 1976, Reel 11.

_____. The Late Religious Commotion in New England. Boston: Green, Busbell, and Allen, 1743.

Chilver, E. M., and P. M. Kaberry. "Sources of the 18th Century Slave Trade: Two Comments." Journal of African History 6, no. 1 (1965): 117-20.

Cleveland, Catharine Caroline. The Great Revival in the West. Gloucester, Mass.: Peter Smith, 1959.

Collins, Robert O. Western African History. Princeton: Markus Wiener, 1997.

_____. African History in Documents: Western African History. Princeton: Markus Wiener, 1990.

Collins, Robert. Essay on the Management and Treatment of Slaves. Boston: Eastburn's Press, 1853.

Connah, Graham. African Civilizations: Precolonial Cities and States in Tropical Africa: An Archeological Perspective. Cambridge: Cambridge University Press, 1975.

Conneau, Theophilus. A Slaver's Log Book or 20 Years Residence in Africa. Englewood Cliffs, N.J.: Prentice Hall, 1976.

Conniff, Michael L., and Thomas J. Davis. Africans in the Americas: A History of the Black Diaspora. New York: St. Martin's Press, 1994.

Curtin, Philip D., and Jan Vansina. "Sources of the Nineteenth Century Atlantic Slave Trade." Journal of African History 2 (1964): 185-208.

_____. Africa Remembered: Narratives by West Africans from the Era of the Slave Trade. Madison, Wisconsin: University of Wisconsin Press, 1967.

_____. "Joseph Wright of the Egba." In Africa Remembered: Narratives by West Africans from the Era of the Slave Trade, ed. Philip Curtin, 317-33. Madison, Wisconsin: University of Wisconsin Press, 1967.

_____. The Atlantic Slave Trade: A. Census. Madison: University of Wisconsin Press, 1969.

Daget, Serge. De la Traite A L'Esclavage. (Actes du Colloque International sur la traite des Noires. Nantes: 1985.

Dalzel, Archibald. The History of Dahomey: An Inland Kingdom Of Africa. London: Frank Cass & Co., 1793 and 1967.

Davenport, Frederick Morgan. Primitive Traits in Religious Revivals. New York: AMS, 1905.

Davidson, Basil. The African Slave Trade: Precolonial History, 1450-1850. Boston, Atlantic: Little, Brown & Company, 1961.

_____. Black Mother: The Years of the African Slave Trade. Boston: Atlantic, Little, Brown & Company, 1961.

Deschamps, Hubert. Les Religions De L'Afrique Noire. Paris: Presses Universitaires Des France, 1960.

Donnan, Elizabeth. Documents Illustrative of the History of the Slave Trade to America. Vol. 2. New York: Octagon, 1969.

Drescher, Seymour. "The Slaving Capital of the World: Liverpool and National Opinion in the Age of Abolition." In De la Traite A L'Esclavage, ed. Serge Daget, 281-95. (Actes du Colloque International sur La traite des Noires): Nantes, 1985.

_____. "The Ending of the Slave Trade and the Evolution of European Scientific Racism." In The Atlantic Slave Trade: Effects on Economies, Societies, and Peoples in Africa, The Americas, and Europe, ed. Joseph E. Inikori and Stanley L. Engerman, 361-96. Durham & London: Duke University Press, 1992.

DuBois, William E. B. The Souls of Black Folk. A. C. McClurg & Co., 1903. Reprint, New York: Penguin Books, 1995.

_____. The Negro Church. Atlanta, Ga.: The Atlanta University Press, 1903.

Edwards, Jonathan. The Great Awakening: Works of Jonathan Edwards, Vol. 4. Edited by C. C. Goen. New Haven and London: Yale University Press, 1972.

Edwards, Paul. Equiano's Teravels. New York, Washington: Praeger, 1966.

Elkins, Stanley M. Slavery: A Problem in American Institutional and Intellectual Life. Chicago: The University of Chicago Press, 1959.

Eltis, David, and David Richardson. "West Africa and the Transatlantic Slave Trade: New Evidence of Long-Run Trends." In Routes to Slavery, ed. David Eltis and David Richardson, 16-35. London: Frank Cass, 1997

_____. Routes to Slavery: Direction, Ethnicity and Mortality in the Transatlantic Slave Trade. London, Portland: Frank Cass, 1997.

Eltis, David, and Lawrence Jennings. "The Trade between Western Africa and the Atlantic World in Pre-Colonial Era." American Historical Review 93 (October-December 1988): 936-59.

Evans-Pritchard, E. E. Witchcraft among the Azande. Oxford: Claredon, 1937.

_____. Nuer Religion. Oxford: Claredon, 1956.

_____. Theories of the Primitive. Oxford: Claredon, 1965.

Fage, J. D. A History of West Africa: An Introductory Survey. Cambridge: Cambridge University Press, 1969.

_____. "Slavery and The Slave Trade in the Context of West African History." Journal of African History 10, no. 3 (1969): 393-404.

Faith, Vibert. "The Society for the Propagation of the Gospel in Foreign Parts: Its Work for the Negroes in North America before 1783." Journal of Negro History 18, no. 2 (1933): 171-212.

Fisher, Humphrey John. "A Muslim William Wilberforce? The Sokoto Jihad as Anti-slavery Crusade: An Enquiry into Historical Causes." In De la Traite A L'Esclavage, ed. Serge Daget, 537-55. (Actes du Colloque International sur La traite des Noires): Nantes, 1985.

Fogel, Robert, and Engerman Stanley. Time on the Cross: The Economics of American Negro slavery. Boston: Little and Brown Company, 1974.

Forde, Daryll. African Worlds. Oxford: Oxford University Press, 1954.

_____. "The Cultural Map of West Africa: Successive Adaptations to Tropical Forests and Grasslands." In Cultures and Societies of Africa, ed. Simon and Phoebe Ottenberg, 116-38. New York: 1960.

Fortes, Meyer. Oedipus and Job in West African Religion. New York: Octagon Books, 1981.

Frazier, Franklin E. The Negro in the United States. Rev. ed. Toronto: Macmillan, 1957 and 1969.

_____. The Negro Church in America: The Black Church since Frazier. Edited by C. Eric Lincoln. New York: Schochen Books, 1974.

Fuller, Lois. A Missionary Handbook on African Traditional Religion. Kaduna: Baraka, 1994.

Fulop, Timothy E., and Albert J. Raboteau. African-American Religion: Interpretive Essays in History and Culture. New York: Routledge, 1997.

Gallay, Alan. "Planters and Slaves in the Great Awakening." In Masters & slaves in the House of the Lord: Race and Religion in the American South, 1740-1870, ed. John B. Boles, 19-36. Lexington: University Press of Kentucky, 1988.

Gaustad, Edwin Scott. The Great Awakening in New England. New York: Harper Brothers, 1957.

_____. Historical Atlas of Religion in America. New York: Harper & Row, 1962.

Geggus, David. "Sex Ratio, Age and Ethnicity in the Atlantic Slave Trade: Data from the French Shipping and Plantation Records." Journal of African History 30 (1989): 23-44.

Gemery, Henry A., and Jan S. Hogendorn. The Uncommon Market: Essays in the Economic History of the Atlantic Slave Trade. New York: Academic Press, 1979.

Genovese, Eugene D. Roll Jordan Roll: The World Slaves Made. New York: Vintage Books, 1976.

George, Carol V. R. Segregated Sabbaths: Richard Allen and the Rise of the Independent African Churches, 1760-1840. New York: Oxford University Press, 1973.

Gewehr, Wesley, Marsh. The Great Awakening in Virginia, 1740-1790. Gloucester, Mass.: Peter Smith, 1965.

Godwyn, Morgan. The Negro's and Indian's Advocate: Suing for Their Admission into the Church. London: Printed for the author, by J. D., 1860. Microfilm BR 515, R43, 1976, Reel 20.

Gravely, Will B. "The rise of the African Churches in America (1786-1822): Rexamining the Contexts." Journal of Religious Thought 41, no. 1 (1984): 58-73.

Grillo, Laura. "African Religions." In Merian-Webster's Encyclopedia of World Religions. Springfield, Mass.: Merian-Webster, 1999, 17-22.

Grove, A. T. Africa. Oxford: Oxford University Press, 1978.

Hair, Paul E. H. "The Enslavement of Koelle's Informants." Journal of African History 6, no. 2 (1965): 193-203.

_____. "Ethnolinguistic Continuity on the Guinea Coast." Journal of African History 8, no. 2 (1967): 247-68.

Handy, Robert T. "Negro Christianity and American Historiography." In Reinterpretation in American Church History, ed. Jerald C. Brauer, 91-113. Chicago: University of Chicago Press, 1968.

Harris, W. T. "The Idea of God among the Mende." In African Ideas Of God: A Symposium, ed. Edwin Smith, 277-300. London: Edinburgh House, 1950.

Hayden, Carlton J. "Conversion and Control: Dilemma of Episcopalians in Providing for the Religious Instruction Of Slaves, Charleston, South Carolina, 1845-1860." Historical Magazine of the Protestant Episcopal Church 40, no. 2 (1971): 143-71.

Herskovits, Melville J. "On the Provenience of New World Negroes." Social Forces 12, nos. 1-4 (October 1933-May 1934): 247-62.

_____. "Social History of the Negro." In A Handbook of Psychology, ed. Carl Murchinson, 207-67. Worchester, Mass.: Clark University Press, 1935.

_____. The Myth of the Negro Past. Boston: Beacon Hill, 1941.

_____. "The Significance of West Africa for Negro Research." Journal of Negro History 21, no. 1 (Sept 1935): 15-30.

Hesse, Philip. "Le Code Noire: De L'Homme et de L'Esclave." In De La Traite a L'Esclavage, ed Daget Serge 185-91. (Actes du Colloque International sur la traite des Noirs) Nantes, 1985.

Higgins, Robert. "The Geographical Origins of Negro Slaves in Colonial South Carolina." The South Atlantic Quarterly 70 (1971): 34-47.

Horton, Robin. Patterns of Thought in Africa and the West: Essays on Magic, Religion and Science. Cambridge: Cambridge University Press, 1993.

Humphreys, David. An Historical Account of the Incorporated Society for the Propagation of the Gospel in Foreign Parts. London: Joseph Downing, 1728.

Hyde, Francis E., Bradbury B. Parkinson and Sheila Marriner. "The Nature and Profitability of the Liverpool Slave Trade." Economic History Review 5 (1953): 368-77.

Idowu, Bolaji E. African Traditional Religion: A Definition. Maryknoll, N.Y.: Orbis Books, 1973.

Ikenga-Metuh, Emefie. The Gods in Retreat: Continuity and Change in African Religion. Enugu: Fourth Dimension, 1986.

_____. Comparative Studies of African Traditional Religions. Ibadan: Claverianum, 1987.

_____. African Inculturation Theology: Africanizing Christianity. Onitsha: IMICO Books, 1996.

_____. God and Man in African Religion. Enugu: Snaap, 1999.

Imasogie O. African Traditional Religion, Ibadan: University Press, 1985.

Inikori, Joseph E. "Measuring the Atlantic Slave Trade: An Assessment of Curtin and Anstey." Journal of African History 18, no. 2 (1976): 197-223.

_____. "The Sources of Supply for the Atlantic Slave Exports from the Bight of Benin and the Bight of Bonny (Biafra)." In De la Traite A L'Esclavage, ed. Daget Serge, 25-43. Actes du Colloque International sur La Traite des Noires: Nantes, 1985.

Inikori, Joseph E., and Stanley L. Engerman. The Atlantic Slave Trade: Effects on Economies, Societies, and Peoples in Africa, the Americas, and Europe. Durham and London: Duke University Press, 1992.

Jackson, Luther P. "Religious Development of the Negro in Virginia from 1760 to 1860." Journal of Negro History 16 no. 2 (1931): 168-239.

_____. "Religious Instruction of Negroes, 1830-1860, with Special Reference to South Carolina." Journal of Negro History 15, no. 1 (April 1931): 72-114.

James, Larry M. "Biracial Fellowship in Antebellum Baptist Churches." In Masters and Slaves in the House of the Lord: Race and Religion in the American South, 1740-1870, ed. John B. Boles, 37-57. Lexington: The University Press of Kentucky, 1988.

Jernegan, Marcus W. "Slavery and Conversion in the American Colonies." Historical Review 21, no. 3 (1916): 504-27.

Johnson, Charles A. The Frontier Camp Meeting. Dallas, Tex.: Southern Methodist University Press, 1955.

Jones, Charles C. The Religious Instruction of the Negroes in the United States. Savannah: Thomas Purse, 1842. Reprint, New York: Negro Universities Press, 1969.

Jones, G. I. "Olaudah Equiano of the Niger Ibo." In Africa Remembered, ed. Philip Curtin, 60-98. Madison, Milwaukee, and London: University of Wisconsin Press, 1968.

Jordan, Winthrop D. White over Black: American Attitudes towards the Negro, 1550-1812. Kingsport, Tenn.: Kingsport, 1968.

Joyner, Charles. "Believer I Know." In African-American Christianity: Essays in History, ed. Paul E. Johnson, 18-45. Berkeley: University of California Press, 1994.

Kelly, Robin D. G., and Earl Lewis. To Make our World New: A History of African-Americans. Oxford, N.Y.: Oxford University Press, 2000.

Klein, Herbert, and Stanley L. Engerman. "Long-term Trends in African Mortality in the Transatlantic Slave Trade." In Routes to Slavery, ed. David Eltis and David Richardson, 38-48 London: Frank Cass, 1997.

Klein, Martin A. "The Impact of the Atlantic Slave Trade on The Societies of the Western Sudan." In The Uncommon Market: Essays in the Economic History of the Atlantic Slave Trade, ed Henry A. Gemery and Jan S. Hogendorn, 25-47 New York: Academic Press, 1979..

Klingberg, Frank J. Anglican Humanitarianism in Colonial New York. Philadelphia: The Church Historical Society, 1940.

_____. An Appraisal of the Negro in Colonial South. Washington D.C.: Associated Publishers, 1941.

Koelle, Sigismond Wilhelm. Polyglotta Africana. London: Church Missionary House, Salisbury Square, Fleet Street, 1963.

Kulp, A. P. A History of Sierra Leone, 1400-1787. Cambridge: Cambridge University Press, 1961.

Lambert, Frank. "The Pedlar in Divinity: George Whitefield and the Great Awakening, 1737-1745." The Journal of American History (Formerly, The Mississippi Valley Historical Review) 77, no. 3 (December 1990): 812-37.

_____. Inventing the Great Awakening. Princeton, N.J.: Princeton University Press, 1999.

Law, Robin. "Slave-Raiders and Middlemen, Monopolists and Free-Traders: The Supply of Slaves for the Atlantic Trade in Dahomey c. 1715-1850." Journal of African History 30 (1989): 45-46.

Lawrence, James B. "Religious Education of the Negro in the Colony of Georgia." Georgia Historical Quarterly 14, no. 1 (1930): 41-57.

Levine, Lawrence. Black Culture and Black Consciousness. New York: Oxford University Press, 1977.

Little, Kenneth L. "The Role of the Secret Society in Cultural Specialization." In Cultures and Societies in Africa, ed. Simon and Phoebe Ottenberg, 199-213, New York: Random House, 1960.

Lloyd, P. C. "Osifekunde of Ijebu." In Africa Remembered, ed. Philip D. Curtin, 217-88. Madison, Milwaukee, and London: The University of Wisconsin Press, 1968.

Long, John Dixion. Pictures of Slavery in Church and State. Philadelphia: John Dixion Long, 1857. Reprint, New York: Negro Universities press, 1969.

Lovejoy, Paul E., and Jan S. Hogendorn. "Slave Marketing in West Africa." In The Uncommon Market: Essays in the Economic History of the Atlantic Slave Trade, ed. Henry A. Gemery and Jan S. Hogendorn, 213-35. New York: Academic Press, 1979.

_____. "The Volume of the Atlantic Slave Trade: A Synthesis." Journal of African History 23 (1982): 473-501.

_____. "The Impact of the Atlantic Slave Trade on Africa: A Review of the Literature." Journal of African History 30 (1989): 365-94.

Lyell, Charles. Travels in North America. Vols. 1 and 2. New York: Wiley and Putnam, 1845.

M'Nemar, Richard. The Kentucky Revival. Cincinnati: The Press Of John W. Browne, 1807. Microfilm: Religion in America, Part I, Early Books & Manuscripts, BR 515, R43, 1976, Reel 27.

Magesa, Laurenti. African Religion: The Moral Traditions of Abundant Life. Maryknoll, N.Y.: Orbis Books, 1997.

Manning, Patrick. "The Slave Trade in the Bight of Benin, 1640-1890." In The Uncommon Market: Essays in the Economic History of the Atlantic Slave Trade, ed. Henry A. Gemery and Jan S. Hogendorn, 107-41. New York: Academic Press, 1979.

Mather, Cotton. Magnalia Christi Americana: The Ecclesiastical History of New England. New York: Russel & Russel, 1967.

Mbiti, John S. African Religions and Philosophy. New Hampshire: Heinemann Educational Books, 1969.

_____. Concepts of God in Africa. New York: Praeger, 1970.

_____. Introduction to African Traditional Religion. London: Heinemann Educational Books, 1975.

Mettas, Jean. Repertoire Der Expiditions Negrieres Francaises Au XVIII siecles. Paris: Societe Francaise D'Histoire Du'Outre-mer, 1978.

Miller, Joseph C. "The Numbers, Origins, and Destination of Slaves in the Eighteenth Century Angolan Slave Trade." In The Atlantic Slave Trade: Effects on the Economies, Societies, and Peoples in Africa, the Americas, and Europe, ed. Joseph Inikori and Stanley L. Engerman, 77-115. Durham and London: Duke University Press, 1997.

Miller, Randall M., and David Smith. A Dictionary of Afro-American Christianity. New York: Greenwood, 1967.

Morgan, Philip D. "The Cultural Implications of the Atlantic Slave Trade: African Regional Origins, American Destinations and New World Developments." In <u>Routes to Slavery</u>, ed. David Eltis and David Richardson, 122-45. London: Frank Cass, 1997..

Murchinson, Carl. <u>A Handbook of Psychology</u>. Worchester, Mass.: Clark University Press, 1935.

Obichere, Boniface. "Slavery and the Slave Trade in Niger Delta Cross River Basin." In <u>De la Traite A L'Esclavage</u>, ed. Sarge Daget, 45-56. (Actes du Colloque International sur la Traite des Noires): Nantes, 1985.

Olmsted, Frederick Law. <u>The Cotton Kingdom</u>. New York: Alfred Knoff, 1966.

Oshinsky, David. "Oral History: Playing by the Rules." <u>The Journal of American History</u>. Formerly: <u>The Mississippi Valley Historical Review</u> 77, no. 2 (1990): 609-25.

Ottenberg, Simon and Phoebe. <u>Cultures and Societies of Africa</u>. New York: Random House, 1960.

Park, Robert E. "The Conflict and Fusion of Cultures with Special Reference to the Negro." <u>The Journal of Negro History</u> 4, no. 2 (1919): 111-33.

Parrinder, Geoffrey. <u>African Traditional Religion</u>. Westport, Conn.: Greenwood, 1962.

_____. <u>Encountering World Religions</u>. New York: Crossroad, 1987.

Parsons, Robert T. "The Idea of God among the Kono of Sierra Leone." In African Ideas of God: A Symposium, ed. Edwin Smith, 260-76. London: Edinburgh House, 1950.

Pascoe, C. F. Two Hundred Years of the S.P.G.: An Historical Account. London: Published by the Society's Office, 1901. Micrifilm: BR.515, R43, 1976, Reel 33.

Phillips, Ulrich B. Plantation and Frontier Documents, 1649-1863. Vols. 1 and 2. New York: Burt Franklin, 1910.

_____. American Negro Slavery. Baton Rouge, La.: State University Press, 1966.

Powdermaker, Hortense. After Freedom: A Cultural Study in the Deep South. New York: Viking, 1939.

Puckett, Newball. "Religious Folk-Beliefs of Whites and Negroes." Journal of Negro History 16, no. 1 (April, 1931): 9-35.

Raboteau, Albert J. Slave Religion: The Invisible Institution in the Antebellum South. Oxford and New York: Oxford University Press, 1978.

_____. "Retelling Carter Woodson's Story: Archival Sources for Afro-American Church History." The Journal of History. Formerly: The Mississippi Historical Review 77, no. 1 (1990): 183-99.

_____. "African-Americans, Exodus, and the American Israel." In African-American Christianity: Essays in History, ed. Paul E. Johnson, 1-17. Berkeley: University of California Press, 1994.

Rattray, R. S. Religion and Art in Ashanti. London: Oxford University Press, 1927.

Rawick, George P. The American Slave: A Composite Autobiography. Vol. 19, God Struck Me Dead. Westport, Conn.: Greenwood, 1972.

_____. The American Slave: A Composite Autobiography. Vol. 16, Kansas, Kentucky, Maryland, Ohio, Virginia and Tennessee Narratives. (Federal Work Project). Westport, Conn.: Greenwood, 1941.

_____. The American Slave: A Composite Autobiography. Vol. 5, Texas Narratives. (Federal Work Project). Westport, Conn.: Greenwood, 1972.

_____. The American Slave: A Composite Autobiography. Vol. 11: From Sundown to Sunup: The Making of the Black Community. Westport, Conn.: Greenwood, 1972.

_____. The American Slave: A Composite Autobiography. Vol. 13, Georgia Narratives Parts 3 & 4. (Federal Work Project) Westport, Conn.: Greenwood, 1972.)

_____. The American Slave: A Composite Autobiography. Vol. 8, Arkansas Narratives Part 1 & 2. (Federal Work Project). Westport, Conn.: Greenwood, 1972.

Richardson, David. "Slave Exports from West and West-Central Africa, 1700-1810: New Estimates of the Volume and Distribution." Journal of African History 30 (1989): 1-22.

_____. "The Eighteenth-Century British Slave Trade: Estimates of its volume and Coastal Distribution in Africa." Research in Economic History 12 (1989): 151-95.

Rodney, Walter. "Upper Guinea and the Significance of the Origins of Africans Enslaved in the New World." The Journal of Negro History 54, no. 4 (1969): 327-45.

Seabrook, Whitemarsh, B. An Essay on the Management of Slaves and Especially Their Religious Instruction. Charleston: A. E. Miller, 1834.

Simpson, Robert Drew. American Methodist Pioneer: The Life and Journals of the Rev. Freeman Garrettson. Madison, N.J.: Drew University Library, 1984.

Sims, Patsy. Can Someone Shout Amen!: Inside the Tents and Tabernacles of American Revivalists. Lexington: The University Press of Kentucky, 1996.

Smith, Edwin W. African Ideas of God: A Symposium. London: Edinburgh House, 1950.

Smith, Timothy L. Revivalism and Social Reform. New York and Nashville: Abingdon, 1957.

_____. "Slavery and Theology: The Emergence of Black Christian Consciousness in Nineteenth-century America." Church History 41 (December 1972): 497-512.

Sparks, Randy J. "Religion in Amite County, Mississippi, 1800-1861." In Masters and Slaves in the House of the Lord: Race Religion in the American South, ed. John B. Boles, 58-80. Lexington: The University Press of Kentucky, 1988.

Stampp, Kenneth M. The Peculiar Institution. New York: Alfred A. Knopf, 1963.

Sweet, William Warren. "Review of The Great Awakening in Virginia, 1740-1790," by Wesley M. Gewehr. American Historical Review 35 (1930): 887-88.

_____. The Story of Religions in America. New York and London: Harper & Brothers 1930.

_____. Religion in the Development of American Culture, 1765-1840. Gloucester, Mass.: Peter Smith, 1963.

_____. Revivalism in America: Its Origin, Growth, and Decline. Gloucester, Mass.: Peter Smith, 1965.

Taylor, John V. The Primal Vision: Christian Presence Amid African Religion. London: SCM Press, 1963.

Thomas, Hugh. The Slave Trade: The Story of the Atlantic Slave Trade, 1440-1870. New York: Simon & Schuster, 1997.

Thompson, Ernest Trice. Presbyterians in the South, 1607-1861. Vol. 1. Richmond, Va.: John Konx, 1963.

Thornton, John. Africa and Africans in the Making of the Atlantic World, 1400-1800. Cambridge: The Cambridge University Press, 1992.

Tienou, Tite. "African Traditional Religion." In Evangelical Dictionary of World Missions, ed. Scott Moreau, 46-48. Grand Rapids, Mich.: Baker Books, 2000.

Touchstone, Blake. "Planters and Slave Religion in the Deep South." In Masters and Slaves in the House of the Lord: Race and Religion in the American South, ed. John B. Boles, 99-126. Lexington: The University Press of Kentucky, 1988.

Tracy, Joseph. The Great Awakening: History of the Revival of Religion. New York: Arno Press and New York Times, 1969.

Turnbull, Colin M. "Initiation among the Bambuti Pygmies of The Central Ituri." In Cultures and Societies of Africa, ed. Simon and Phoebe Ottenberg, 421-42. New York: Random House, 1960.

Van Horne, John C. Religious Philanthropy and Colonial Slavery: The American Correspondence of the Associates of Dr. Bray, 1717-1777. Urbana and Chicago: University of Illinois Press, 1985.

Van Woodward, C. Review Article: "History from Slave Sources." American Historical Review 79, no. 2 (1974): 470-81.

Walvin, James. An African's Life: The Life and Times of Olaudah Equiano, 1745-1797. London and New York: Cassell, 1998.

Weimer, Cecil G. "Christianity and the Negro Problem." Journal of Negro History 16, no. 2 (1931): 67-78.

Westermann, Diedrich. Africa and Christianity. London: Oxford University Press, 1937.

Woodson, Carter G. The History of the Negro Church. Washington D.C.: Associated Publishers, 1921.

_____. The Education of the Negro Prior to 1861. New York: Arno Press and New York Times, 1968.

Zahan, Dominique. The Religion, Spirituality, and Thought of Traditional Africa. Chicago and London: University of Chicago Press, 1979.

Printed in the United States
By Bookmasters